PENGUIN CLASSICS

FROGS AND OTHER PLAYS

ARISTOPHANES was born, probably in Athens, *c.* 447–445 BC and died between 386 and 380 BC. Not much is known about his life, although there is a sympathetic portrait of him in Plato's *Symposium*. Early in his career, during the 420s, he was prosecuted for attacks on the prominent politician Cleon, but later, in 405, he was awarded public honours for promoting Athenian unity in *Frogs*. Aristophanes wrote forty plays in all. Of these the eleven surviving plays are *Acharnians* (425), *Knights* (424), *Clouds* (423), *Wasps* (422), *Peace* (421), *Birds* (414), *Lysistrata* (411), *Women at the Thesmophoria* (411), *Frogs* (405), *Assemblywomen* (*c.* 392) and *Wealth* (388).

DAVID BARRETT (1914–98) was born in London where he attended the City of London School, having already learnt Greek by the age of ten. He studied Classics at Peterhouse, Cambridge, and then worked at the British Museum Library where he developed a particular interest in the Finnish collection. After the Second World War he became a lecturer in English at Helsinki University. Over the years he translated many classic Finnish texts and was later made a Knight, first class, of the Order of the White Rose of Finland. On his return to England in 1965 he joined the staff of the Bodleian Library, Oxford. He was quite well versed in over thirty languages, some of them little known, and at the Department of Oriental Books he specialized in Georgian and Armenian books and manuscripts. As well as the plays in the present volume David Barrett's translations of *The Birds* and *The Assemblywomen* are also published by Penguin Classics.

SHOMIT DUTTA was educated at the Royal Grammar School, High Wycombe, University College, Oxford, King's College, London, and Lady Margaret Hall, Oxford. He has taught classics at various schools and universities. Besides working as a freelance arts reviewer, he has published a translation of Sophocles' *Ajax* and a volume of Greek tragedy for Penguin Classics.

T0176235

ARISTOPHANES

Frogs and Other Plays

Translated by DAVID BARRETT
Revised Translation with an Introduction and Notes by SHOMIT DUTTA

PENGUIN BOOKS

PENGUIN CLASSICS

Published by the Penguin Group
Penguin Books Ltd, 80 Strand, London WC2R 0RL, England
Penguin Group (USA) Inc., 375 Hudson Street, New York, New York 10014, USA
Penguin Group (Canada), 90 Eglinton Avenue East, Suite 700, Toronto, Ontario, Canada M4P 2Y3
(a division of Pearson Penguin Canada Inc.)
Penguin Ireland, 25 St Stephen's Green, Dublin 2, Ireland
(a division of Penguin Books Ltd)
Penguin Group (Australia), 250 Camberwell Road, Camberwell, Victoria 3124, Australia
(a division of Pearson Australia Group Pty Ltd)
Penguin Books India Pvt Ltd, 11 Community Centre, Panchsheel Park, New Delhi – 110 017, India
Penguin Group (NZ), 67 Apollo Drive, Rosedale, North Shore 0632, New Zealand
(a division of Pearson New Zealand Ltd)
Penguin Books (South Africa) (Pty) Ltd, 24 Sturdee Avenue, Rosebank, Johannesburg 2196, South Africa

Penguin Books Ltd, Registered Offices: 80 Strand, London WC2R 0RL, England

www.penguin.com

This translation first published by Penguin Books 1964
Revised translation with new Introduction and Notes published in Penguin Classics 2007

029

Copyright © David Barrett, 1964
Revised translation, Introduction and Notes copyright © Shomit Dutta, 2007
All rights reserved

The moral right of the editors has been asserted

Set in 10.25/12.25 pt PostScript Adobe Sabon
Typeset by Rowland Phototypesetting Ltd, Bury St Edmunds, Suffolk
Printed and bound in Great Britain by Clays Ltd, Elcograf S.p.A.

Except in the United States of America, this book is sold subject to the condition that it shall not, by way of trade or otherwise, be lent, re-sold, hired out, or otherwise circulated without the publisher's prior consent in any form of binding or cover other than that in which it is published and without a similar condition including this condition being imposed on the subsequent purchaser

ISBN 978-0-140-44969-3

www.greenpenguin.co.uk

MIX
Paper from responsible sources
FSC™ C018179
FSC www.fsc.org

Penguin Books is committed to a sustainable future for our business, our readers and our planet. This book is made from Forest Stewardship Council™ certified paper.

Contents

Introduction

The plays of Aristophanes, the oldest surviving genre of comedy in Western literature, still have much to tell us. As recently as 2003, a thousand one-off performances of *Lysistrata* – the play in which the women of Greece mount a sex-strike to bring about peace – were staged across the world (including one in every US state) as a protest against the invasion of Iraq.

Aristophanic comedy's enduring relevance in spite of its antiquity is just one way in which it may be seen as simultaneously old and new. The tension between old and new is itself a prominent theme in several plays; none more so than *Frogs*, where the comic hero Dionysus is asked, in his capacity as the god of theatre, to judge a contest between the old-fashioned Aeschylus and the avant-garde Euripides. But while *Frogs* appears to condemn Euripides as a debaser of tragic convention, we should not infer from this that Aristophanes was an unequivocal conservative. The same Euripides is portrayed as the tirelessly innovative hero of *Women at the Thesmophoria*.[1] Aristophanes is also at pains to emphasize his own innovativeness as a dramatist. The Chorus of *Wasps*, speaking on the poet's behalf, openly berates the audience's conservatism in failing to appreciate his previous, highly original and unconventional play *Clouds*.

Even Aristophanes' method of constructing his plays reflects a preoccupation with the old and the new. As a poet and dramatist he borrows, plunders and parodies from earlier writers remorselessly and yet, as his recycling of Euripidean tragedy in *Women* shows, he transforms what he appropriates into something utterly new. For Aristophanes, as for T. S. Eliot, tradition and novelty (or originality) are not in conflict but rather complementary elements of artistic creation; this is evident in his implicit attempt in *Frogs* to incorporate the once-modern Euripides into an evolving tragic canon.

It is often said that classic works are both of their time and timeless. This is true of Aristophanic comedy. The plays are highly topical and firmly located in contemporary Athens, but in creating their own autonomous blend of fact and fiction they attain universal scope. Aristophanes is also the earliest canonical writer to use comedy systematically to examine and contest core cultural values – artistic, social, religious, political and philosophical – of the society to which he belonged.

Critical judgement of Aristophanes' writing crosses the whole spectrum. Many have hailed him as an artist of the highest order, some damned him with faint praise, others condemned him unequivocally. One reason for such a mixed reception is Aristophanic comedy's seemingly contradictory characteristics: ceaselessly innovative and irrepressible yet rooted in tradition and generic convention; unashamedly highbrow and yet inordinately fond of slapstick and vulgarity. Still, critical differences notwithstanding, most scholars across the ages agree on two things. First, Aristophanes has few rivals for sheer ingenuity. Secondly, he is one of the greatest exemplars of the grace, charm and scope of Attic Greek – the dialect of fifth- and fourth-century Athens in which its drama, history, philosophy and oratory were composed. Hopefully, the former of these qualities and something of the latter come across in these revised translations of three of his finest plays.

Today we may read Aristophanes simply for entertainment. Over and above this, however, there have been three main approaches to his work. The first is to treat Aristophanic texts as documents for understanding the cultural life of fifth-century Athens. This idea can be traced back to Plato who, when asked by the tyrant Dionysius of Syracuse to explain the Athenians' system of governance, responded by sending him the complete works of Aristophanes. The second is to regard Aristophanes as a comic *writer*. From such a perspective his work may be studied in its own context, compared with other comic literature, or considered in terms of its influence on later forms of comedy. The third is to see Aristophanes as a comic *dramatist*. Aristophanes may well have intended his work to be read (the fact that we have the second, unperformed version of *Clouds*, and evidence in the plays themselves, such as Dionysus' recollection of perusing a play of Euripides in *Frogs* 52–3, suggest that play texts existed in Aristophanes' day), but it primarily was through spectacular one-off performances in dramatic festivals that his plays made their impact on the culture of fifth-century Athens.

Performance radically enhances, or alters, our understanding of any dramatic text. With Aristophanes the gap between the texts and their realization as performances is especially wide. The aspects of performance about which we know very little include delivery, stage action and theatrical effects. We do know from vase-paintings depicting theatrical scenes that various kinds of scenery and props were used in the ancient theatre (according to Aristotle, scene-painting was introduced by Sophocles), although the exact configuration of the stage for original performances of particular comedies remains conjecture. We can also tell where stage machinery – a crane (*mēchanē*) for aerial appearances and a revolving platform (*eccyclēma*) for showing indoor scenes – was used. In Aristophanes such occasions, which often parody stage practice in tragedy, are usually alluded to openly in the text (e.g., *Women* 96, 265).

A significant proportion of ancient drama involved musical accompaniment. Some such passages were lyric and would have been sung, others would have been recited, or chanted, as opposed to spoken as dialogue or monologue. The Chorus danced during some, though not all, of their lyric passages. While we can usually tell at what points musical accompaniment would have occurred in Aristophanes, we know almost nothing of what it might have sounded like. Likewise with dancing, we can generally tell when it would have occurred, but only occasionally are there any specific clues about the movements involved; one such instance is Philocleon's burlesque of tragic dancing in the finale of *Wasps*, where he gives a running commentary on his series of highly demanding manoeuvres.

There are considerable obstacles to reconstructing fully the original performance of a specific Aristophanic comedy, but we are better placed to gain an idea of the general theatrical experience of Aristophanes' fifth-century Athenian audience, and, firstly, the life of Aristophanes.

The Life and Times of Aristophanes

Little is known for certain about the life of Aristophanes: even the dates of his birth and death are speculative. His birth date is somewhere between 447 and 445 BC, as his first play, *Banqueters* (427), was performed when he was young but probably no less than eighteen. The date of his death, probably not long after 386, is conjectured on the basis of his having written two plays after his last surviving play, *Wealth*, staged in 388.

Aristophanes was born and educated in Athens, and belonged to the deme (city district) of Cydathenaeum. His father was Philippus and his mother Zenodora. His family may have had some connection with the island of Aegina (Aristophanes hints at this in *Acharnians* 653–4). If his family did own property there, it may have been acquired after Athens' defeat of the Aeginetans in 431. Other biographical facts are few and far between. He had three sons: Philippus, Araros and Nicostratus (or Philetaerus). All three seem to have embarked on the same career as their father, and we know that Araros put on Aristophanes' last two works, *Cocalus* and *Aeolosicon* (both lost), early in his career. As for Aristophanes' physical appearance, humorous remarks in *Clouds* and *Peace* suggest that he went bald at an early age, although some sculptural portraits show him, in early middle age, as having ample hair.

In a writing career spanning forty-odd years, Aristophanes is known to have had forty comedies produced. Of these, apart from numerous fragmentary quotations, eleven plays survive: *Acharnians* (425), *Knights* (424), *Clouds* (a revised version of the play that was produced in 423), *Wasps* (422), *Peace* (421), *Birds* (414), *Lysistrata* and *Women at the Thesmophoria* (411), *Frogs* (405), *Assemblywomen* (probably 392) and *Wealth* (388). Comedy, like tragedy, was performed as part of state-sponsored competitions (on which see below). Of his surviving works, Aristophanes is known to have won first prize in the comic competition with *Acharnians*, *Knights* and *Frogs*; second prize with *Birds* and *Wasps*; and third prize with *Clouds*. We do not have results for the other five. Of his lost plays, we know that he won first prize with *Babylonians* (426) and *Preview* (422).

It was probably in the 380s that Plato (*c*. 427–347 BC) wrote his *Symposium*, a fictional dramatic account of a drinking party given by the tragedian Agathon in 416 to celebrate his first victory in the tragic competition. Among the guests are Aristophanes and Socrates. Though written several years after its supposed date, *Symposium* is our only source for what Aristophanes may have been like in person. It presents him as sociable. Socrates suggests that he 'devotes all his time to Aphrodite and Dionysus'.[2] He seems on friendly terms with the other guests and his host. Indeed, the first thing he says is that he has a hangover from drinking with Agathon on the previous day.

Though *Symposium* is a Platonic dialogue, it is largely made up of speeches aimed at defining love. Aristophanes, in his speech, contends that love is the desire and pursuit of spiritual and physical wholeness. The myth he invents to support this claim is amusing and absurd. People, he suggests, were originally one of three genders: male, female or hermaphrodite. They possessed two sets of everything – head, arms, legs, genitalia. However, the gods, feeling threatened by mankind, split them into two. This condition of being incomplete explains why people feel the urge to find, and conjugate with, their respective other halves (whether a different gender or the same). While Aristophanes aims to amuse by his speech, he does not expect to be dismissed as trivial; Plato makes him say as much himself. *Symposium* ends just as Agathon, Aristophanes and Socrates – the only guests still conscious – are about to discuss whether the technique of composing tragedy and comedy is fundamentally the same. What they might have said, according to Plato at any rate, we shall never know.

In Aristophanes' lifetime the political circumstances of Athens changed considerably. During his childhood and early career the city was at its zenith. Radical democracy meant that all citizens could vote in the Assembly on all major policy decisions. They also stood a reasonable chance of gaining public office since a number of positions were appointed by lot. But generals and ambassadors were elected, and usually came from aristocratic or otherwise wealthy families; it was such men who tended to dominate politics. Pericles, one of the men responsible for establishing radical democracy in 462–461 BC, emerged as Athens' single most powerful political leader. Through a mixture of diplomacy and aggression, and by building up naval supremacy, he turned an existing alliance of Greek states (against the threat from Persia) into a virtual Athenian empire. But Athens' expansionism and harsh treatment of its former allies (now effectively subject states) caused other Greek city-states to fear for their independence. In 431 Sparta, the dominant military power in the Peloponnese, drew Athens into war.

When Pericles died in 429 BC he was soon succeeded by Cleon, a self-made man who was an unscrupulous, pro-war demagogue. Only after Cleon and the bellicose Spartan general Brasidas were killed at the battle of Amphipolis was an opportunity for peace seized in 421 (this is celebrated in Aristophanes' play *Peace*). But this did not last. Athens soon resumed its imperialism, setting its sights on subjugating Sicily. The Spartans again endeavoured to thwart Athenian ambitions. A vast Athenian naval expedition to Sicily ended in catastrophic defeat. Meanwhile the Spartans, advised by Pericles' nephew Alcibiades (who had defected), fortified their base at Deceleia, deep within Athens' own territory. In 411, the year *Women* and *Lysistrata* were produced, dissatisfaction with the handling of the war led to Athens' democratic system being replaced by an oligarchy, although democracy was restored the following summer. By this time, however, most of Athens' subject states had either revolted or gone over to the Spartans, who had also secured Persian support. A costly Athenian naval victory at Arginusae in 406 did little to ward off final disaster, which came in 405 in the form of a crushing defeat at sea off Aegispotami (when *Frogs* was first performed early in 405 the city's situation was desperate but this final blow had not yet been dealt). This cut off Athens' grain supplies through the Hellespont and forced unconditional surrender in the spring of 404. Athens was stripped of all overseas territories and power was seized by oligarchs who established a reign of terror. As in 411–410 BC, democracy was soon restored, and lasted until Philip of Macedon's conquest of Athens in 338. But defeat in the Peloponnesian War (404 BC), and the corresponding loss of empire, meant that the former intimate relationship between citizens and the state, a vital condition for Aristophanes' highly politicized and topical comedy to flourish, was irrecoverably lost.

The Cultural Context of Old Comedy

Theatre in fifth-century Athens was one of the principal and most popular art forms. It was firmly rooted in its religious origins. Drama was composed for performance at two major festivals held in the city, the City Dionysia and the Lenaea, both in honour of Dionysus, the god of theatre.[3] These festivals were major public events of civic as well as artistic and religious importance. Going to dramatic festivals was seen by Athenian citizens not just as a privilege but a duty and a right; there was even a 'theoric' fund for those unable to afford the price of tickets (two obols in Aristophanes' day).

The festivals of the City Dionysia and Lenaea were each held over four days every year, the former around the beginning of March, the latter in January. The City Dionysia took place in the Theatre of Dionysus on the southern slope of the Acropolis. The location of the Lenaea is disputed. Originally it was probably held at a sanctuary called the Lenaeon, located by some scholars outside the city walls but identified by others with the precinct of 'Dionysus in the Marshes'. The festival may have relocated after the building of the Theatre of Dionysus, as it would be surprising if a makeshift theatre were preferred to an available permanent one. In Aristophanes' *Acharnians* (line 504), the hero Dicaeopolis speaks of himself and the audience as being 'at the Lenaeon', but this is not conclusive, as the phrase (also used by Plato and Demosthenes) may refer to the festival irrespective of its location.

Athenian comedy and tragedy were performed as part of separate competitions (albeit at the same festivals). In the comic competition rivalries were fierce. Aristophanes, for instance, described his venerable elder contemporary Cratinus as an incontinent, drunken has-been, and was himself accused of plagiarism by another contemporary, Eupolis. At the City Dionysia, where the primary focus was on tragedy, three tragedians competed, each offering three tragedies and a satyr-play (a relatively simple, humorous genre involving a Chorus of drunken, lascivious satyrs in a mythological setting). These plays were performed on the first three days of the festival. On the fourth and final day there were single plays by five comic playwrights. The Lenaea appears originally to have had just single comedies by five playwrights. But at some point around the end of the 430s, tragedies were introduced, with two tragedians each putting on two tragedies (but no satyr-plays); the tragedies were performed before the comedies. Evidence suggests that during certain years of the Peloponnesian War the comic competition was reduced from five competitors to three for financial reasons (comic choruses tended to involve elaborate and expensive costumes).

The process by which playwrights were invited, or selected, to put on plays was complex. For the City Dionysia, the Eponymous Archon (the principal magistrate of the nine elected annually), upon taking up office, had to nominate wealthy citizens to be the sponsor, or *chorēgos*, of a comic or tragic chorus. For the Lenaea, this duty was performed by another of the magistrates, and it was possible to nominate wealthy resident foreigners (as non-citizens could participate as chorus members). The *chorēgos* was responsible for recruiting the twenty-four members of the comic chorus (the tragic chorus in Aristophanes' day numbered only fifteen). He had to pay for costumes and masks, and also for professional voice trainers and choreographers. He would probably also have paid for any professional singers, musicians, dancers and minor actors or extras the play required. Sponsoring a chorus, while mandatory, was also considered a great civic honour. Nevertheless, if someone felt that another citizen could afford to fund a chorus more easily, the nominee could challenge this person either to be *chorēgos* in his stead or make a complete exchange of property and goods. Such exchanges, while not common, are attested.

Playwrights wishing to compete in the City Dionysia or Lenaea had to apply formally to the appropriate archon to be 'granted a chorus'. The archon would then see samples of their respective plays before reaching his decision. Besides being granted a chorus, successful playwrights were given a principal actor, or 'protagonist', at public expense; it is unclear how the other two main actors were recruited and paid. The granting of choruses took place shortly after archons came into office in July. This meant that playwrights and their *chorēgoi* had ample time to prepare and rehearse before the following January or March for the Lenaea or City Dionysia respectively.

The playwright was known officially as the *didaskalos* (literally, 'teacher' or 'instructor'), a role that falls somewhere between author and director. Playwrights before Aristophanes' day also performed other roles including writing the music and choreography, and training the Chorus to sing and dance. By Aristophanes' day, however, it was common to employ a special chorus master, or *chorodidaskalos*. In some cases, the whole play was handed over by the playwright to another person, who would act as *didaskalos*. Aristophanes did this with his early plays up to and including *Acharnians*, all of which had his older friend Callistratus as their *didaskalos*. Aristophanes also used another friend Philonides as *didaskalos* for his lost play *Preview*, which beat *Wasps* (produced/directed by Aristophanes himself) at the Lenaea in 422. Where someone other than the playwright acted as *didaskalos*, authorship would almost certainly have been an open secret.

*

Actors were highly skilled professionals who were also capable of singing and dancing. The actor playing Philocleon in *Wasps*, for example, had to sing a solo aria (316–33) and perform an elaborate burlesque of tragic dance (1482–1515); and the actor playing Agathon in *Women* had to imitate, and parody, Agathon's innovative singing and play solo and choral parts in alternation (101–29). Actors also had to perform elaborate 'stage business'. Besides slapstick scenes, such as Philocleon popping up from various parts of the house in *Wasps*, there were scenes involving the use of stage machinery. In *Women*, for example, the actor playing Euripides (dressed as the tragic Perseus) has to swing across the stage aerially attached to a stage crane.

Comedy, like tragedy, observed a three-actor rule.[4] Aristophanic comedy is, for the most part, performable with three actors; although odd scenes do require a fourth actor, there is no play in which the fourth actor would have to speak more than a few lines.[5] The general observation of the three-actor rule ensured that comic playwrights competed on level terms and kept a check on production costs. Conforming to the three-actor rule cannot have been easy, especially in comedies which often involved large numbers of minor characters. Typically, the principal actor would play the lead character. This would involve being onstage for the majority of the play, but when the lead character was not onstage the principal actor may also have had to play one or two minor characters. The second actor would usually play two or three other major parts, although again he may also have had to play the odd minor character (particularly in scenes where a string of characters come onstage only to be rebuffed by the hero, as happens in *Acharnians*, *Peace* and *Birds*). The third actor would play the majority of minor characters but possibly one major character as well.

The actors' parts are relatively easy to determine in the case of *Women*. The protagonist must play Mnesilochus, who is onstage for almost the entire play. The second actor must play Euripides (in all his disguises) and the First Woman (Mica). This leaves the third actor to play Agathon's servant, Agathon himself, the Second Woman, Cleisthenes, Critylla and the Scythian. There are two minor parts remaining. The first is the Magistrate, who comes on at 922, only one line after Euripides exits and while the other two actors, playing Mnesilochus and Critylla, are still onstage; this part must be played by a fourth actor. The other part is Echo. It is unclear how this part was played, and by which actor (the second or the fourth); still, the number of lines involved is small, and all the lines are repetitions, making them easy to perform. *Frogs* requires a little more of its fourth actor. The protagonist must play Dionysus, who is onstage throughout. The second actor plays Xanthias and either Aeschylus or Euripides. The third actor plays Heracles, Charon, Aeacus, a Maid, First Landlady, the Old Slave (who may be Aeacus) and either Euripides or Aeschylus. This leaves the fourth actor with the part of Second Landlady, when the three main actors are playing Dionysus, Xanthias and the First Landlady, and the part of Pluto, when the three main actors are present playing Dionysus, Aeschylus and Euripides.

There were also conventions concerning masks and costume. Masks were grotesque. Most were generic – the old man (e.g., Philocleon, Mnesilochus), the young man (e.g., Bdelycleon), the slave, the old woman, and so on – but individual masks could be used for well-known individuals. Socrates in *Clouds*, for example, was probably recognizable by a mask portraying his well-known snub-nose and satyr-like features. It is also possible that the mask worn by 'The Dog' in the trial scene in *Wasps* was identifiable as Cleon. Mythological figures, such as Dionysus and Heracles in *Frogs*, would be recognized by traditional attributes – Dionysus by his ivy, fennel wand and effeminate clothing, and Heracles by his club and lion-skin. Conventions were sometimes deliberately infringed for comic effect (e.g., Dionysus dressed as Heracles in *Frogs*). Women's masks were white, while men's masks were darker and bearded, but it is clear from remarks made by other characters onstage that in *Women* the masks of Agathon and Cleisthenes, who are both portrayed as very effeminate, are beardless and, probably, paler than usual.

The comic actor's costume typically comprised tights worn

over thick padding that exaggerated the stomach and buttocks, complementing the grotesqueness of the mask. He would also wear a tunic (or *chitōn*), which was short enough to reveal a large phallus. An outer garment was often worn, which allowed the phallus to be shown or concealed as required. Aristophanic comedy is rife with comic business involving the phallus. In *Women*, for instance, the disguised Mnesilochus goes to great lengths to conceal his phallus when Cleisthenes and the women seek to expose him (643–8).

Members of the Chorus were not specialists, as the actors and playwrights were. Still, between them the Chorus and Chorus-Leader usually had a sizeable quantity of lines, sung and spoken. The Chorus's costume and appearance were also very important. Along with their dancing and singing they were significant factors in the judging of performances. The importance of the Chorus is evident partly from the fact that comic dramatists had to be 'granted a chorus' to enter a play. As ordinary citizens, the Chorus members also represented a strong link between the performers and the audience.

What remains today of the Theatre of Dionysus belongs to the theatre rebuilt in the fourth century BC by Lycurgus. Any account of the theatre as it was in Aristophanes' day therefore remains largely speculative. The capacity of the Theatre of Dionysus was approximately 14,000 to 17,000. It was outdoors, and performances ran from morning to evening. Prior to its rebuilding in stone by Lycurgus, the seating area (*theatron*) was not semi-circular but a more irregular shape, and the rows of seats were movable and wooden. Important officials sat in the front row, in seats of honour called *prohedria*, with the priest of Dionysus in a throne-like seat at the centre. At the foot of the seating area was a circular pit, the *orchestra*, where the Chorus performed. In the middle of this was the altar of Dionysus. Behind this was the stage-building, or *skēnē*, with a raised stage in front of it for the actors. In Aristophanes' day the building was a long wooden structure with a painted façade. Inside it were rooms in which actors could change costumes, and in which props and costumes were stored. The stage-building contained central doors and two further doors stage left and right. The flat roof of the stage-building offered a higher level for actors and could, as in *Wasps*, represent the upper floor, or roof, of a house (this is where Bdelycleon is sleeping at the start of *Wasps*, and it is from here that Philocleon attempts his first ploy to escape). To each side of the stage were wings or side-entrances (*eisodoi*). By these the Chorus could enter the orchestra. There were also ramps, for actors, leading up from the wings to the stage.

The composition of Aristophanes' audiences may have been affected by various factors. One was place of residence. Many outlying parts of Attica were about thirty miles from Athens. The journey may have been too arduous for many poorer rural folk, who would have had to walk to the city (the better-off would probably have had a second home in the city). Assuming some plays were re-performed, such people may have preferred to attend rural Dionysia festivals instead. This said, during the war much of the rural population moved into the city, making it easier for them to go to the theatre. Cost was also an issue. Despite the theoric fund for those unable to afford theatre tickets, the money may not have covered the full expense; moreover, those who claimed the fund may have kept the money and not attended.

Another significant factor was status. Throughout the fifth century there were many non-citizens living in Athens (metics). While these people could attend the theatre, they could not claim the theoric fund. Some slaves seem to have attended; these presumably came from well-off families, as their masters would have had to pay for them. One imagines that if demand for tickets was higher than availability, citizens would get preference over slaves and, probably, metics; if so, it is unclear how such matters were handled. There are references in Aristophanes suggesting that some boys were among the audience. It is not known from what age they were allowed, or encouraged, to attend. Given that their fathers would have to pay for their tickets, we may reasonably suppose that only boys from relatively wealthy families attended.

Evidence about whether women attended is inconclusive. The situation may even have been different for tragedy and comedy. In Aristophanes there are two remarks possibly suggesting that women went to see tragedy (*Women* 386 and *Frogs* 1050–51). As regards comedy, the often-cited remark in *Peace* 966 about women never getting the free food thrown to the audience is inconclusive: while it may mean that women sat towards the back, it may equally mean that they were not present. A more suggestive piece of evidence is the Chorus's remark, in *Birds* 793–6, that having wings would allow a man to fly off and visit a woman whose husband was in the audience and return before the end of the day's performances. This implies that women did not attend the theatre, at least not in significant numbers.

A separate but related issue is whether the composition of the audience differed for the Dionysia and Lenaea respectively. One passage from Aristophanes' *Acharnians* suggests a difference. The hero Dicaeopolis, seemingly speaking on behalf of Aristophanes himself, declares that he need have no fear of being accused by Cleon of maligning the city (something that appears to have happened after Aristophanes' previous play *Babylonians*). Dicaeopolis says he can address the audience freely because there are 'no foreigners present' at the Lenaea, adding that Metics are *de facto* citizens. This clearly implies that some foreigners came to the City Dionysia, and it is not unreasonable to suppose, on this basis, that Greeks from other states may also have been in attendance. Still, despite the possible presence of Metics, slaves, boys, women, foreigners and other Greeks, the vast majority of the audience, at the City Dionysia and the Lenaea, would have been adult male Athenian citizens.

The most important members of the audience, as far as playwrights were concerned, were the judges. Athenian drama was, it must be remembered, performed as part of a competition. The judging process for the Dionysia is known up to a point, and the procedure for the Lenaea may, in the absence of any evidence to suggest otherwise, be supposed to have been similar. Ten judges were chosen by lot, by the Archon, from a larger group of citizens chosen previously by the Council (the basis on which this prior selection was made is unclear). Before taking up their special seats at the front, these ten judges had to take an oath to vote for the best performance. After all the performances were over the judges wrote down their votes on tablets. These votes were then used to determine the victorious play and the second and third prizes.

Aristophanes and Old Comedy

Athenian comic drama began in 486 BC, half a century after the establishing of the tragic competition in 534. The genre may be divided into two strongly contrastive periods, Old and New Comedy. Old Comedy, as represented by Aristophanes, stands completely apart from other kinds of dramatic and narrative fiction in the ancient Greek world. (His surviving plays are our only complete examples of Old Comedy.) It flouts the principles of causality and probability; it disregards rules of space and time; it has little interest in creating or maintaining dramatic illusion; its action and characterization are neither consistent nor lifelike. By contrast, its older contemporary tragedy and its successor New Comedy share a common set of fictional conventions and practices which may be traced back to Homeric epic (this is pretty much what Aristotle does, with tragedy, in his *Poetics*): they are both plotted with strict economy according to rules of causality and probability; and they both strive to create characters who are convincing and lifelike in speech, reasoning and action.[6] Old Comedy does not reject the rules to which tragedy and New Comedy subscribe in their entirety, but it does feel free to deploy or discard them at will. Aristophanes belonged to the third generation of writers of Old Comedy. Writing during the latter stages of the form, he arguably presided over its zenith, although his final surviving work reflects a decisive turn from Old Comedy's spirit of cheerful irreverence towards the restrained spirit of New Comedy.

Aristophanic Old Comedy is topical and satirical. In confronting socio-political and cultural issues of the day, it pokes fun at well-known figures onstage, sometimes benignly (e.g., Euripides in *Women*) but often with vitriol (e.g., Cleon in *Wasps*). It is unpredictable and readily embraces fantasy, contradiction and absurdity. Hence in *Wasps* it is possible for a dog to prosecute another dog while calling on kitchen utensils as witnesses. It is also self-consciously literary, with a fondness for parodying, imitating, assimilating and alluding to other texts – not only poetry (e.g., tragedy, epic or lyric poetry) but also songs and certain specialized uses of language (e.g., oracles, philosophical jargon, prayers and oratory). Thus in *Women* the women parody the procedural language of the Athenian assembly, while Mnesilochus and Euripides extensively parody Euripidean tragedy. Old Comedy also frequently draws attention to itself both as comic fiction and as a theatrical performance, paying little heed to the notional boundary between stage and audience. A memorable example of this is when a distressed Dionysus in *Frogs* appeals for help directly to the priest of Dionysus sitting in the front row of the audience, reminding him that he – the actor playing Dionysus – will be having a drink with him after the show. But for all its ridicule, abuse and absurdity, Old Comedy also engages with contemporary political, philosophical and artistic thought at the highest intellectual level: as a piece of sophisticated literary criticism about tragedy, the preposterous contest between Aeschylus and Euripides in *Frogs* is no less valuable than Aristotle's *Poetics*.

It is unclear exactly how Greek comic drama originated. Even in the ancient world the issue was a disputed one. Aristotle (384–322) offers a few suggestions. He says that comedy (like tragedy) came about through improvisation, tracing its origins, in part at least, to fertility songs sung in honour of Phales (a divine companion of Dionysus, represented by a pole, or phallus); an example of such a song occurs in Aristophanes' *Acharnians* (263ff.). He links comedy to invective or lampoons (*iamboi*). He also implies that comedy was derived from the *kōmos*, a ritual act of revelry. Aristophanes' surviving plays suggest that there is probably some truth in all of these propositions.

In terms of their broad areas of interest there are, perhaps, five notional types of play in Old Comedy. These were not recognized categories in the ancient world, and do not necessarily cover all Old Comedy – in any case, individual plays are not restricted by these types since they tend to fall under several categories – but they do help to describe and distinguish Aristophanes' surviving plays.

The first is political comedy. While all of Aristophanes' plays are 'political' inasmuch as they concern the city, or *polis*, of Athens, not all confront pressing political issues directly. Of his surviving works, the earlier plays show a more pronounced political dimension. *Knights* and *Wasps*, for example, target a particular, deeply loathed politician, Cleon, who rose to prominence after Pericles' death. A similar hostility against the later demagogue Cleophon is present in *Frogs* but only surfaces in passing. Other strongly political comedies involve responses to the Peloponnesian War. In *Acharnians* the hero makes a controversial, if implausible, private peace with Sparta at a time when the general mood was for continued hostilities. *Lysistrata*, written when Athenian fortunes were low, shows the women of Athens (and elsewhere in Greece) achieving a fanciful peace by mounting a sex-strike. Such plays, which confront political issues head on, may be contrasted with *Women*, which is conspicuously free of political concerns.

The second type of play is the comedy of manners, or social comedy. According to Aristotle, the comic playwright Crates developed this type of play a generation before Aristophanes. Several of Aristophanes' plays involve elements of social comedy. His first play, *Babylonians* (lost), involved two differently schooled sons vying for their father's affection. *Wasps* and *Clouds* both present conflicts between urbane sons and their unsophisticated fathers. The double-act in the first half of *Frogs* with Dionysus as dim-witted master and Xanthias as clever slave anticipates the kind of situation-based social comedy that occurs throughout New (and Roman) Comedy, as does the 'below-stairs' scene in which Xanthias and Pluto's slave gossip about their masters.

The third category is comedies about specific topical cultural issues. Plays that may be placed in this group include *Clouds*, which polemically examines modern education and its transformation by philosophers, or sophists, such as Socrates; *Women*, which explores Euripides' presentation of female characters in his tragedies; and *Frogs*, which surveys tragedy retrospectively from Aeschylus to Euripides. Other playwrights do not appear to share Aristophanes' preoccupation with tragedy but they did write plays about other kinds of poetry. Plays about cultural issues are often couched in terms of a wider conflict of Old and New. We see this in *Frogs*, in the contest between old-fashioned Aeschylus and the innovative Euripides, and *Clouds* with its conflict between traditional and new education. Significantly, in *Clouds* the contrast between the father who is at heart old-fashioned and the son who has been educated by the avant-garde Socrates is expressed in terms of the former's fondness for Aeschylus and the latter's newfound enthusiasm for Euripides.

The fourth category is comedies involving utopias or fantastic locations. Common settings include the underworld and the Golden Age. There are many lost plays of this kind by other Old Comic playwrights. Of Aristophanes' plays, *Frogs* is set in the underworld, while *Birds* is set in *Nephelococcygia* (Cloud-cuckooland). The fifth and final category is plays involving mythological or tragic burlesque. There were a surprisingly large number of such plays, which are often identifiable by their use of the titles of tragedies or mythological characters. Aristophanes, however, seems only to have written a very small number of such plays, none of which survive.

We have very little by way of literary criticism on Aristophanic comedy from his contemporaries. Indeed, Aristophanes' own *Frogs*, which tells us a great deal about contemporary perceptions of tragedy, is one of the first major pieces of ancient literary criticism. There is, however, one interesting fragment from Old Comedy, written by Aristophanes' contemporary Cratinus (fr. 342). It involves one character referring to another as 'a pedantic purveyor of niceties, a real Euripidaristophanes'.[7] This conflation of Euripides and Aristophanes into a single name suggests that they are alike in their love of verbal precision and cleverness. The quality of being *dexios* ('clever' or 'talented') is not just one that Aristophanes claims for himself and, flatteringly, his audience (e.g., *Clouds* 521–48); Dionysus, in *Frogs* 71, explains his quest for Euripides as a yearning for a tragedian who is *dexios*. Aristophanes' insistence that he is always introducing new ideas into his comedies (*Clouds* 547) is also something that implicitly aligns him with Euripides, the innovative tragedian par excellence.

Plato in his *Apology* complains about Aristophanes' presentation of Socrates in *Clouds*. Plato's main gripe, however, is the negative effect of the portrayal upon the popular perception of Socrates; there is no pejorative criticism of *Clouds* on artistic grounds. Besides, while complaining of Aristophanes' treatment of Socrates in particular, Plato acknowledges that Old Comedy as a whole was negative towards philosophers and philosophy.

Aristophanes' last surviving play, *Wealth*, shows signs of the shift in taste away from the uninhibited excesses of Old Comedy towards greater restraint, consistency and uniformity (of action, characterization, style, tone and so on). In the fourth century Old Comedy quickly went out of fashion. While tragedies of Euripides and Sophocles were regularly re-performed from 386 BC onwards (those of Aeschylus were re-performed from sometime after his death in 456), there is no evidence for revivals of fifth-century comedies.

The clearest indication of Old Comedy's fall from grace lies in Aristotle's verdict in his *Poetics*. Aristotle expresses a general distaste for Old Comedy's crudeness, excess and fondness for the ridiculous. He also suggests that Old Comedy's habit of satirizing particular individuals onstage means that it is not universal. Part of his definition of poetry is that it deals with the hypothetical, or universal, rather than the actual, or particular; this sets poetry above other disciplines such as history and alongside philosophy.[8] To accuse Old Comedy of not being universal is tantamount to claiming that, while it may be verse, it does not count as poetry at all. Aristotle further criticizes Old Comedy for neglecting plot. Only one Old Comic playwright, Crates, is described as structuring action satisfactorily (i.e., in accordance with causality and probability). This criticism, however, is misguided. Old Comedy, for the most part, *chooses* to construct its action in a way that neglects causality and probability in favour of the absurd and the improbable.

Aristotle's negative verdict notwithstanding, the plays of

Aristophanes continued to be read, despite being difficult texts to follow (they had no stage directions, often lacked indications of speaker and were full of obscure topical references). Interest lay not so much in their merits as comic drama but in their exemplification of the expressiveness and charm of Attic Greek (which had by this time given way, along with other regional dialects, to a common dialect known as *koinē*). Alexandrian scholars, more sympathetic to Old Comedy than Aristotle, gradually established a consensus that Aristophanes, Cratinus and Eupolis were the greatest exemplars of the genre.[9]

Later responses to Old Comedy are mixed. While Cicero (106–43 BC) saw Aristophanes as 'the wittiest poet of Old Comedy', Horace (65–8 BC), in his *Ars Poetica*, suggests that although the free speech enjoyed by the poets of Old Comedy was notionally a good thing, in practice it degenerated into unfettered abuse. In his *Satires*, however, he praises Old Comedy for its use of laughter (as opposed to outright abuse) as a means of exposing hypocrisy in the public sphere. This more favourable view of Old Comedy may in part be attributed to Horace's having regarded the genre as a distant precursor of his own satires.

A far less positive judgement is offered by Plutarch (AD *c.* 45–*c.* 125) in a comparison of Aristophanes and Menander. He accuses Aristophanes of vulgar action, general boorishness and uncouth language. He also decries what he considers poor puns (e.g., 'where shall flick you, cursed pot, when you're the one who's given me the flick'), weak associations ('he's so harsh to us. I suppose it comes of being brought up on his mother's bitter potherbs') and laboured jokes (e.g., 'I'm laughing so much, before I know it I'll be in Chortleton').[10] Plutarch may have a point – Aristophanic characters do sometimes make bad jokes – but by ignoring context he risks overlooking the underlying purpose of his examples. The remark about potherbs, for instance, one of many jokes in *Women* about Euripides' mother being a seller of greens, is part of a broader characterization of the women of Athens as implacably hostile to Euripides.

Plutarch also criticizes Aristophanes for stylistic inconsistency, particularly combining the tragic and the comic, the elevated and the prosaic, and the erudite and the everyday. Characters, he suggests, often do not speak as befits them. He further claims that Aristophanes lacks his much-touted verbal 'ingenuity'; that his roguish characters are simply malicious; that his rustics are idiotic rather than simple; that he avoids romantic love in favour of pure lust. Like Aristotle, Plutarch is guilty of criticizing Aristophanic comedy simply because it differs from the New Comedy more akin to his conservative sensibilities. Ironically his criticisms, taken as a whole, are almost as excessive and inconsistent as the works they disparage.

The Roman rhetorician Quintilian (AD *c.* 35–*c.* 95), writing a little earlier, offers a more positive, less judgemental view:

> Old Comedy is almost alone in preserving the genuine grace of the Attic tongue; moreover, it has a most eloquent freedom of speech: and if it is especially notable for its attacks on vices, it has a great deal of strength in other departments also. It is splendid, elegant, graceful; and nothing else after Homer (who, like Achilles, must always be the exception) is more like oratory, or more suitable for training orators. It has many exponents, but Aristophanes, Eupolis and Cratinus stand out. (*The Orator's Training* 10.1.65–6)

The Formal Structure of Old Comedy

By Aristophanes' day Old Comedy had well-established formal elements and conventions, although Aristophanes (and most likely other comic playwrights) felt free to modify, omit or depart from these up to a point.

A fundamental structural pattern found at expected points in Aristophanes' plays is a scheme of alternation known as the *syzygy*.[11] While it may vary in length, order and complexity, its simplest form is A B A′ B′, where A and A′ are lyric passages corresponding in metre and their number of lines, while B and B′ are similarly corresponding blocks of lines that are spoken or recited.[12]

The plays of Old Comedy contain certain formal units, or elements, appearing in customary sequence. Among Aristophanes' surviving plays these units are most fully represented in *Wasps*. They are as follows:

1. *Prologue*

The prologue, as defined by Aristotle, is all that precedes the entry of the Chorus. Unlike most other elements it has no strict formal requirements. It generally comprises spoken iambic trimeters, although lyric passages may be inserted (e.g., the servant's prayer and Agathon's song in *Women*, 39–57 and 101–29). The prologue may open with dialogue between major characters (e.g., *Women*, *Frogs*, *Birds*, *Lysistrata*) or minor characters (e.g., *Wasps*, *Knights*, *Peace*). Alternatively, it may consist of a speech or monologue by the protagonist (e.g., *Acharnians*, *Clouds*, *Assemblywomen*) or another major character (e.g., *Wealth*). It may then proceed variously. In *Wasps*, a slave addresses the audience directly and explains the situation in Philocleon's house, after which there is a slapstick scene with Philocleon trying to escape. In *Women* and *Frogs* there are encounters with a character who provides advice or assistance (Agathon and Heracles respectively), followed by scenes of buffoonery.

The prologue establishes the opening situation, introduces the main characters and indicates the play's main topical and thematic concerns. Thus in *Wasps* the two slaves discuss their dreams about the deluded Athenian public and its corrupt political leaders, and then describe Philocleon's delusional condition; in *Frogs* we hear one discussion between Dionysus and Xanthias about comic conventions and another between Dionysus and Heracles about tragedy past and present. The prologue may include a change of location. The whole prologue of *Wasps* takes place before Philocleon's house, but in *Women* the action shifts from Agathon's house to the site of the Thesmophoria festival, while in *Frogs* we move from Heracles' house to the underworld.

2. *Parodos*

This is the Entry-Song of the Chorus. The comic Chorus, which numbered twenty-four, would enter via the wings (*eisodoi*). Its arrival is often anticipated in the text. In *Wasps*, for example, Philocleon's old friends, who comprise the Chorus, appear soon after Bdelycleon remarks that they are later than usual (*Wasps* 217–21). The metre and mood of the *parodos* can vary. In *Wasps* the Chorus enters singing in plodding iambic tetrameters to indicate their age and sluggishness. The Choruses of *Acharnians* and *Knights*, by contrast, enter singing bustling trochaic tetrameters to reflect their vigour and aggression. The Initiate-Chorus of *Frogs* sing their *parodos* mainly in the ionic metre associated with their patron god Iacchus. The *parodos* in *Women*, unusually, is in prose.

3. *Agōn*

This is a formal 'contest' or 'debate' in which the Chorus, or a major character, chooses between two parties (*agōn* is the Greek word for 'trial'). In *Wasps* the Chorus decides between Philocleon and Bdelycleon; in *Frogs* Dionysus chooses between Aeschylus and Euripides. Not all plays have an *agōn*. The absence of an *agōn* in *Peace*, for instance, perhaps suggests in formal terms that no arguments for war remain. *Knights*, by contrast, has two proper *agones*. In the convention of the formal *agōn*, the contestant who speaks second is victorious. There are other kinds of competitive scene besides the formal *agōn*. In *Wasps*, for example, after the *agōn* proper there is a trial scene in Philocleon's kitchen. In *Frogs* the whole contest between Euripides and Aeschylus, even outside the *agōn* proper, resembles an expanded *agōn* (*agōn* is also the Greek word for the dramatic competition). Another situation resembling the *agōn* is where a major character presents a case before a hostile audience, such as Mnesilochus' speech before the women in defence of Euripides in *Women*.

The *agōn* is recited rather than spoken. In its fullest manifestation, as in *Wasps*, it comprises nine components arranged in the form A B C D A′ B′ C′ D′ E (the examples are all from *Wasps*):[13]

A. *Ode* (526–45, 'The speaker who will . . . ghosts of parchment-cases'): a stanza sung by the Chorus to encourage both participants.

B. *Katakeleusmos* (546–7, 'Be bold . . . glib persuasive art'): a brief invitation to the first contestant to begin.
C. *Epirrhema* (548–619, 'Well, to get off to . . . scarcely greater than my own!'): the first contestant's speech; in tetrameters (usually anapaestic).
D. *Pnigos* (620–30, 'When people speak . . . damned if I fear you'): a short climactic end to the speech, supposedly recited in a single breath (hence its name, the 'choker').
A′. *Antode* (631–47, 'A most sensible speech . . . convert a hostile jury'): a stanza corresponding to the earlier *ode*, usually praising the first speech.
B′. *Antikatakeleusmos* (648–9, 'You'd better think . . . countering our fury'): an invitation to the second contestant to reply.
C′. *Antepirrhema* (650–718, 'It is a difficult undertaking . . . keeping you shut up'): the second contestant's speech; also in tetrameters.
D′. *Antipnigos* (719–24, 'I want to look after . . . the paymaster's milk'): see D.
E. *Sphragis* (725–9, 'You should never decide . . . whatever you say'): the announcement of the victor, sealing the result (*sphragis* means 'seal').

4. *Parabasis*

The parabasis (literally, 'the stepping forward'), in which the action of the play is suspended, occurs at a point when the stage is empty (although in *Women* two characters remain). It involves the Chorus suspending its dramatic identity – by temporarily removing masks and some elements of costume – and stepping forward to address the audience directly in recitative mode. The parabasis usually occurs somewhere near the middle of the play, but may vary in complexity and length. The parabasis of *Women* is relatively short, and that of *Clouds* simply a single block of lines, while in *Wasps* not only is it fully developed but there is a second, shorter parabasis. The full parabasis has seven parts and may be expressed in the form A B C D E D′ E′. The parabasis proper (B) is a sizeable block of lines in tetrameters (usually anapaestic), with a corresponding introduction, or *kommation* (A), and conclusion, or *pnigos* (C). This is followed by a *syzygy* (D E D′ E′).

The parabasis typically involves praise of the author and the play – most commonly in the parabasis proper (B) – and abuse of well-known public figures to whom the author is ill-disposed. Usually there is some humorous play on the Chorus's identity. In *Wasps*, for example, the Chorus liken their irascible nature and cohesiveness to the behaviour of wasps; in *Birds* the Chorus threaten to defecate on the judges from on high if the play is not awarded first prize. The parabasis also allows the Chorus-Leader seemingly to speak on the playwright's behalf.

5. *Miscellaneous scenes*

The parabasis is followed by a series of scenes, usually farcical, for which there is no technical term. These are generally in iambic trimeters. In some cases, particularly where the protagonist's outrageous plan has turned out well, we see a string of impostors who hope to gain by his success but are promptly drubbed (e.g., *Acharnians*, *Peace*, *Birds*). In such plays we also see the fruits of the hero's plan: usually a celebration and some kind of ritual marriage. In plays where the outcome is still in doubt at the end of the parabasis, the action is more varied. In *Wasps*, Philocleon is re-educated and launched into more glamorous society with hilarious results; in *Women*, Euripides has to intervene in person to rescue his ill-fated relative; and in *Frogs*, Dionysus has yet to decide which tragedian to rescue.

6. *Exodos*

This is the final scene or, more strictly, the actual finale. There are no specific formal requirements for the *exodos*. Some final scenes imitate tragic formal features. In *Wasps* and *Birds*, for example, a tragic-style 'messenger-speech' heralds the return of the protagonist. Usually there are festivities of some kind, although not in *Women* or *Clouds*, both of whose endings are oddly subdued. The actual finale, in which the Chorus makes its exit, varies considerably. In *Wasps* we find a riotous dance, with the characters leading off the Chorus (a first according to Aristophanes). In *Frogs*, by contrast, the closing dactylic hexameters (the metre of epic, but also common in Aeschylean tragedy) suggest a more dignified exit.

An aspect of Old Comedy that contrasts with both its generic rival tragedy and its descendant New Comedy is the active role of the Chorus. In tragedy the Chorus, though present, does not as a rule actively influence the play's action but rather looks on helplessly.[14] In New Comedy the Chorus, which only sings non-dramatic odes between certain scenes, has no physical presence in the play's action. The Chorus of Old Comedy is far more prominent both in the dramatic and non-dramatic parts of the play. The *parodos* usually involves the Chorus interacting significantly with major characters. In some plays the Chorus is integrated into the dramatic action by having the protagonist defend himself before them (*Acharnians*, *Birds* and *Women*). The parabasis, which reinforces some of the play's topical or thematic concerns, is also delivered by the Chorus-Leader and Chorus.

It is almost impossible for us to gain a precise sense of what Aristophanes' Old Comedy meant as an overall experience to its original audience. The Greek dramatic festival was a civic, religious event experienced by citizens far more closely linked to the community as a whole than is remotely possible in our larger, more ethnically and culturally diverse modern democracies. Even in classical Athens, after the city's defeat in the Peloponnesian War, Old Comedy declined rapidly as a genre, as the closeness of the relationship between individual citizens and their city-state decreased. For us the nearest thing to the experience of Aristophanic comedy's original audiences – in feel if not in form or scale – is probably a school or college revue, insofar as it presents strongly topical material to a close-knit community and involves a palpable sense of participation among audience, writer(s) and performers alike.

There are, however, other useful modern parallels for many aspects of Aristophanic comedy. The scholar Ian Storey, for example, asks the reader of Aristophanes to imagine a combination of 'the slapstick of *The Three Stooges*, the song and dance of a Broadway musical, the verbal wit of W. S. Gilbert or of a television show like *Frasier*, the exuberance of Mardi Gras, the open-ended plot line of *The Simpsons*, the parody of a Mel Brooks movie, the political satire of *Doonesbury*, the outrageous sexuality of *The Rocky Horror Picture Show*, and the fantasy of J. R. R. Tolkien wrapped up in the format of a Monty Python movie.'[15] While this farrago of modern comparisons represents a fair attempt to capture the confection of farce, variety, carnival, fantasy, parody, satire, vulgarity and absurdity in Aristophanes' plays, it seems to downplay Aristophanic comedy's form and character as highbrow comic drama. Perhaps the nearest single modern parallel with Aristophanic comedy from contemporary theatre is the work of Tom Stoppard. His *Rosencrantz and Guildenstern are Dead*, for instance, parodies and imitates other texts, most obviously *Hamlet* but also *Waiting for Godot*. It has inconsistency of characterization and action, and involves its own absurd logic (at the start of the play, a coin in a coin-tossing game lands 'heads' eighty-five times in a row and yet Rosencrantz shows no surprise). It indulges in reflexive theatrical games; part of the text is identical to *Hamlet*, while most of it complements its Shakespearean model by presenting the action that might have happened offstage. As with Aristophanes, several of Stoppard's plays are plays of ideas that polemically explore major cultural issues often while presenting comic versions of well-known figures onstage (e.g., Joyce and Lenin in *Travesties*; the philosopher George Moore in *Jumpers*; Wilde and Housman in *The Invention of Love*). If we add Stoppard to Storey's list, we perhaps gain a fuller idea of the form, variety and ingenuity of Aristophanic comedy.

What makes Aristophanic comedy seem so contemporary in its outlook, and gives it enduring relevance, is that its defining qualities – a spirit of inquiry, a determination to question the democratic powers that be, a penchant for extensive cultural reference, a willingness to entertain new ideas, a healthy sense of self-criticism and, of course, a readiness to see the funny side of things – are ones that we generally endorse. What is more, the core values that Aristophanic comedy affirms seem very much to chime with our own. Foremost among these are the freedom of expression, the independence of the human spirit and – last but by no means least – the therapeutic power of laughter.

NOTES

1. Henceforth abbreviated to *Women*.
2. My own translation.
3. Another major festival, the Rural Dionysia, was celebrated within Attica but outside Athens itself. It took place in various towns and villages, such as Piraeus and Eleusis, on different days in the month of Poseidon (late December/early January). The festival comprised various fertility rites, including songs to Dionysus and a procession with a large phallus (as seen in Aristophanes' *Acharnians*), but it also included dramatic performances. While Aristophanes and both Sophocles and Euripides are known to have had plays put on at the Rural Dionysia, it is probable that these were not first performances of new plays (which would very likely have taken place at the City Dionysia and Lenaea).
4. According to Aristotle, Sophocles raised the number of actors from two to three (*Poetics* 1449a), just as Aeschylus had earlier raised the number from one to two. The likely date for the introduction of the third actor is 468 BC, or some time shortly after it.
5. For a detailed discussion of the issue, see D. Bain, *Actors and Audiences* (Oxford, 1977).
6. Indeed Menander's New Comedy takes its illusionistic credo to such lengths that one ancient scholar felt compelled to write, 'Oh life, Oh Menander! Which of you imitates the other?'
7. My translation.
8. It is their universality that makes poetry and philosophy *theoretical*; *theoria* ('contemplation') is described by Aristotle, in his *Nichomachean Ethics*, as man's highest form of activity.
9. In the handbook *On Style*, wrongly attributed to fourth-century scholar Demetrius of Phaleron (it is probably from the second or first century BC), Aristophanes is praised on a number of occasions for his charm (*charis*) and wit.
10. The translations are my own.
11. Various scholars have tried to trace this structural pattern back to a prototypical comic revel or *kōmos*.

12. Recited (as opposed to spoken) lines would have been delivered with some kind of musical accompaniment in a manner generally termed 'recitative'.
13. In formal terms the English translation does not correspond exactly to the Greek components of the *agōn*. Thus the *katakeleusmos* appears to belong with the *ode* that precedes it in the English, but is in a different metre (anapaestic rather than the iambo-choriambic of the *ode*) in the Greek; conversely, the *epirrhema* and *pnigos* appear metrically different in the English but are in the same (anapaestic) metre in the Greek.
14. While this is true of extant tragedy from the 430s and 420s, the period at which tragedy seems to have conformed most strictly to what we might call tragic conventions, it is not as true of Aeschylus. In *Eumenides*, for example, the eponymous chorus, who are non-human and aggressive towards the hero, seem much more like an Old Comic chorus than a typical tragic chorus.
15. I. C. Storey, 'Poets, Politicians and Perverts: Personal Humour in Aristophanes', *Classics Ireland* 5 (1998), p. 85.

Further Reading

Greek Texts of Aristophanes and Commentaries

There are editions of all eleven plays with Greek text, translation and commentary by A. H. Sommerstein (Warminster, 1980–2001). There are very good individual editions (Greek text and detailed commentary) of *Wasps* by D. M. MacDowell (Oxford, 1971), *Women at the Thesmophoria* by S. Olson (Oxford, 2004) and *Frogs* by K.J. Dover (Oxford, 1993).

Aristophanes and his Plays

K. J. Dover, *Aristophanic Comedy* (London, 1972)

K. McLeish, *The Theatre of Aristophanes* (London, 1980)

E. W. Handley, 'Comedy' in P. E. Easterling and B. M. W. Knox (eds.), *The Cambridge History of Classical Literature*, vol. 1 (Cambridge, 1985), pp. 355–498

R. Harriott, *Aristophanes: Poet and Dramatist* (Oxford, 1986)

K. J. Reckford, *Aristophanes' Old-and-New Comedy I: Six Essays in Perspective* (Chapel Hill, 1987)

A. M. Bowie, *Myth, Ritual, Comedy* (Cambridge, 1993)

P. A. Cartledge, *Aristophanes and his Theatre of the Absurd* (3rd edn; Bristol, 1995)

D. M. MacDowell, *Aristophanes and Athens* (Oxford, 1995)

E. Segal (ed.), *Oxford Readings in Aristophanes* (Oxford, 1996)

Aristophanes and Ancient Theatre Production

C. W. Dearden, *The Stage of Aristophanes* (London, 1976)
D. Bain, *Actors and Audiences* (Oxford, 1977)
L. M. Stone, *Costume in Aristophanic Comedy* (New York, 1981)
A. W. Pickard-Cambridge, *The Dramatic Festivals of Athens* (3rd edn, revised by J. Gould and D. M. Lewis; Oxford, 1988)
C. F. Russo, *Aristophanes: An Author for the Stage* (London, 1994)
E. G. Csapo and W. J. Slater, *The Context of Ancient Drama* (Ann Arbor, 1994)
D. Wiles, *Greek Theatre Performance: An Introduction* (Cambridge, 2000)

A Note on the Revised Translations

For the translator, attempting to capture the poetry and humour of Aristophanes' plays is a formidable challenge. First, one must work under the shadow of Robert Frost's famously negative pronouncement, 'poetry is what gets lost in translation'. Secondly, as everyone knows, jokes are notoriously difficult to put into another language. In addition, one is often at a loss as to what to do with some of the more obscure topical references of Aristophanic comedy. In spite of all this, David Barrett's 1964 translations are outstanding for their accessibility, wit and charm. They succeed, with a remarkable lightness of touch, in capturing the freshness, the comic spirit and the poetic qualities of Aristophanes' original plays.

Barrett's translations have received only minor alterations. My primary aim in revising them has been to update them where necessary for the contemporary reader in terms of idiom, topical reference and jokes. I have also pursued a few specific objectives. One is to reflect, wherever possible, the stylistic pitch of the original Greek in the English, particularly where Aristophanes uses the language of tragedy (while Barrett has done this with most specific quotations, he has not with a small number of more general, or subtle, imitations of tragic or other kinds of poetic language). I have also tried, in a few cases, to render the Greek more accurately in English where it is possible to do so without sacrificing readability or losing the underlying sense of the original. Finally, I have restored the line order of the translation, and very occasionally the attribution of speakers (this is not indicated in the manuscripts), in the few instances where Barrett departs from the general consensus. To this end, with one or two exceptions, I have followed Alan Sommerstein's excellent editions of the individual plays published by Aris & Phillips: *Wasps* 1983; *Thesmophoriazusae* (translated here as *Women at the Thesmophoria*) 1994; and *Frogs* 1996. The line numbers of the original Greek text are indicated in the margin of the translations at ten-line intervals. Inevitably, there are some instances where, because of the word order in the translation, such numbering is approximate.

WASPS

PREFACE TO *WASPS*

When *Wasps* was performed at the Lenaea festival of 422 BC, Aristophanes was still only in his early-to-mid twenties. At the time, Athens and Sparta, and their respective allies, had been at war for nine years. For the moment, though, actual fighting was restricted primarily to northern Greece, where the energetic Spartan general Brasidas was hoping to relieve his beleaguered garrison at Scione, a situation to which the play alludes (210). Like many of Aristophanes' early comedies, *Wasps* focuses on a single political issue, namely the abuse of the judicial system by Cleon, the demagogue whom Aristophanes had savagely attacked in his *Knights* two years previously.

At the time of the play the Athenian judicial system worked as follows. Every year a list of 6,000 jurors was drawn up from volunteers, who had to be citizens over the age of thirty. Juries for each trial were selected from this list by lot. The size of the jury varied from a minimum of two hundred up to five hundred, but in certain important cases it could be larger. There were several courts each having assigned to it a specific magistrate (*archōn*) and set of jurors. Magistrates were not legal specialists but ordinary citizens chosen by lot for one year; they simply chaired the proceedings. In the cases themselves, the prosecutor spoke first and then the defendant. Neither party was represented by a lawyer, but witnesses and friends could be called (and usually were). The time limit for each side was fixed by a water-clock, a vessel with a small hole. After speeches, the jury voted by placing a pebble in one of two urns marked for conviction and acquittal respectively. The majority vote carried, with a tie counting as an acquittal. Some offences entailed fixed penalties, otherwise the prosecution and defence would both propose a penalty (the defence's would naturally be lighter) and make supporting speeches. The jury would then vote again. *Wasps* itself offers the only evidence for this procedure: jurors each had a wax tablet on which they would draw a long line for the prosecution's sentence or a short one for the defence's.

Jurors were paid. The amount was three obols per day. This was not a good rate of pay but it was enough to attract older citizens with little other means of income. What is so amusing about Philocleon's obsessive jury service is the indiscriminate zeal with which he convicts those who come before him. The main reason Bdelycleon wants to dissuade his father from jury service is that he fears Philocleon and his fellow jurors are controlled by unscrupulous demagogues, in particular Cleon, who had raised jury pay from two obols per day to three. The argument runs as follows: most jurors are so dependent on their pay that they become extremely suggestible, particularly when men such as Cleon either personally prosecute or publicly decry defendants who are their political opponents (the farcical trial of the dog Labes in Philocleon's kitchen humorously illustrates the point). Bdelycleon does not blame the jurors themselves – Aristophanes emphasizes the poverty of the Chorus, who do not have a wealthy son to support them, as Philocleon does – but he does expose their irresponsible role in a corrupt process.

Wasps is not just an attack on Cleon and the jury system. While the jury system forms the background to the first two-thirds of the play's action, the final third is effectively a comedy of manners. The sophisticated Bdelycleon tries to teach the simple, old-fashioned Philocleon how to behave in refined social circles; we then see the amusing consequences. Some hints of earlier topical concerns remain. The fellow guests at the drinking party Philocleon attends are in fact the loathsome Cleon and his cronies. Philocleon also ends up having a court summons issued against him for violent conduct. But the prospect of going to court in no way dampens the play's riotous, exuberant conclusion.

What unites the two parts of the play is the sustained conflict between unruly father and concerned son. As Aristophanes himself suggests, the play, pared down to its essentials, works like 'a little fable' (64). Philocleon starts the play as a juror possessed. When Bdelycleon finally cures this compulsive disorder, he tries to turn his father into a respectable man-about-town. Philocleon, however, ends up as an equally compulsive reveller. Proving himself to be utterly incorrigible, Philocleon ends the play literally spiralling out of control (in a dancing competition) and off the stage. Ironically, for a play that begins as a fable about an obsessive juror, we are left not so much with a moral as an open verdict: both Bdelycleon and Philocleon are caught in a vicious circle, at once disquieting and comical, in which the former keeps failing to learn that the latter is incapable of reform.

The play starts with two drowsy slaves talking about their recent dreams. This opening exchange contains significant clues about how *Wasps* works. Both dreams are premonitions about the city's future, and involve the kind of phenomena we find in the play itself, particularly the symbolic transformation of prominent political figures and ordinary Athenian citizens into animals. The play too is presented as something of a cautionary tale, with Athenian war veterans appearing as wasps and the demagogue Cleon thinly disguised, in the kitchen trial, as 'The Dog' (a well-known soubriquet of Cleon's). The two antithetically named main characters – Philocleon means 'Cleon-lover' and Bdelycleon 'Cleon-loather' – carry an allusive, metaphoric significance. Bdelycleon's fruitless endeavours to correct the delusional Philocleon seemingly reflect the vain efforts of the young, well-meaning poet Aristophanes to enlighten his older, blinkered fellow citizens. The parallels between Aristophanes and Bdelycleon and between Philocleon and Aristophanes' largely pro-Cleonian audience – Cleon was, after all, in office at the time – are reinforced in the play's formal debate. Bdelycleon describes his attempt to turn Philocleon from supporting Cleon in terms of the wider efforts of comic playwrights to convince a deluded Athenian public (650–51).

But for all its hints about Aristophanes' own frustration with the political short-sightedness of (most of) his audience, *Wasps* remains sanguine in its outlook. By making Bdelycleon something of a killjoy and presenting Philocleon as a lovable rogue, Aristophanes is careful to coax as well as to censure his audience. Philocleon is one of Aristophanes' most likable creations. A protean figure, he is likened to various animals, including a rat, a limpet, a jackdaw, a mouse and a honeybee. He is wily and tireless. When we first see him, he pops out of various parts of the house, like a jack-in-the-box, in his numerous bids to escape. He then tries to get out by tying himself under a donkey, emulating Odysseus' escape from the Cyclops. While he sometimes behaves like certain tragic figures who share his delusional condition – Euripides' love-stricken heroines Phaedra and Stheneboea, and Sophocles' possessed, stubborn, suicidal hero Ajax – what distinguishes Philocleon from such tragic counterparts is his capacity to bounce back. Of all Aristophanic heroes, he is arguably the fullest embodiment of the comic spirit – triumphantly and defiantly incorrigible, imperishable and irrepressible.

CHARACTERS

SOSIAS, XANTHIAS } *slaves of Philocleon and Bdelycleon*

BDELYCLEON, *a youngish Athenian*

PHILOCLEON, *his father*

FIRST DOG

A REVELLER

A BAKING WOMAN

A CITIZEN

CHORUS OF OLD MEN, *the 'Wasps' of the play*

SUBSIDIARY CHORUS OF BOYS

Silent Characters

MIDAS, PHRYX, MASYNTIAS } *slaves of Philocleon and Bdelycleon*

SECOND DOG, *called Labes*

DARDANIS, *a flute-girl*

CHAEREPHON, *the philosopher*

WITNESS, *brought by the Citizen*

COOKING UTENSILS, *witnesses at the trial of Second Dog*

PUPPIES, *belonging to Second Dog*

REVELLERS

THREE SONS OF CARCINUS, *all tragedians (like their father)*

ACT ONE

Scene 1: *Outside a house in Athens.*

[*The scene opens just before dawn. Makeshift barricades have been placed in front of the doors and windows, and the house is enveloped in an enormous net. There is an outside staircase to the flat part of the roof (not covered by the net) where* BDELYCLEON *is sleeping. The two slaves,* XANTHIAS *and* SOSIAS, *sit propped up against the wall of the house asleep. Suddenly* SOSIAS *stirs and yawns. He tries to wake* XANTHIAS.]

SOSIAS Xanthias, you old rascal, what do you think you're doing?

XANTHIAS [*waking*] Relieving the night watch, they call it.

SOSIAS Earning yourself a beating, more like. Don't you realize what kind of creature we're guarding?

XANTHIAS I know, but I feel like shaking off dull care for a bit.

SOSIAS Well, that's your look out. Though, oddly enough, I'm feeling deliciously drowsy myself.

[*They both settle down and fall asleep again. Soon* SOSIAS *begins to toss and turn in his sleep.* XANTHIAS *stirs. He then tries to wake* SOSIAS.]

XANTHIAS Have you gone mad? Or have you become a Corybant?[1]

SOSIAS No, just asleep. Though I won't deny there was something Bacchic about it. [*He displays a wine flask.*]

XANTHIAS Looks as if we're fellow devotees [*displaying another*]. Talk about sleep assailing the eyelids, it was like trying to hold off the whole Persian army. Funny dream I had just now.

SOSIAS Me too! Like none I've ever had before. But tell me about yours first.

XANTHIAS I dreamt that I saw an enormous eagle swoop down into the Agora, and it snatched up a copper-coloured snake and flew off with it up to the sky. And then suddenly the eagle turned into Cleonymus. Then the snake turned into his shield, and he dropped it![2]

SOSIAS So Cleonymus is just like a riddle.

XANTHIAS How so?

SOSIAS One might ask of him, 'What creature is it that drops its guard, on land, at sea and in the sky?'[3]

XANTHIAS Seriously, I'm worried. It doesn't bode well, a dream like that.

SOSIAS Don't give it another thought. There's no harm in it, I'm sure.

XANTHIAS No harm, in a man losing his equipment?[4] What was *your* dream, anyway?

SOSIAS Oh, mine was a big one. About Athens itself – the whole ship of state.

XANTHIAS Well, anchors away! Let's hear it.

SOSIAS Soon after I'd fallen asleep I saw a whole lot of sheep, and they were holding an assembly on the Pnyx;[5] they all had little cloaks on, and staves in their hands, and these sheep were all listening to a rant by a rapacious-looking creature with a figure like a whale and a voice like a scalded sow.

XANTHIAS No, no!

SOSIAS What's the matter?

XANTHIAS Don't tell me any more, I can't bear it. Your dream stinks of a tanner's yard.[6]

SOSIAS And this disgusting whale-creature had a pair of scales and it was weighing out bits of fat from a carcass.

XANTHIAS Dividing up the body politic[7] – I see it all. Horrible!

SOSIAS And then I noticed that Theorus[8] was sitting on the ground at the creature's feet, only he had the head of a raven. And Alcibiades turned to me and said, 'Look, Theolus is tlansformed into a laven!'[9]

XANTHIAS You've got Alcibiades' lisp down to a tee.

SOSIAS Yes, but isn't it a bit sinister, Theorus turning into a raven?

XANTHIAS On the contrary. It's a very good sign.

SOSIAS How so?

XANTHIAS Well, first he's a man, then he suddenly turns into a raven. Isn't it obvious what that means? He's going to croak.

SOSIAS I should make you my personal dream-interpreter, at two obols a day!

XANTHIAS Now look, I'd better tell the audience what this is all about. Just a few words by way of introduction. [*To the audience*][10] You mustn't expect anything too grand from us, but you won't get any crude Megarian stuff either. And I'm afraid we can't afford a couple of slaves with baskets full of nuts to throw to you. You won't see Heracles being cheated of his dinner; we're not going to hurl abuse at Euripides; and we don't intend to make mincemeat of Cleon this time – even if he *has* covered himself in glory[11] lately. No, this is just a little fable, with a moral; not too highbrow for you, we hope, but a bit more demanding than the usual knock-about stuff. The big man asleep up there on the roof,[12] he's our master. He's ordered us to stand guard over his father and keep him locked inside, so that he can't escape. You see, the old man's suffering from a very peculiar disease.[13] I'm sure none of you has heard of it, and you'll never guess what it is unless we tell you. Still, would you like to try? [*He pretends to wait for suggestions from imagined spectators.*] What's that Amynias?[14] A compulsive dice player? No, it's not 'cubomania'.

SOSIAS He's judging by his own failing.

XANTHIAS You're right though, it is a kind of mania, an addiction of sorts. What's that Sosias is telling Dercylus? That he's an alcoholic?[15]

SOSIAS No, no! Only the best people suffer from that.

XANTHIAS Nicostratus[16] here wants to know if he's a 'xenophile'.

SOSIAS Good god no, Nicostratus! He doesn't accommodate strangers the way Philoxenus[17] does.

XANTHIAS No, you're all wrong, you'll never get it. Keep quiet then, and I'll tell you what the old man's trouble is. He's what they call a 'trialophile' – the worst case I've ever come across. He *yearns* to sit in judgment, and *pines*[18] if he's denied a front-row seat. He never sleeps a wink at night – or if he does drop off, his spirit flutters round the courtroom clock till he wakes up again. He's so used to clutching his voting-pebble that he wakes up with his thumb and two fingers glued together, as though he'd been sprinkling incense for a new-moon[19] sacrifice. If he goes past Demos' house and sees what someone's written on the gatepost – you know the sort of thing, 'O Demos, how I dote on you!' – he goes and writes underneath: 'O urn, how I vote in you!'[20] It's no joke. Once he complained that the cock was late calling him – and it was well before midnight! He said the retiring magistrates must have bribed it because their accounts were coming up for review the next day. Oh, he had it bad: as soon as supper was over he'd shout for his shoes, and off he'd go to court, sleeping through the small hours at the head of the queue, clinging to the doorpost like a limpet. And he's so harsh! He scratches a long line on his tablet every time they get a conviction – full damages.[21] Honestly, he comes home with enough wax under his fingernails to stock a beehive. He's so afraid of running out of voting pebbles that he keeps a whole beach of them inside the house. Such is his madness: the more you warn him, the more he goes to court.[22] That's why we've had to bolt him in and guard the house, in case he gets out. His son can't cope with this disease of his. He tried talking to him, he tried all kinds of arguments to stop him wearing his juryman's cloak or to get him to stay at home, but he just wouldn't listen. So then he tried all the usual treatments for madness. He gave him a ritual washing and carried out all the purification rites: no use at all. After that he took him to the priests of Bacchus, to see if they could work him up into a Corybantic frenzy, and cure him that way, but the old man just escaped and burst back into the courtroom, drum in hand, to hear a trial. In the end, as none of these rites seemed to do him any good, the young master sailed him over to

Aegina and booked him into the Temple of Asclepius[23] for the night: but next morning, at the crack of dawn – there he was at the courtroom door! Since then we haven't been letting him out at all. But he kept slipping out through the drains or chimneys, so we've had to stuff every hole we could find with bits of old rag. Then he drove little pegs into the courtyard wall and hopped up them like a jackdaw and then over the top. So now we've covered the whole house with netting and we're guarding him day and night. The old man's name, by the way, is Philocleon – I kid you not! And his son's called Bdelycleon;[24] he's all right, although he can be a bit high and mighty.

[BDELYCLEON *stirs.*]

BDELYCLEON Xanthias! Sosias! Are you asleep?

XANTHIAS Oh god! [*He shakes the dozing* SOSIAS.]

SOSIAS What is it?

XANTHIAS It's Bdelycleon. He's up.

BDELYCLEON Come round to the back, one of you, quickly! My father's got into the kitchen and he's scurrying about like a rat. Keep an eye on the waste pipe, and see that he doesn't get out that way.

[SOSIAS *runs up the stairs.*]

And, you, stand close to the door.

XANTHIAS Yes, boss.

BDELYCLEON Good god, what's that noise in the chimney?

[PHILOCLEON *pokes his head out through the chimney.*]

Who's there?

PHILOCLEON A puff of smoke.

BDELYCLEON Smoke? Why, what are they burning?

PHILOCLEON Figwood.[25]

BDELYCLEON That accounts for the acrid smell. Phew! Go on, get back inside. Where's the cover? [*He replaces the chimney cover, ramming it down on the old man's head.*] Down you go. I'd better put this log on top as well. You'll have to think up another bright idea. Puff of smoke indeed! Now they'll really call me 'son of Smoke'.[26]

XANTHIAS Look out, he's pushing at the door.

BDELYCLEON Hold him, push as hard as you can – I'll come

and help. [*He heads back down.*] Hold on to the latch – and mind he doesn't pull the peg out.

PHILOCLEON [*from within*] What are you doing? Let me out! I have to get to court, or Dracontides[27] will get off.

XANTHIAS And you couldn't bear that, could you?

PHILOCLEON When I went to Delphi, the oracle said that if ever I acquitted a man, I would shrivel up and wither away.

XANTHIAS Apollo save us, what a prophecy!

PHILOCLEON Come on, please let me out, or I'll explode!

XANTHIAS Never, by god, you Cleon-lover!

PHILOCLEON I'll gnaw through the net.

XANTHIAS You haven't got any teeth.

[BDELYCLEON *returns from the roof.*]

PHILOCLEON Alas! If only I could slay you? But how? Someone give me a sword this instant – or a juryman's tablet! [*A scuffling noise follows.*]

BDELYCLEON The man is planning something truly drastic![28]

PHILOCLEON No, no. I just thought I'd take the donkey down to the market and sell him – the panniers too; it's the first day of the month.[29]

BDELYCLEON Couldn't I do that for you?

PHILOCLEON Not as well as I could.

BDELYCLEON Not as well – better. All right, you can let the donkey out.

XANTHIAS That was a sly excuse to get out.

BDELYCLEON Ah, but it didn't come to anything: I saw through it. I think I'd better go in and fetch the donkey myself, in case the old boy slips out. [*He goes in and tries to come out with the donkey, but it seems reluctant to move.*] Why do you weep? Because you're going to be sold? Come on! Why these groans?[30] Anyone would think you had some Odysseus clinging to your underside.[31]

XANTHIAS My god, he has too! There's someone under there!

BDELYCLEON Where? Let me see.

XANTHIAS Here he is, up this end.

BDELYCLEON Now then, what's going on? Who on earth are you?

PHILOCLEON No-man.[32]

BDELYCLEON No-man, eh? Where are you from?

PHILOCLEON Ithaca.

BDELYCLEON Well, No-man, you can get yourself back to No-man's-land, sharpish. Pull him out from under there, quickly. Oh, the dirty old sod – look where he's stuffed his head. I never thought we'd see our old donkey[33] discharge a juryman!

PHILOCLEON Let me be, or we'll come to blows.

BDELYCLEON What is there to fight about?

XANTHIAS He'll fight you over the proverbial 'donkey's shadow'.[34]

BDELYCLEON You're a rotten, devious, wayward old man.

PHILOCLEON Rotten? Me? You don't realize just how tasty I am! Wait till you've sampled stuffed juryman's belly.

BDELYCLEON Get that donkey back into the house, and yourself too.

PHILOCLEON [*as he and the donkey are pushed back inside*] Help, help! My fellow jurors, Cleon, help!

BDELYCLEON Shout as much as you like once I get this door shut.

[XANTHIAS *helps him to close and relock the door.*]

Now, pile a load of those stones up against the door. And get that peg back into its socket properly. That's right. Now, up with the bar. Heave! That's it. And now, quickly, roll that big mortar up against it.

[*They mop their brows.*]

XANTHIAS Hey, where did that come from? A great chunk of dirt hit me right on the head!

BDELYCLEON [*looking up at the eaves*] Perhaps there's a mouse up there, knocked a bit of rubble down.

XANTHIAS Some mouse! Somebody's pet juryman, more like. Look, there he is, coming up through the tiles.

BDELYCLEON Oh no, he thinks he's a sparrow. He'll take flight any minute now. Where's that bird-net? Shoo, shoo, get back inside! [*They clamber up and push the old man's head back, replacing the tiles.*] I'd as soon keep guard over Scione[35] as try to keep my old man indoors!

XANTHIAS Well, we've shooed him in again. He can't slip past us any more. Now couldn't we just have a tiny bit of sleep?

BDELYCLEON What! Don't you realize that all the other jurymen will be along any minute now to call for him?

XANTHIAS But it's only just beginning to get light!

BDELYCLEON Then they must have got up late this morning. They usually turn up soon after midnight, carrying lamps and crooning old easy-listening favourites by Phrynichus.[36] That's how they call him out.

XANTHIAS Well, we'll soon get rid of them. We can throw stones at them, if need be.

BDELYCLEON You poor deluded fool, if you provoke this gang of old geezers it'll be like stirring up a wasps' nest. They've all got sharp stings in their butts – and they know how to use them! They whirr and dart around and fly at you like sparks from a bonfire.

XANTHIAS Don't you worry – as long as I've got enough stones I can scatter a whole swarm of jurymen, sting or no sting.

[*Despite what they say, both characters quickly fall asleep again. Very soon afterwards a curious buzzing sound is heard. This gradually becomes the wheezing and murmuring of a group of aged jurymen, who form the Chorus. They are guided by their sons, who are small boys,*[37] *carrying dim lamps. The jurymen are dressed as wasps, with stings protruding behind them. Over their wasp-costumes they wear tattered jurymen's cloaks. As they advance, the* CHORUS-LEADER *encourages his frail companions.*]

CHORUS-LEADER Come along, quick march![38] Commias, old friend, you're getting left behind. You've changed a bit since the old days – you used to be as tough as old boots. Now even Charinades can walk better than you. Ah, Strymodorus, there you are. My dear fellow juryman, how are you? And what about Euergides, is he with us? And Chabes from Phlya? Ah, here they come – well, well. All that's left of the old battalion, eh? Remember that night in Byzantium, when you and I were on sentry duty together – we snitched the old girl's kneading trough and used it for firewood, remember? Nice bit of pimpernel we had for supper that night. Cooked it up ourselves over the fire. Well, men, we'd better hurry up – Laches is on trial today.[39] They say he's got wads of money tucked away, that Laches. And you heard what Cleon, our Great Protector, said yesterday: 'Come in good time, with three days' supply of bile in your knapsacks. You're the ones he's wronged,' he said, 'and you're the ones who are going to make him pay.' Well, comrades, we'd best be pushing on, if we're going to get there by dawn. And mind how you go – you still need your lamps. There may be a stone lurking somewhere, waiting to trip you up.

BOY Father, father, look out, it's muddy here.

CHORUS-LEADER Get a twig and trim that wick a bit, son. I can't see a thing.

BOY But I can pull it up with my finger, see.

CHORUS-LEADER What are you thinking of, reckless boy, using your finger like that? Don't you realize there's an oil shortage? [*He clouts the boy.*] It's all very well for you, you don't have to pay for it.

BOY If you're going to start using your knuckles on us, we'll blow the lamps out and go home – and you can find your own way in the dark, splashing around in the mud like a load of old peewits.

CHORUS-LEADER I've punished bigger people than you in my time, son, and don't you forget it. [*He slips in a puddle.*] Ugh! Now I've gone and tramped right through the mud. There's rain on the way. Mark my words, within the next four days there'll be a real downpour. See that snuff on the wick? It's a sure sign. Oh well, it'll be good for the fruit trees. They want bringing on a bit. A bit of rain and a north wind is what they need. That's funny: here we are at Philocleon's house and there's no sign of him. Not like him to be a shirker. He's usually first in the line, singing tunes by Phrynichus – he's a great one for the old songs.[40] Let's stop and sing to him now. That ought to bring him out.

CHORUS

Is there no one at the door?
This has not occurred before!
What has happened to him overnight?

Some disaster, it is clear –
Did his slippers disappear?
Did he stumble, fumbling for the light?

Did he stub his little toe?
That's a nasty thing, you know,
And can give you problems, if you're old.
If the toe is badly maimed,
And the ankle gets inflamed,
It may harm the groin, so I've been told.

It's extremely hard to say
What is keeping him away;
He's the keenest stinger of us all.
No appeal can make him blench.
When he's sitting on the bench –
Might as well make speeches to a wall!

But if I am not mistaken
It's because he was so shaken
By the plea submitted yesterday.
Naturally it was all lies,
Still it brought tears to our eyes,
And the villain nearly got away.

But we nailed him in the end;
So get up, my dear old friend,
Do not punish yourself any more:
There's a very juicy case,
A conspirator from Thrace,
And we must not let him flee the law.

CHORUS-LEADER Come along, boy, come along.

BOY Father, may I ask you for something?

CHORUS-LEADER Of course, what is it you want, son? Marbles, eh?

BOY No, papa, I'd like some figs – they're much nicer.

CHORUS-LEADER Figs! I'll see you hanged first!

BOY All right, then, I won't come any further. I'm going home.

CHORUS-LEADER Figs indeed! Don't you realize I have to buy porridge and firewood and meat for the three of us, all out of my jury pay? And you ask me for *figs*!

BOY

Father, what if no jury sits today?
How, in that case, are we to feed ourselves?
Would we not then be in the direst straits?

CHORUS-LEADER Ye gods, what a dreadful thought. I don't know where our dinner would come from.

BOY

Wherefore, o mother, didst thou give me birth?

CHORUS-LEADER To give your father misery.

BOY

What profit dost thou bring, o empty purse?
Alas, alas! Ours is but to weep.[41]

[*At this point* PHILOCLEON *appears at a small upper window, from which he has removed part of the barricade.*]

PHILOCLEON

Oh with what anguish in my soul
I've heard you through my tiny hole!
How inexpressibly I yearn
To join you at the voting-urn!

I long to come to court with you
Some solid, lasting harm to do;
But now, alas, it cannot be,
For I am under lock and key.

Would that some god, with blinding stroke,
Convert me to a cloud of smoke!
Like politicians' words I'd rise
In gaseous vapour to the skies.

In pity for my sufferings dire
Scorch me, Zeus, with heavenly fire!
Breathe on me with your breath divine –
And serve with vinegar and brine.

Or turn me, if it be thy will,
To stone – that suits me better still.
Part of the courthouse wall I'd be
And then they'd count the votes on me.[42]

CHORUS Who is it that keeps you shut up in there?
[PHILOCLEON *remains silent.*]
Tell us, we're your friends.

PHILOCLEON My son, but don't talk so loud. He's asleep out the front there. So keep your voices down.

CHORUS But why is he doing it? What's his motive?

PHILOCLEON He won't allow me to go to court: he won't let me do harm to anybody. He wants to give me an easy life, he says. I've never heard such nonsense. I don't want an easy life.

CHORUS Outrageous! It's a threat to democracy! He'd never dare say such things unless he was plotting to overthrow the constitution. Traitor! Conspirator! You must try to find a way out. Can't you get down without him seeing you?

PHILOCLEON What way out is there? See if you can find one – I'll do anything. I'm desperate. If only I could get to court! I long to file past the screens again, with the pebble in my hand!

CHORUS Couldn't you tunnel a way through the wall and come out disguised in rags, like wily Odysseus?

PHILOCLEON They've stopped up all the holes: there isn't a chink a gnat could squeeze through. You'll have to think of something else – I'm not made of cream cheese.

CHORUS Remember the Naxos campaign, and the way you stole those spits and climbed down the wall?

PHILOCLEON Yes, but things were different then. I was a young man, quick-footed and light-fingered – at the peak of my powers. And I wasn't under guard; it was easy to get away.

This place is besieged: it's crawling with heavy infantry blocking my line of retreat. There are two of them down by the door, watching every move I make. They've got spits. Anyone would think I was the cat making off with tomorrow's meat!

CHORUS Come on, you've got to think up some way of getting out, quickly – it's getting light.

PHILOCLEON I'll have to gnaw through the net, I suppose. May Dictynna[43] forgive me!

CHORUS Spoken like a true soldier! Onward to freedom! By the right, close jaws!

[PHILOCLEON *gets to work on the net with what teeth he has left. He manages to remove a bit more of the wooden barricade, and can get his head and shoulders through.*]

PHILOCLEON I've gnawed a hole in it, but don't make a sound. We must make sure Bdelycleon doesn't catch us.

CHORUS Don't worry about him. One grunt out of him and we'll give him something to grunt about. We'll make him run for his life. That'll teach him to disrespect the ballot box! Now, tie that cord to the window, and the other end round yourself, and let yourself down. Be brave! Be a regular Diopeithes![44]

PHILOCLEON But what do I do if they spot me when I'm halfway down, and try and haul me back inside?

CHORUS Don't worry, we'll come to the rescue – won't we, boys? Hearts of oak are we all, and we'll fight till we fall. They'll never be able to keep you in. We'll show them a thing or two.

PHILOCLEON All right. [*He attaches the cord.*] Here I come. I'm relying on you. And . . . if anything should happen to me, lift me gently, and spare a tear for my corpse. Then bury me under the dear old courtroom floor.

CHORUS Nothing's going to happen to you. Come on down bravely, with a prayer to your very own patron god.

PHILOCLEON

O Lycus,[45] lord and hero, let me turn to you in prayer:
It really is remarkable how many tastes we share.
You love the tears of suppliants, no sound pleases you more,

And that is why you choose to live beside the courtroom door.
Have pity on your neighbour now, and lend your aid divine,
And I will swear no more to piss or fart behind your shrine.
[*He climbs out and begins to descend.*]

BDELYCLEON [*waking suddenly*] Hey you, wake up!

XANTHIAS What's the matter?

BDELYCLEON I thought I heard a sort of noise. Is the old man trying to give you the slip again?

XANTHIAS [*looking up and seeing* PHILOCLEON] No, by heaven, he's letting himself down on a rope!

BDELYCLEON Hey, what are you doing, you utter rascal? Don't you dare come down! [*To* XANTHIAS] Quick, get up the rope and whack him with the harvest wreath. That'll make him beat a retreat.

PHILOCLEON [*now halfway down*] Stop him! Anyone got a case coming up this year? Smicythion! Tisiades![46] Chremon! Pheredeipnos![47]

[BDELYCLEON, *meanwhile, has entered the house by the front door. He now appears at the upper window and starts to tug at the rope.*]

Quick, to the rescue, or they'll have me back inside!

[*The* CHORUS *prepare for battle as* XANTHIAS, *halfway up the rope, whacks* PHILOCLEON *from below with the harvest wreath while* BDELYCLEON *tugs him from above.*]

CHORUS

Comrades, why are we delaying
When we should be up and slaying?
Turn, your deadly stings displaying,
  Wave them in the air!

Let no reckless fool provoke us,
From our nest attempt to smoke us –
We will brook no hocus pocus!
  Let our foes beware!

Retribution we agree on!
Run, boys, run along to Cleon!
We all know whose side he'll be on!
  Go on, fetch him out.

Here's a man who's roused to fury –
Stops us sitting on the jury –
But we wasps will soon make sure he
  Never sits again!

[*The* BOYS *run off, shouting. The* CHORUS *mill around like angry wasps, buzzing noisily.*]

BDELYCLEON [*trying to make himself heard*] Gentlemen! *Gentlemen*! Listen to me! And stop all that buzzing!

CHORUS We'll buzz all we like!

BDELYCLEON I am not going to let him go.

CHORUS Shame! This is scandalous! It's bare-faced tyranny. O my city! O vile Theorus, and every other brownnoser who champions us!

XANTHIAS Look sir, they've got stings.

BDELYCLEON They have indeed – as Philippus found out at his trial.[48]

CHORUS-LEADER And as *you're* going to find out in a minute. Wasps! About *turn*! Present *stings*! By the right, in reverse, quick march! Keep in line there! [*They close in on* XANTHIAS.] Now then, let him have it! Put some gall into it! Show him what a wasps' nest he's stirred up!

[XANTHIAS *hastily drops to the ground.* PHILOCLEON *follows him down, but* XANTHIAS *grabs him and uses him as a shield.*]

XANTHIAS I don't fancy a fight with this lot. I don't like the look of those stings of theirs one bit.

CHORUS-LEADER Let go of the man, or – I warn you – you'll be envying tortoises for their hard shells.[49]

[XANTHIAS *releases* PHILOCLEON.]

PHILOCLEON Now then, my fellow jurymen, my savage-hearted wasps! Some of you go for his backside: let him have it, that's the way! You others, surround him. Jab at his eyes and fingers!

[*The* CHORUS *attack*. XANTHIAS *tries to seize* PHILOCLEON, *but is surrounded.* PHILOCLEON *makes a dash for freedom.*]

BDELYCLEON [*from the window*] Midas, Phryx, Masyntias! Here, quickly, get hold of him!

[*Three* SLAVES *rush from the house and grab* PHILOCLEON.]

And don't let him go, d'you hear, or it's chains and no dinner for you. Don't mind them – they make a lot of noise, but it doesn't mean anything. All sizzle and splutter, like rissoles in a frying-pan.

[*He withdraws from the window.* PHILOCLEON *struggles wildly, but is overpowered by the* SLAVES.]

CHORUS-LEADER Let him go, or we'll run you through.

PHILOCLEON O Cecrops,[50] lord and hero! As a true Athenian, with serpent's blood in your veins – from the waist down, at least – are you going to stand by and see me mauled by these barbarians? Men who've had nothing but the best from me – six of the best every time.

CHORUS-LEADER Such are the miseries of old age. Look at these two now, laying violent hands on their old master, without a thought for all he's done for them: the leather jackets, the shirts, the caps he's bought them, and all the care he's shown for their feet in the wintertime, making sure that they're nice and warm. No respect at all for their old . . . footwear.

PHILOCLEON [*to one of the slaves holding him*] Let me go, you brute! Have you forgotten what happened when I caught you stealing grapes? Didn't I tie you to the nearest olive tree and give you a hiding that made you the envy of the neighbourhood? Have you no gratitude? Come on, let go of me, both of you, before that son of mine comes out again.

CHORUS-LEADER You wait, my lads, you're going to pay heavily for this. And you won't have to wait long either. You'll find out what it is to come up against men like us – sour-faced, stern and fiery.

[BDELYCLEON *rushes from the house with an armful of smoking torches, which he distributes to the* SLAVES.]

BDELYCLEON Attack, Xanthias, drive them back, away from the house!

XANTHIAS Just watch me!

BDELYCLEON [*to one of the other slaves*] Come on, you too! Smoke 'em out!

XANTHIAS Shoo, shoo! Go away! Buzz off!

BDELYCLEON Go on, let them have it! What we really need is Aeschines[51] to gas them into a coma.

[*The* CHORUS *are beaten back.*]

XANTHIAS There, I knew we'd beat them off in the end.

BDELYCLEON Lucky for you they've been training on Phrynichus and not on some of these modern songs – or you'd have been overcome by the fumes!

CHORUS

Treason and treachery! Now it is clear!
Tyranny, as ever, strikes from the rear!
See how this criminal glories in wrong:
We have our hair cut short, he has his long![52]

Who do you think you are? Simply because
You think you're somebody, you flout the laws!
Totalitarian, that's what you are!
Down with all tyranny! Shame on you, sir!

BDELYCLEON Couldn't we drop all this fighting and shouting? Why don't we negotiate? Perhaps we could come to some arrangement.

CHORUS-LEADER Arrangement? With you? You enemy of the people! You monarchist! You long-haired Amynias! You tassel-fringed pro-Spartan, in cahoots with Brasidas![53]

BDELYCLEON Honestly, I'd just as soon do without a father altogether as embroil myself in this kind of altercation day after day.

CHORUS-LEADER 'Embroil myself' – hark at him! If it's fancy talk you're after, let me tell you this: you haven't got past the trimmings yet, son – you're still picking at the parsley. Just wait till the prosecutor flings these same charges at you in court: 'conspiracy' is the word he'll use.

BDELYCLEON Will you go away and leave me in peace, or are you going to stand here bickering all day?

CHORUS-LEADER I won't leave while I've still got a drop of blood left in my body. You're plotting to establish a monarchy.

BDELYCLEON It's always 'tyranny' and 'conspiracy' with you people, isn't it? However trivial the offence, the charge is the same. The word 'tyranny' hasn't been heard in Athens for fifty years,[54] and now it's suddenly become as common as pickled fish. You can't even walk through the market without having it flung at you. If you buy a perch instead of sprats, the man at the sprat stall mutters, 'Bloody monarchist!' If you ask the sardine man to throw in a couple of spring onions, the woman at the vegetable stall gives you a filthy sideways look. 'A monarchist, that's what you are,' she says. 'Do you expect the city to pay you a tribute of onions?'

XANTHIAS Like that tart I paid for yesterday, down town. I just happened to say, 'How about having a ride on top?' 'No riding, buster,' she says, 'we're democrats here.'

BDELYCLEON And these people [*pointing to the* CHORUS *and audience*] lap it all up. Just because I want my father to give up leading the life of a miserable-prying-litigious-early-morning-stirrer and live like Morychus,[55] I'm accused of being a conspirator and a monarchist.

PHILOCLEON Well, that's what you are. I wouldn't give up the life I'm leading, not if you fed me on peacock's milk for the rest of my days. I'm not interested in your lampreys and your eels in aspic – give me a nice juicy lawsuit, done to a turn.

BDELYCLEON I know – you've developed a taste for such things. But if only you'd keep quiet and listen to me for a minute, I'm sure I could convince you that you're quite wrong.

PHILOCLEON Wrong? To sit as a juryman?

BDELYCLEON Worse than wrong: you don't realize how you're being taken in by these men you almost worship. You're a slave without realizing it.

PHILOCLEON Oh, I'm a slave now am I? I who hold supreme power.

BDELYCLEON You think you do, but you don't. You're just a lackey. I know – as an Athenian you can squeeze the rest of the Greek world dry, but can you tell us what *you* get out of it personally?

PHILOCLEON Certainly I can. Let these gentlemen decide between us.

BDELYCLEON All right. I'll agree to that. Let him go.

[PHILOCLEON *is released by the slaves.*]

PHILOCLEON And fetch me a sword.

[*One of the slaves fetches a sword and hands it to* PHILOCLEON.]

I swear that if I lose to you in this debate, I shall fall upon this sword.[56]

BDELYCLEON And if you fail to abide by the whatever-they-are, the stipulations?

PHILOCLEON May I never quaff neat jury-pay again.

CHORUS

The speaker who will plead our case, the champion of our school,
If he would be advised by us, must keep this simple rule:
Say something new, and say it well, and you will then appear –

BDELYCLEON

Go in and fetch my writing case and quickly bring it here!

[*A* SLAVE *goes off on this errand.*]

Yes, what will he appear to do, if he's advised by you?

CHORUS

To speak with more politeness than some younger people do.
You see what you are up against: the contest will be tense;
Such mighty matters are at stake, the issues are immense.
If he should chance to beat you (which the gods forbid he should) . . .

[*The* SLAVE *returns with* BDELYCLEON*'s writing materials.*]

BDELYCLEON
I'm going to write down every word: his speech had best be good!

PHILOCLEON
Oh, please go on: if he should win – what were you going to say?

CHORUS
Why, that would mean admitting that old men have had their day.
There'd be no further use for us, they'd mock us to our faces
And call us affidavit-husks, the ghosts of parchment-cases.
Be bold! Our sovereignty's at stake, and you must play your part
With every trick of oratory and glib persuasive art.

PHILOCLEON Well, to get off to a flying start, I propose to prove to you that this power of ours amounts to nothing short of absolute sovereignty. Can you think of any living creature that is happier, more fortunate, more pampered, or more feared than a juror? No sooner have I crawled out of bed in the morning than I find great hulking fellows waiting for me at the bar of the court. As I pass, one slips his delicate hand into mine – the very hand that has dipped so deeply into the public funds. And they all bow down low, and plead with me in pitiful tones: 'Have mercy, venerable sir,' they cry; 'Have you never made a bit on the side yourself? When you held some high office, or went shopping for your mess-mates?' That's how they talk to me – people who've never known of my existence till that moment, unless they've been tried before, and acquitted.

BDELYCLEON Point one. Supplicants at bar of court. I'm noting that. [*He writes on his tablet.*]

PHILOCLEON Then, after they've all crawled to me and tried to butter me up, I go behind the bar and take my seat, and forget all about any promises I may have made. I just listen to what they say – and there's nothing they won't say to flatter the jury in their efforts to get acquitted. Some of them bewail their poverty and exaggerate their troubles; one will start quoting the legends, another comes out with funny stories from Aesop, or starts cracking jokes to make me laugh and put me in a good mood. And if he can't win me over that way, he drags his children out in front – all his little girls and boys – and I just sit and listen while they all grovel, bleating in unison. Meanwhile their father stands over them and pleads with me to ratify his accounts as if I were a god. 'Master,' he cries, 'if you delight in the bleating of the lamb, hear my son's cries and have mercy. Or if your preference is for pork,[57] let my daughter persuade you.' And after that, I relax my severity a little. Isn't that power for you? Doesn't it make mere wealth look silly?

BDELYCLEON [*writing*] 'Make – mere – wealth – look – silly.' And now tell me what advantages you gain from your dominion over all Greece.

PHILOCLEON Well, for one thing we see all the boys in the nude when they come up for inspection. And then, say we have Oeagrus[58] up on a charge, he won't get off till we've heard him recite the big speech from *Niobe*.[59] Or suppose we have a flute-player, and he wins his case, he'll show his gratitude by playing a nice tune for us on his way out. Suppose a man dies: he may have named a husband for his heiress, but what do we care for wills and solemn seals and signatures? We give her to the suitor who puts up the best show in court.[60] And what's more, we can't be held to account afterwards, as the magistrates are. Theirs isn't real power – that belongs to us.

BDELYCLEON [*making a further note*] No, you're not held to account, and that's the first thing you've mentioned that I can really congratulate you on – though it's wrong to be tampering with heiresses' seals.

PHILOCLEON And another thing: if the Council or the Assembly can't reach a decision on some big case, they hand the prisoner over to the jury courts. We also have Evathlus[61] and Toady-onymous[62] coming along to tell us that they'll never betray us, they'll fight for the people. And no one has ever had a motion carried in the Assembly unless they've arranged for the courts to close down early so that we can attend. As for Cleon himself, the Great Screamer, we're the only people he never dares to nibble at: we lie safely in his arms and he keeps the flies off us. Which is a lot more than you've ever done for your old dad. Whereas a man like Theorus – a man who ranks . . . no lower than Euphemius[63] – comes crawling to us with his jar and sponge to shine our shoes. So you see what kind of advantages you're trying to cut me off from. And you claim to be able to convince me that they amount to slavery and servitude!

BDELYCLEON Go on, have your say; you can't go on for ever. And when you've finished, I'll show you where you can stick your precious power.

PHILOCLEON I haven't mentioned the best thing of all yet: when I get home with my pay, they're all over me. Because of the money, you see. First my daughter comes to give me a wash and rub my feet with oil, and it's 'dear papa' this and 'dear papa' that. Then she leans over to give me a kiss – and fish out those three obols with her tongue![64] And my little wife brings me out a barley loaf to tickle my appetite, and sits down beside me and presses me to eat: 'Do have some of this, do try one of these!' I love it! I don't want to have to depend on you and that steward of yours, and wait for him to bring me my lunch, muttering curses under his breath. As it is, if lunch is late, I've got this to stave off hunger [*pointing to his money, or perhaps a squashed morsel of food he carries with him*]. And if you don't pour me any wine, I've got my donkey here. [*He brings out a donkey-shaped wine-flask.*] Just tilt and pour. [*He demonstrates and wine gargles out.*] You see what he thinks of you and your goblets! A fine martial bray!

The power of Zeus upon his throne
    Is scarcely greater than my own.
When people speak of me and Zeus,
    The same expressions are in use:
For when the court's assembled there
    Our angry murmurs fill the air,

And passers-by, in fear and wonder,
Exclaim, 'By heaven, how they thunder!'
And when I flash, they cringe and cower
In dread at my almighty power,
And, hoping that they won't be struck,
They click their tongues to bring good luck.
The rich and powerful fear my frown
And tremble lest I bring them down;
And you fear me, by god, you do –
But I'll be damned if I fear you.
[*The* CHORUS *applaud enthusiastically*.]

CHORUS-LEADER
A most sensible speech:
I enjoyed every word.
As frank an oration
As ever I heard.

PHILOCLEON
He thought he'd get by
Though his case was the weaker:
He never imagined
I'd shine as a speaker!

CHORUS
A splendid performance,
Without any doubt
He touched on each point,
And left nothing out.
With pride and contentment
I felt myself swelling,
So fine were his words,
And his style so compelling.
I honestly could not
Have been more impressed
If I'd been in a court
In the Isles of the Blest.[65]

PHILOCLEON
You see the way he's fidgeting: he's clearly ill at ease.

BDELYCLEON

Before the day is over you'll be beaten to your knees.

CHORUS

You'll have to weave a crafty web to make that boast come true.
The person who gets beaten is more likely to be you.
It takes a clever speaker to convert a hostile jury:
You'd better think of ways and means of countering our fury.

[BDELYCLEON *clears his throat and takes up the posture of an orator.*]

BDELYCLEON It is a difficult undertaking, requiring a degree of skill and understanding far beyond that of comic poets in general, to cure the city of such a chronic and endemic sickness. [*He looks heavenwards.*] But you, O Lord and Father . . .

PHILOCLEON [*thinking himself addressed*] Now don't start Lord-and-fathering me – it won't get you anywhere. What you've got to do is prove that I'm a slave, and you better hurry up about it. Otherwise I'll have to kill you. I suppose they'll debar me from the sacrificial feasts for it, but it can't be helped.

BDELYCLEON All right then, daddy dearest. Listen to me, and stop looking so stern. For a start, just count up, roughly – on your fingers will do – how much tribute we get altogether from the subject cities. Add to that the revenue from taxes, percentages, deposits, the mines, market and harbour dues, rents and confiscations. Add these up, and we get a total of nearly twelve million drachmas[66] a year. Now work out how much of that annual sum goes to the jurors – six thousand of them, taking the maximum. And the total is . . . nine hundred thousand – am I right?

PHILOCLEON [*checking over the figures in amazement*] But that means – our pay doesn't even amount to ten per cent of the national income.

BDELYCLEON That's right.

PHILOCLEON Where does all the rest of the money go?

BDELYCLEON To those fellows you mentioned just now: 'I will never betray the Athenian riff-raff! I will always fight for the rabble!' The people you elect to rule over you, because you're taken in by their speeches. And on top of that there are the bribes they get from subject cities: three hundred thousand drachmas at a time, extorted by threats and intimidation: 'If you don't pay up, I'll ruin your city with a single thunderous speech!' While you, apparently, are quite content to chew on the leftovers – so much for your precious power. The subject states take one look at the scrawny rabble, feeding on scraps and living it up on . . . bugger all, and conclude that you're not worth a damn. Meanwhile they ply these other men with gifts of pickle, wine, cheese, honey and sesame, rugs and cushions, cups and bowls, fancy clothing and jewellery, and every other conceivable luxury. And what do *you* get out it, this empire you've toiled and fought for on land and sea? Not so much as a bulb of garlic to flavour your fish soup.

PHILOCLEON True enough! Only yesterday I had to send out for three measly cloves. But when are you going to get to the point and prove I'm a slave? I'm getting impatient.

BDELYCLEON Well, isn't it slavery when these men, and their cronies, all hold overpaid executive posts, while you're over the moon with your three obols? Obols which you yourself have laboured and rowed and battled and sieged into existence? Furthermore, you're entirely at their beck and call. What infuriates me is seeing some affected little toff come mincing up to you – like this – and start ordering you around. 'You're to be in court first thing tomorrow morning. Anyone who isn't in his seat when the flag goes up will lose his three obols.' Rest assured, he'll be getting his prosecutor's fee all right – an entire drachma – however late he arrives. And they work together, too, did you know that? If a defendant comes up with a bribe, the prosecution and defence will share it, and then they'll play up to each other convincingly, like two men with a saw – one gains a point, the other gives way. You never spot what they're up to because you're too busy gaping at the paymaster.

PHILOCLEON No, no! They don't do that to me! What are you

saying? How you shake me to my inmost core and win me over! You do I know not what to me![67]

BDELYCLEON Well then, just think how rich you and everybody else could be, if it wasn't for this gang of demagogues who keep you trapped just where they want you. Yes, I know you rule over a vast number of cities from the Black Sea to Sardinia. But what do you get out of it, apart from this absolute pittance? And even that they squeeze out like little drops of oil, just enough at a time to keep you going. They *want* you to be poor, and I'll tell you why: they're training you to know the hand that feeds you. Then, when the time comes, they let you loose on some enemy or other: 'Go on, good dog! Bite him! That's the way!' If they really wanted to give the people a decent standard of living, they could do it easily. At the moment we have a thousand cities paying tribute to Athens; if you gave each of them twenty men to feed, you'd have twenty thousand ordinary Athenians lording it up on jugged hare and cream cakes every day, with garlands on their heads, leading lives worthy of the land they belong to, worthy of the victors of Marathon.[68] Instead of which you have to queue up for your pay like a bunch of olive-pickers.

PHILOCLEON What's come over me? I feel unusual. An eerie numbness has spread over my hand. I can't hold up my sword any more, I've gone all limp.

BDELYCLEON Whenever they're really worried, they offer you the whole of Euboea,[69] and promise you seventy-five bushels of wheat all round. But you've never got that, have you? Five bushels is all they give you, and barley at that – a quart at a time, and only if you can prove your ancestry. Do you see now why I've been keeping you shut up? I want to look after you properly. I don't want you made a mockery of by these unscrupulous ranters. You only have to ask and I'll give you anything you want – except the paymaster's milk.

[PHILOCLEON *remains silent.*]

CHORUS

'You should never decide till both sides have been heard'
Is a saying both ancient and true:

We are happy to state that you've won the debate
  And converted us all to your view.
We freely admit we were hostile at first,
  But our anger has melted away;
So we'll lay down our staves (we don't want to be slaves)
  And agree to whatever you say.

CHORUS-LEADER [*addressing* PHILOCLEON][70]
Give in, give in to his words, dearest friend!
  Be not too headstrong or unbending!
If only I had relatives with such sense,
  Whose care for me was so unending.
Now surely some god has determined your fate,
  And you should accept such amending.

BDELYCLEON
No pains will I spare: on appropriate fare
  I shall see that he's lavishly fed;
A shawl he shall have, and a rug for his knees,
  And a woman to warm him in bed.

But why is he silent? I don't like his look;
  He ought to have spoken by now,
If only to mutter. But no, not a word –
  And look at his glowering brow![71]

CHORUS-LEADER
I fancy he's feeling the pangs of remorse;
  His eyes are now open at last.
No doubt he's resolving to pay you more heed –
  To atone for his faults in the past.

[PHILOCLEON *utters a piercing tragic wail.*]

BDELYCLEON What on earth is the matter?

PHILOCLEON [*in a quasi-tragic manner*]
Alas, what mean these promises to me?
What I long for is *there* – there would I be,[72]
Sitting once more among the things I love,
Hearing the chairman calling loud and clear:
'If any juror has not voted yet,
Will he come to the urns immediately?'

And I would take my time – I always made
A point of voting last.
[*He raises his sword and tries to take his own life with it.*]
Godspeed, my soul!
Where *is* my soul? It must be under here.
Part, part, ye shady folds, and let me pass![73]
[*The sword falls.*]
I'd ten times sooner die, by Heracles,
Than take my seat upon the bench again
And find my Cleon in the dock for theft!

[*He sinks to the ground, sobbing, as* BDELYCLEON *removes his fallen sword.*]

Scene 2: *The same.*

BDELYCLEON Father, I beg you, do as I ask.

PHILOCLEON What is it? Ask what you will except for one thing.

BDELYCLEON What's that?

PHILOCLEON To give up jury work. 'May death receive me before I do that.'[74]

BDELYCLEON If you're so set on trying cases, why bother going all the way to court to do it? Why not stay here and try your own household?

PHILOCLEON Try them? For what? You're raving, boy.

BDELYCLEON You can do exactly what you do in court. Say one of the slave girls leaves the door on the latch – you can give her a stiff . . . sentence. That's the usual procedure, isn't it? And just think: if it's a fine sunny morning you can dispense 'summery' justice; if it's snowing, you can sit by the fire; if it's wet, you don't have to go outside. And if you don't wake up till midday, there'll be no court officer to bar you from court.

PHILOCLEON I like the sound of that.

BDELYCLEON What's more, if you get one of these speakers who just go on and on and on, you won't have to sit there starving, and then take it out on the defendant.

PHILOCLEON But I wouldn't be able to judge as well if I was eating the whole time.

BDELYCLEON Nonsense! You'd be much better. Don't they always say, 'After chewing over the facts, the jury decided that the witnesses were lying'?

PHILOCLEON You know, I'm beginning to warm to this idea. But there's one thing you haven't mentioned. Who's going to pay me?

BDELYCLEON I am.

PHILOCLEON Good. That means I'll get the right change; I hate that sharing business. Do you know what that joker Lysistratus did to me once? They hadn't got change so he and I were given a drachma between us. We went to the fish market to change it, but what he put in my mouth was three fish scales.[75] I just stood there and let him do it, thinking they were obols. Ugh, they smelt foul! I had to spit them out, but then I went for him.

BDELYCLEON And what did he say?

PHILOCLEON He laughed and said, 'You've got a stomach like a cockerel: I bet you'd digest the silver pretty quickly, anyway.'

BDELYCLEON You see how much you stand to gain by all this.

PHILOCLEON A lot, I agree. All right, do what you will.

BDELYCLEON Wait here, then, while I fetch the things.

[BDELYCLEON *goes into the house.*]

PHILOCLEON It seems the oracles are coming true. I'd always heard that one day the Athenians would judge cases in their own homes; and that every man would have a tiny lawcourt in front of his house, like the little shrines of Hecate we have on our porches.[76]

[BDELYCLEON *returns with several* SLAVES *carrying tables, benches, kitchen utensils and other equipment, including a cockerel in a wooden cage. When the domestic 'courtroom' has been arranged to* BDELYCLEON*'s satisfaction the* SLAVES *leave.*]

BDELYCLEON There, what more could you want? I've brought you everything as promised, and a lot more. Here's a potty for you: let's hang it up here on the peg. Then it won't be far away when you need it.

PHILOCLEON Now that's what I call a handy arrangement: just what an old man needs.

BDELYCLEON Right, here's your fire [*he puts down a brazier*], and I've put a bowl of soup on to keep hot, in case you get hungry.

PHILOCLEON That's a good idea: now I can get my pay even if I've got a temperature – just stay where I am and sip my soup. But what's the bird for?

BDELYCLEON To wake you up, of course, in case someone makes a long speech for the defence and you nod off in the middle of it.

PHILOCLEON It all seems fine, except for one thing.

BDELYCLEON What's that?

PHILOCLEON No shrine of Lycus.

BDELYCLEON Yes, there is [*pointing to the stage altar*]. And here's the hero in person [*motioning one of the slaves to pose as a statue on the altar*].

PHILOCLEON O hero Lycus, I didn't see you there!

BDELYCLEON He's as visible as Cleonymus to me!

PHILOCLEON He's lacking his equipment, I'll grant you that.[77]

BDELYCLEON Now, the sooner you sit down, the sooner we can call the first case.

PHILOCLEON [*sitting down*] I've been sitting down for ages. Call away, I'm ready.

BDELYCLEON Well now, what's the first case going to be? Has anyone in the house been misbehaving lately? Let's see – Thratta[78] burnt the soup yesterday.

PHILOCLEON Wait a minute! What are you playing at? You can't call a prisoner if you haven't got a bar to call them to! That's the most sacred thing of all.

BDELYCLEON You're right, we've forgotten that.

PHILOCLEON I'll run inside and get one right away. [*He leaps to his feet and runs into the house.*]

BDELYCLEON Now what's he up to? Dreadful the way some people get homesick!

[*Scuffling and shouting is heard from the kitchen, and a flustered* XANTHIAS *emerges, brandishing a kitchen knife.*]

XANTHIAS To hell with you! I don't know why we keep him!

BDELYCLEON What's the matter?

XANTHIAS It's that mutt Labes. He came flying into the kitchen, then snapped up a fresh piece of Sicilian cheese, and wolfed the lot.[79]

BDELYCLEON That'll do nicely for the old man's first case. You'll have to attend as prosecutor.

XANTHIAS Actually, sir, our other dog has expressed a desire to open for the prosecution, if the case comes to court.

BDELYCLEON Very well then, bring them both here.

XANTHIAS Right, sir.

[*He goes in. Meanwhile* PHILOCLEON *comes back out dragging a large wooden pig-pen with him.*]

BDELYCLEON And what, may I ask, is that?

PHILOCLEON The pig-pen from our inner sanctum.

BDELYCLEON Isn't that sacrilege?

PHILOCLEON [*setting it up and taking his seat behind it*] Nothing like starting from scratch,[80] I always say. Well, let's get on with it: I'm in the mood for fining.

BDELYCLEON Wait a second while I go and get the notice-boards and charge-sheets. [*He goes into the house.*]

PHILOCLEON You're driving me mad with all these delays. My nails are itching to furrow the wax once more.

[BDELYCLEON *returns with two wooden dishes, which he hangs up as notice-boards, and a bundle of documents. He sits at a table.*]

BDELYCLEON There you are.

PHILOCLEON Call on the case.

BDELYCLEON Right. [*In an official tone*] Who appears before the court?

PHILOCLEON [*to himself*] Damn, what a fool I am! I forgot the urns. [*He gets up again.*]

BDELYCLEON Where are you off to now?

PHILOCLEON To fetch the urns.

BDELYCLEON [*picking up two large ladles and placing them on the table*] No need. That's what I brought these ladles for.

PHILOCLEON [*resuming his seat*] Splendid! Now we really have got all we need. Hang on, we don't have a water-clock.

BDELYCLEON [*pointing to the potty*] What do you think that is?

PHILOCLEON You really have thought of everything – and using local resources too.

BDELYCLEON [*calling out*] Someone bring me a taper. And we'll need some myrtle and incense. We must offer a prayer to the gods before we begin.

[*One slave brings out a taper, incense and a libation cup; another brings myrtle wreaths, which he places on the heads of all present.*]

CHORUS

We trust that by means
Of these prayers and oblations
The seal may be set
On your friendly relations;
And since you've decided
To cease being foemen,
We'll gladly pronounce
A few words of good omen.

BDELYCLEON First let there be silence.

[PHILOCLEON *and the* SLAVES *stand silent as* BDELYCLEON *pours the libation and burns incense before the shrine of Apollo in the porch.*[81] The CHORUS *then chant their prayer.*]

CHORUS

Phoebus Apollo, grant that the transactions
Soon to take place here, on your very doorstep,
May to your servants, lately saved from error,
Prove beneficial.

BDELYCLEON

Master and neighbour, watcher of my doorway,
Deign to accept the rites I now perform,
Newly devised, sketched out and made to measure
For my old father.

Teach him to change his harsh and bitter nature,
Soften his heart, and give over his sourness:
Mix with his gall a tiny drop of honey,
Just as a sweetener.

Oh, may he lose his nettle-sting of anger,
Look upon men with eyes more sympathetic,
So that his tears may flow for the defendant –
Not the accuser!

CHORUS

Hear, hear! And now we'll sing an ode to start this novel session:
The chairman's opening words have made an excellent impression.
He seems to treat the People with a deep consideration
Not often found in members of the younger generation.

BDELYCLEON [*calling out as Court Officer*] All jurors take their places in the courtroom! No admittance after proceedings have begun.

[*The* TWO DOGS, *as plaintiff and defendant respectively, make their entry, the latter escorted by two slaves in their capacity as guards.*]

PHILOCLEON Which is the defendant?

BDELYCLEON [*pointing to* LABES] This one.

PHILOCLEON Ha, wait till he hears the sentence!

BDELYCLEON Attention, please, for the indictment. Prosecution initiated by The Dog of Cydathenaeum against Labes of Aexone,[82] on the grounds that the said Labes did wilfully and feloniously wrong and injure the one Sicilian cheese by eating it all himself. Penalty proposed: a figwood collar.[83]

PHILOCLEON No, no! Death – if he's convicted.

BDELYCLEON The defendant, Labes, stands before the court.

[LABES *is led forward.*]

PHILOCLEON The filthy scum! Look at his furtive look! Trying to get round me with a cheeky grin. Where's the plaintiff, The Dog from Cydathenaeum?

[*The* DOG *leaps forward fawningly.* PHILOCLEON *strokes him.*]

FIRST DOG Bow-wow!

BDELYCLEON [*interpreting*] Present!

PHILOCLEON This one's another Labes, good at barking and licking his bowl clean!

BDELYCLEON Silence in court! Be seated! [*To the* DOG] Proceed with the charge.

PHILOCLEON [*ladling out some soup*] I think I'll have some soup while this is going on.

FIRST DOG [*taking the prosecutor's 'stand', an upturned pot*] Gentlemen of the jury, you have heard the terms of the indictment filed by me against the defendant. He has committed the most atrocious offences, not only against me, but against every sailor in the fleet, namely by running away into a corner, *siciliating*[84] a large quantity of cheese and stuffing himself with it under cover of darkness.

PHILOCLEON The case is beyond doubt. A moment ago he belched in my general direction. The malodour of cheese was unmistakable. Disgusting creature!

FIRST DOG When I asked for a share, he refused point blank. I put it to you, gentlemen, how can anyone claim to be serving your interests if I, The Dog, am not given my proper share?

PHILOCLEON I, the public, wasn't given my share either. It seems he's hot-tempered and fiery – a bit like this soup!

BDELYCLEON Now, father, I beg you, don't decide against him before you've heard both sides.

PHILOCLEON My dear boy, the thing's as plain as a pikestaff. It screams out at you.

FIRST DOG [*at the top of his voice*] Don't you dare acquit him, do you hear? This man is the most confirmed wolf-it-all-yourself-merchant in the history of houndkind. He even cruised round the whole island gnawing plaster off the cities.[85]

PHILOCLEON And here I am without enough plaster to mend my potty.

FIRST DOG He must be punished for this. There's no room for two thieves in one patch. I don't see why I should go on barking in vain. So convict him, or else you'll not get another yap out of me.

PHILOCLEON Good god! What a lot of crimes you've accused him of. He's an utterly thieving piece of work! [*He turns to the cock*] Isn't he, my old rooster? Look, he's winking – he agrees. Officer! Where's the man got to? I want my potty!

BDELYCLEON Get it yourself. I have to call the witnesses.

[PHILOCLEON *gets the potty and relieves himself.*]

Witnesses for the defendant's character, come forward!

[*As their names are called, the* WITNESSES *file out of the house and take up their positions at the defendant's side.*]

Citizen Bowl! Citizen Pestle! Citizen Cheese-Grater! Citizen Brazier! Mistress Pot! And the rest of you burnt utensils! [*To* PHILOCLEON] Have you still not finished pissing?

PHILOCLEON [*resuming his seat and pointing at* LABES] I think I'll have someone shitting themselves in a minute.

BDELYCLEON Must you always be so harsh and implacable with the poor fellows who are in the dock? You're always sticking the knife in. [*To* LABES] Prisoner, stand up and make your defence!

[LABES *mounts the 'stand', another upturned pot, but remains tongue-tied.*]

BDELYCLEON Why don't you speak? Get on with it?

PHILOCLEON He doesn't seem to have anything to say.

BDELYCLEON Thucydides had the same problem at *his* trial:[86] a case of sudden paralysis of the jaw. [*To* LABES] All right, stand down: I'll conduct the defence myself. [*He takes* LABES' *place on the 'stand'.*]

Gentlemen. Ahem . . . It is a difficult undertaking to reply on behalf of a slandered dog, I shall proceed all the same. Er . . . He is a good dog. He chases away the wolves.

PHILOCLEON You mean he's a thief and a conspirator.

BDELYCLEON Not at all. He's the finest dog alive. Capable of guarding any number of sheep.

PHILOCLEON What's the good of that, if he wolfs all the cheese himself?

BDELYCLEON Why, he fights for you and guards the house. What's more, he's a noble creature in every way. What if he did filch something? Can't you overlook it? After all, he was never taught to play the harp.[87]

PHILOCLEON Personally I'd rather he hadn't been taught to read and write. Then he wouldn't have known how to fiddle the books.

BDELYCLEON Sir, will you please listen to my witnesses? Citizen Cheese-Grater, will you come up and testify? And speak up.

[CHEESE-GRATER *steps forward.*]

You were serving as a quartermaster, I understand?

[CHEESE-GRATER *nods.*]

And was what you grated for the troops?

[CHEESE-GRATER *nods again.*]

He says it was.

PHILOCLEON He's lying!

[CHEESE-GRATER *and other witnesses leave the 'court'.* BDELYCLEON *wraps up in emotive tones for the defence.*]

BDELYCLEON Kind sir, have pity on a creature in distress. This dog, Labes, slaves away tirelessly, feeding on giblets and fish-bones, always on active service. His opponent, meanwhile, stays at home as a mere watchdog, although he still demands his share of anything that's brought in. And takes a bite, if he's not given it.

PHILOCLEON Good god, what's happening to me? I feel myself softening! Something must be wrong – I'm being won over![88]

BDELYCLEON Come, father, I implore you, have pity on him, don't send him to his downfall. Where are his children?

[*A slave goes into the house and returns with a family of puppies.*[89]]

Poor creatures, come up here and plead. Entreat him, pray to him, with tears and whimpers.

[*The* PUPPIES *crowd round* BDELYCLEON*'s feet and whine piteously.*]

PHILOCLEON [*reduced to tears*] Enough, enough! Step down, step down!

BDELYCLEON All right. Though many a man has heard those words in the past and been deceived, nevertheless, I will step down.

[BDELYCLEON *stands down and the* PUPPIES *leave.*]

PHILOCLEON It's this damned soup. I knew it was a mistake. I'd never have started weeping like that if I hadn't been bloated with soup.

BDELYCLEON You're going to acquit him, then?

PHILOCLEON [*hardening*] It's hard to say.

BDELYCLEON Come on, daddy dearest, now's your chance to turn over a new leaf. Take this pebble, shut your eyes, rush straight over to that second urn and acquit him.

PHILOCLEON No! I was never taught to play the harp either.

BDELYCLEON Come on, then. I'll take you round the quick way.

[PHILOCLEON, *still clouded by tears and confusion, allows* BDELYCLEON *to help him over towards the urns.* BDELYCLEON *takes his father's arm and leads him via a circuitous route so as to reach the acquittal urn first.*]

PHILOCLEON Is this the first urn?

BDELYCLEON It is.

PHILOCLEON In she goes.

[*He drops the pebble into the urn and* BDELYCLEON *helps him back into his seat.*]

BDELYCLEON [*aside*] Foiled! He's acquitted him unwittingly. [*To the* SLAVES] Let's empty them out now.

PHILOCLEON Well, how did it go?[90]

BDELYCLEON We shall see in a minute.

[*With an air of officialdom the* SLAVES *present the contents of the 'urns' to* BDELYCLEON, *and retire.*]

Labes, you are . . . acquitted!

[PHILOCLEON *collapses.* BDELYCLEON *rushes across to him.*]

Father, father! What's the matter? Someone, bring some water – quick! Lift yourself up.

PHILOCLEON Just tell me this, was he really acquitted?

BDELYCLEON He was.

PHILOCLEON Then I am no more![91]

BDELYCLEON Don't take it to heart. Sit up.

PHILOCLEON How can I bear to live on after this? Now that

I've let an accused man escape? You gods, forgive me, I was not myself! I didn't mean to do what I just did.[92]

BDELYCLEON Look, there's nothing to get upset about. From now on I'm going to look after you properly. I'll take you out to all kinds of places, we'll go out to dinners and drinking parties, and you'll have a really good time – with no Hyperbolus[93] to trick you and laugh at you behind your back. Let's go in.

PHILOCLEON [*resignedly*] All right, if you say so.

[BDELYCLEON *leads his father into the house. Meanwhile the* SLAVES *clear away the 'courtroom' paraphernalia and leave the* CHORUS *alone onstage.*]

CHORUS-LEADER In you go, then, and good luck to you.

CHORUS

Now, you countless tens of thousands,
  Seated on the benches round,
Do not let our pearls of wisdom
  Fall unheeded on the ground.
Not that you would be so stupid,
  So devoid of common sense –
What it is to have enlightened
  People in the audience!

[*The* CHORUS-LEADER *comes forward and addresses the audience.*]

CHORUS-LEADER

Now once again, spectators, if you like
To hear plain speaking, pay attention, please!
The author has a bone to pick with you
For treating him unfairly when, he says,
You've had so many splendid things from him.
Not always openly: in earlier days[94]
A number of his jokes came from the lips
Of other poets, while he lurked unseen,
Speaking through them, like a ventriloquist;
Till finally one day he ventured forth,
Driving a team of Muses of his own,
And won great honour, such as none before

Had been accorded. Yet he did not rest
Upon his laurels with inflated pride,
Or flounce around the wrestling schools, like some
Successful poets we have known, nor yet
Would he consent to prostitute the Muse
And hold some feeble stripling up to scorn
To satisfy a jealous lover's whim.
Indeed, when he first staged a play himself
He didn't bother to attack mere men.
Disdaining such small fry, our Heracles
Took on the greatest monster in the land.[95]
Jag-toothed it was, and from its staring eyes
Shot rays more terrible than those of Cynna;[96]
And in a grisly circle round its head
Flickered the tongues of servile flatterers,
Condemned to groan; its voice was like the roar
Of mighty floods descending from the hills,
Bearing destruction: heinous was the stench
That issued from the beast as it slid forth,
With camel's arse and stinking unwashed balls.[97]
Undaunted by the sight, he stood his ground
(In spite of all attempts to buy him off)
And fought on your behalf – and still fights on.
And then, last year, he says, he did attack
The many plagues and fevers, nightmare forms
That came and hovered by your beds at night,
Smothering fathers, choking grandfathers,
Inflicting lawsuits, summonses and writs
On harmless, peaceful folk, till many leapt
In terror from their beds, and formed a queue
Outside the office of the Polemarch.[98]
So once again your Champion fought for you
And sought to purge the land of grievous ills.
But what did you do then? You let him down.
For when he tried last year to sow a crop
Of new ideas, you failed to see the point
And all was wasted; yet, with hand on heart,
He swears by Dionysus that, in truth,

There never was a better comedy.[99]
The shame is yours for being so obtuse.
No man of sense will think the worse of him
If, driving so much better than the rest,
He passed them all – and overshot the goal.
So if ever in future
A poet appears
Who gives you a play
That's full of ideas,
With thoughts that are fresh
And a slant that's new,
I advise you to give him
The praise that's his due.
Yes, save up his phrases
And put them in store,
Like fruit, in your clothes box
For twelve months or more.
And so when next year
On these benches you sit,
Why, all of your clothes
Will be scented with wit.

CHORUS

In days when men were men
(And you should have seen us then)
We were noted for our vigour and agility;
We carried all before us
Both in battle and as chorus,
And no one could have questioned our virility.

Those days, alas, are gone,
And the feathers of the swan
Are no whiter than our hair, for we are old;
And yet, as you can see,
Feeble relics though we be,
In spirit we're still manly, young and bold.

Yes, we may be poor old crocks,
But the whiteness of our locks

Does the city better credit, I would say,
Than the ringlets and the fashions
And the rectum-widening passions
Of the namby-pamby youngsters of today.

CHORUS-LEADER

Should it strike you, dear spectators, as a somewhat curious thing
To find me thus embellished with a wasp-waist and a sting,
A word will be sufficient to complete your education
And elucidate the meaning of our costume and formation.
Allow me, then, to mention that I feel a certain pride
In the very handy weapon that protrudes from my backside;
For the warriors who possess it are of native Attic birth,
As stubborn and as brave a breed as ever trod the earth.
It was we who served the city best when those barbarians came
To try to smoke us from our nests, and filled the streets with flame.[100]
Inflamed with rage, we ran straight out with warlike spear and shield;
Our hearts were set on battle, and we faced them in the field.
All day we went on fighting, but Athena's owl had flown
Above our ranks that morning, and we knew we weren't alone:
So thick with arrows was the air, we couldn't see the sun,
But when the shades of evening fell we had them on the run.[101]
We stung them in eyebrows and we stung them on the cheeks;
We jabbed them in the buttocks through their baggy Persians breeks.[102]
And among barbarian nations we're respected to this day –
'There's nothing so ferocious as an Attic Wasp,' they say.

CHORUS

Yes, we were dreaded in our day!
The Persians tried to get away,
But that was not to be;
For after beating them on land
Our gallant three-tiered ships we manned
And, closing in on every hand,
We hammered them at sea.[103]

Not one of us could make a speech,
Denounce, arraign, inform, impeach,
Nor yearned such arts to master.
From these endeavours we forbore:
A question that concerned us more
Was how to ply a lusty oar
And make our ships go faster.

This being so, we rowed with ease
To cities far across the seas
And took them from the Persians;
And if the tribute-money still
Flows into the Imperial till
(From which the young now filch their fill)
It's thanks to our exertions.

CHORUS-LEADER:

Now anyone who studies us from various points of view
Will find that we resemble wasps in everything we do.
No creature, to begin with, is more savage or irate,
When once provoked, than we are, or less easy to placate.
Observe our social structure and you'll see that it conforms
To that of wasps exactly – we are organized in swarms;
And according to the jury that we're privileged to be on
We buzz about the Archon's Court, or nest in the Odeon.[104]

And some, like grublets in the cells, are packed around the wall:
They nod their heads, but otherwise they scarcely move at all.
Our economic system, too, is practical and neat:
By stinging all and sundry we contrive to make ends meet.
Of course we have our drones as well, the stingless brutes who shirk
Their military duties, letting others do the work –
And sure enough they gobble up as much as they can get
Of income *we* have earned them with no end of toil and sweat.
It drives us mad to think that those who've never raised a hand
Or risked a single blister to defend their native land
Can draw their pay with all the rest: I think the rule should be
That if you haven't got a sting, you get no jury fee.

ACT TWO

Scene I: *The same. Two couches have been placed outside the house.*

[PHILOCLEON *comes out of the house followed by* BDELYCLEON, *who is trying to pull the tattered juryman's cloak from his father's shoulders. In attendance is a slave carrying a heavy woollen gown and a pair of smart shoes.*]

PHILOCLEON Nobody's going to strip me of this, not while there's breath in my body. We've stood shoulder to shoulder against many a cold north wind, my cloak and I.

BDELYCLEON Don't you want to be treated well?

PHILOCLEON No, I don't. Treats are not good for me. Last time it was those grilled sprats, and look what happened afterwards. I spent a whole three obols on the cleaning bill.

BDELYCLEON Now, look – you've put yourself in my hands for your own good. You might at least make an effort.

PHILOCLEON What is it you want me to do?

BDELYCLEON Take off that tattered old cloak and put on this gown.

PHILOCLEON Fat lot of good having sons and bringing them up, if all they do is try and suffocate you!

BDELYCLEON Come on, get on with it, and don't talk so much.

[*The* SLAVE *holds up the gown as* BDELYCLEON *removes* PHILOCLEON*'s cloak.*]

PHILOCLEON [*wriggling away*] What, in god's name, *is* this horrible thing?

BDELYCLEON It's a Persian gown. Some people call it a 'full-waister'.

PHILOCLEON I thought it was one of those goatskin things from the country.

BDELYCLEON You would. If you'd ever been to Sardis,[105] you'd have known what it was; but it would seem you don't.

PHILOCLEON I most certainly don't. Looks to me like one of Morychus' knapsacks.

BDELYCLEON No, these are made in Ecbatana.[106]

PHILOCLEON [*inspecting the lining*] What from? Tripe?

BDELYCLEON You really are hopeless! It's an extremely expensive Persian weave – at least sixty pounds of wool went into making this.

PHILOCLEON Then they should have called it a 'wool-waster' not a 'full-waister'.

BDELYCLEON Now stand still, and let's get it on.

[*Helped by the* SLAVE, BDELYCLEON *manages to get his father halfway into the gown.*]

PHILOCLEON [*wriggling away*] My god, it's belching hot steam at me!

BDELYCLEON Come on, put it on.

PHILOCLEON No! If I'm going to be roasted, I'd rather you put me straight in the oven and be done with it.

BDELYCLEON Here, I'll help you myself. [*To the* SLAVE] All right, you can go.

[BDELYCLEON *takes the gown from the* SLAVE *and puts it over* PHILOCLEON*'s shoulders. The* SLAVE *retires.*]

PHILOCLEON [*staggering under the weight of the gown*] I hope you've got a fork handy?

BDELYCLEON What for?

PHILOCLEON To fish me out when I'm baked to pieces.

BDELYCLEON Now, take off those dreadful felt shoes and put on these Spartans[107] instead.

PHILOCLEON Do you really think I could put up with wearing 'foe leather'?

BDELYCLEON Come along, be brave and stick your foot in.

PHILOCLEON It's a crime to make me tread on enemy sole!

BDELYCLEON Now the other one.

PHILOCLEON No, no, not that foot! The big toe's a rabid anti-Spartan.

BDELYCLEON Can't be helped. On with it!

PHILOCLEON This is terrible! Now I won't have a single chilblain to comfort me in my old age.

BDELYCLEON Get it on quickly – that's right. Now let me see you walk. No, no! Like this – with an elegant, affluent swagger.

[PHILOCLEON *begins to warm to his new outfit.*]

PHILOCLEON I know, I'll strike a pose. Tell me which of your well-heeled friends I look like now.

BDELYCLEON You look like a boil with a garlic plaster on it.

PHILOCLEON I was trying to show you the 'butt-wiggle'.

BDELYCLEON Now, look, if you're going to mix with clever, educated men, you'll have to be able to produce a refined anecdote.

PHILOCLEON Of course.

BDELYCLEON Which one will you tell them?

PHILOCLEON Oh, I know loads. There's that story about Lamia farting[108] when she got caught; or the one about Cardopion[109] giving his mother a –

BDELYCLEON No, not folktales. Something with human interest: the kind of thing people usually talk about, with a domestic feel.

PHILOCLEON Domestic, eh? How about this? Once upon a time there was a cat and it met a mouse, and –

BDELYCLEON You benighted ignoramus – as Theogenes[110] retorted to the dung-collector! You can't start talking about a cat and a mouse to men of quality.

PHILOCLEON What kind of thing do they want, then?

BDELYCLEON Something impressive. You know – 'Once, when I was on a State mission with Androcles[111] and Cleisthenes[112] . . .'

PHILOCLEON The only State mission I've ever been on was to Paros – at two obols a day.

BDELYCLEON Then tell them how you remember seeing old Ephudion and how he wiped the floor with Ascondas. Say what a fine figure of a man he still was, for all his white hair: great strong hands; powerful flanks; and his arms.[113]

PHILOCLEON How was he allowed to fight a wrestling match if he was armed?

BDELYCLEON [*ignoring him*] That's the kind of conversation sophisticated people go in for. Now, here's another thing. If you're drinking with strangers, they'll want to know something about you. You could tell them about some daring exploit from your younger days.

PHILOCLEON Like the time I pinched all the vine-props from old Ergasion's vineyard!

BDELYCLEON You and your vine-props, you'll be the death of me! No, you want to tell them how you went boar-hunting or hare-coursing, or ran in the torch race – some dashing deed.

PHILOCLEON Well, the most dashing thing I ever did was to take on the runner Phayllus. I beat him too – sued him for slander, and won the case by two votes.

BDELYCLEON All right. Come and lie down over here. [*He points to the two couches.*] I'll show you how to behave at a fashionable drinking party.

PHILOCLEON Lie down? How am I supposed to lie?

BDELYCLEON Just recline gracefully.

[PHILOCLEON *tries lying down on his back with his knees up.*]

PHILOCLEON Like this?

BDELYCLEON No, no, not like that, for heaven's sake!

PHILOCLEON How, then? Show me.

BDELYCLEON You have to straighten your knees – that's it – and sort of 'pour' yourself into the cushions with poise and grace.

[BDELYCLEON *demonstrates, taking up a reclining position on the other couch.* PHILOCLEON *practises 'pouring' himself into the cushions until* BDELYCLEON *is satisfied.*]

Good. Now you should say something complimentary about the bronze ornaments – look up at the ceiling – admire the rugs on the wall.

[PHILOCLEON *mimes all this as instructed.* BDELYCLEON *now claps his hands to summon the* SLAVES, *who have been briefed in advance. At each stage of the imaginary party* BDELYCLEON *demonstrates the correct procedure and table manners.* PHILOCLEON *attempts to imitate his gestures.*]

Bring the finger-bowls! [*The* SLAVES *do so.*]
Bring in the tables! [*The* SLAVES *do so.*]
Now we eat . . . now wash hands again . . . now a libation.

[*The* SLAVES *whisk away the tables.*]

PHILOCLEON Gods above, are we dreaming this dinner!

BDELYCLEON Now, the flute-girl has played her piece, and you are drinking with – let's say – Theorus, Aeschines, Phanos,[114] Cleon and that foreign type, the son of Acestor.[115] He's at Cleon's head. Can you take up the singing when it comes to your turn?[116]

PHILOCLEON Oh, yes, I'm good at that.

BDELYCLEON Well, we shall see. Now, I'm Cleon: suppose I start off with 'Harmodius' and you have to follow it.

[*Sings*]

Such a man was never seen in Athens . . .

PHILOCLEON [*sings*]

Such a low-down, thieving little bastard . . .

BDELYCLEON If you sing that, you'll never survive the uproar. Cleon will swear to have your blood; he'll threaten to ruin and drive you out of the city.

PHILOCLEON If he threatens me, I've got another song for him:

[*Sings*]

Take care, for if too high in the city you rise,
You'll make her top-heavy and then she'll capsize![117]

BDELYCLEON And supposing Theorus, lying next to Cleon, takes his right hand and starts up with this:

[*Sings*]

It's wise, as Admetus found out in the end,
To choose a courageous man as your best friend.[118]
How will you follow that?

PHILOCLEON I've got something very poetic for that.

[*Sings*]

It isn't as easy, old boy, as it sounds
To run with the hare and to hunt with the hounds.[119]

BDELYCLEON And now it's Aeschines' turn. He's a very

learned, cultured sort of man. He'll probably start off with [*singing boisterously*]

Power, wealth and property
We enjoyed in Thessaly,
Clitagora, you and me . . .

PHILOCLEON [*singing*]

And bragged about it merrily.

BDELYCLEON Well, you seem to have got the gist of it. All right, let's go and have dinner at Philoctemon's. [*He claps his hands.*] Boy! Pack food for two – at last we can go and get drunk![120]

PHILOCLEON I don't approve of drinking! I know what boozing leads to: breaches of the peace, assault and battery – and a big fine while you've still got a hangover.

BDELYCLEON Not if you're drinking with gentlemen. They'll placate the victim for you, or else you can calm him down yourself. Just come out with a neat quotation from Aesop, or one of those stories about Sybarites[121] – something you've heard at the party. Make a joke of the whole thing, and the victim will just go away quietly.

PHILOCLEON I see I'm going to have to learn a lot of those stories, if I want to avoid getting fined. Well, son, what are we waiting for? Let's go.

[XANTHIAS *brings out a basket of food.* PHILOCLEON *and* BDELYCLEON *set out for the party with* XANTHIAS *in attendance.*]

CHORUS [*addressing the audience*][122]

I flatter myself I'm a bit of a wit,
And I've learnt all the tricks of the trade;
But there's one man I know – he's in the front row –
Who can put even me in the shade.
Can you guess who I mean? He has upper-class hair
It's done up in a bun at the top:
And he gambles with dice, a gentleman's vice
Provided you know when to stop.
But Amynias didn't. You'd think, with no cash,
He would starve on an apple a day;
Yet he dines like the wealthy, and keeps very healthy –

Just how does he manage it, pray?
If you mention his recent Thessalian jaunt
He does get a little bit testy;
But it can't have been that – for a person so poor
Would only have met the *Penestae*.[123]

Automenes,[124] you happy man,
How proud you needs must be
To have three sons of such renown
And such ability!
The eldest is a friend to all
And plays upon the lyre;
The second plays upon the stage
With passion and with fire.
But young Ariphades is much
The brightest of the three.
In one respect, at least, he was
An infant prodigy.
He taught himself, his father swore,
To use his tongue with flair.
For when he goes to brothels he'll
Lick all the girls with care.

[*The* CHORUS-LEADER *now speaks on behalf of the poet.*]

CHORUS-LEADER

Some people have been saying that since Cleon tanned my hide
I've made a coward's peace with him and let my wrath subside.[125]
They heard me scream blue murder when the dirty deed was done,
And rolled up in their hundreds – it was their idea of fun.
They didn't give a damn for me: they shouted 'Treat him rough!
He may say something funny if you squeeze him hard enough.'
And so I bluffed them for a while, but now it's time to stop;
And won't the vine look foolish when I pull away the prop!

Scene 2: *The same, a few hours later. It is now evening.*

[XANTHIAS *enters from the street, rubbing his bruises and complaining.*]

XANTHIAS O happy tortoises, that have so hard a shell! Oh, creatures full of sense! What wisdom to cover your bodies with a plate to shield it from blows! As for me, I've been beaten black and blue with that stick.[126]

CHORUS-LEADER What is it, child? It's fair to call you 'child', despite your age, if you've received a beating.

XANTHIAS The old man's been making a terrible nuisance of himself: he's drunker than any of them. And that's saying something, considering who the others are. There's Hypillus, Antiphon, Lycon, Lysistratus, Thuphrastus and Phrynichus[127] – all that crowd. But he's worse than anybody. Once he'd got a bit of food and drink inside him, he started leaping about like a young ass after a feed of barley; jumping up and down, laughing and farting. You should have seen him. Then he started knocking me about. 'Boy! Boy!' he kept shouting. And Lysistratus saw what was happening and started the comparison game. He told the old man he reminded him of a nouveau-riche Phrygian or a donkey let loose in a hayloft. 'Oh, I do, do I?' he shouted back. 'Well, you remind me of a locust when it's just shed its old wings, or Sthenelus[128] shorn of his stage props.' Well, everyone applauded – except Thuphrastus, who pursed his lips; he fancies himself as a wit. So the old man turns on Thuphrastus: 'And who are you to give yourself airs, thinking you're so smart – you who always suck up to the man of the moment?' And that's how he went on, insulting them all one after the other, making crude jokes and telling crass stories, utterly unsuited to the occasion. Then, when he was properly drunk, he left, knocking down everyone he met on the way home. Here he comes, reeling. I'm going to make myself scarce, before I get pasted again.

[*Shouting is heard offstage, and* XANTHIAS *hurries into the house as* PHILOCLEON *staggers into view, still wearing his party garland. He has one arm round a* FLUTE-GIRL *whom he has abducted from the party. In his other hand he carries a torch to ward off indignant protesters in his wake.*]

PHILOCLEON Stop! Make way! You people chasing after me will rue the day! Sod off, you lousy scabs, or I'll fry the lot of you with this torch!

REVELLER That's all very well, but you'll pay for these youthful pranks tomorrow. We'll all be round in the morning, and you'll answer for this in court.

PHILOCLEON Bah! In court? You old fogies! I can't even bear to hear the place mentioned. Balls to the voting urn! I prefer these [*groping the* FLUTE-GIRL*'s breasts*]. Are you still here? Where's this juryman? Get out of my sight!

[*The* REVELLER *leaves reluctantly.*]

Come up here, my little cockchafer. Here, grab this bit of rope. Careful, it's a bit old and tattered, but you'd be surprised how much wear and tear it can stand.[129] Did you see how I whisked you away just as you were about to have to suck off the guests? Well, now you can show this old chap here your gratitude. But no, you won't. You'll let me down. You'll tease me, just as you've left many a man standing. But listen, you be nice to me now, and when my son dies, I'll buy you your freedom and have you as my mistress. How would you like that, my little beaver? I've got the money, it's just that I'm not allowed to handle it yet – not till I'm a bit older. It's my son – he watches me like a hawk. He's a dreadful old skinflint, and very stern. You see, I'm his only father. Sh! Here he comes. Looking for us, probably. Quick, take this torch and stand completely still. I'm going to wind him up a bit – like he did to me before I was initiated in the Mysteries.[130]

[BDELYCLEON *enters. He has been running.*]

BDELYCLEON There you are, you dirty old muff-chaser! What are you doing, trying to screw yourself into the grave? You'll never get away with this.

PHILOCLEON I can see you'd like a nice lawsuit dressed in vinaigrette!

BDELYCLEON It's no laughing matter, kidnapping a flute-girl.

PHILOCLEON Flute-girl? What flute-girl? Have you taken leave of your tomb?

BDELYCLEON Here she is – Dardanis.[131]

PHILOCLEON Oh, you mean this – a sacrificial torch from the marketplace.

BDELYCLEON [*prodding the* GIRL] A torch, did you say?

PHILOCLEON Of course. Can't you tell by the markings?

BDELYCLEON What's this dark patch in the middle?

PHILOCLEON Oh, they leak resin sometimes, when they get hot.

BDELYCLEON And what's this bulge at the back? Feels remarkably like an arse to me.

PHILOCLEON That's just the shape of the wood.

BDELYCLEON What rubbish! [*To the* GIRL] You, come with me!

PHILOCLEON Here, what are you doing?

BDELYCLEON Taking her away from you. In any case, I don't think you'd have got anywhere with her; you're too old for that.

PHILOCLEON Am I indeed? Well, let me tell you something. Once when I was on a State mission to the Olympic Games, I saw Ephudion fight Ascondas, and – believe you me – the old man fought very well. I'll never forget the way he drew back his arm, like so, and then, with a telling punch, he floored the young man . . . like so. [*He hits* BDELYCLEON.]

BDELYCLEON [*staggering back to his feet*] Well, you certainly seem to remember that lesson!

[*Enter a* BAKING-WOMAN *with an empty tray and a witness in tow, who turns out to be the philosopher* CHAEREPHON.[132]]

BAKING-WOMAN [*to* CHAEREPHON] Come here, stand by me, please. [*Pointing to* PHILOCLEON] There's the man who almost did me in, whacking me with his torch. Ten obols' worth of loaves he knocked off this tray, plus four more loaves.

BDELYCLEON You see what you've done? More trouble, more fines to pay – all because of your drinking.

PHILOCLEON Nonsense! This affair can be settled straightaway with little storytelling. Leave her to me, I'll soon straighten this out.

BAKING-WOMAN No one's going to treat me like this and get away with it, I can tell you. I'm a respectable baking-woman. Myrtia, daughter of Ancylion and Sostrate. You've destroyed my entire batch.

PHILOCLEON Listen, old girl, have you, by any chance, heard this story? It's very amusing.

BAKING-WOMAN I don't want to hear it.

PHILOCLEON One night Aesop was walking home – he'd been out to dinner – when he was barked at by a mouthy, drunken bitch. 'Look, bitch,' said Aesop, 'instead of standing there yapping, why don't you go and buy some more flour!'

BAKING-WOMAN On top of everything else, he has the gall to laugh in my face. All right then, whatever your name is, I'm summoning you before the Market Court for damages. Chaerephon here will act as my witness.

PHILOCLEON No, no, listen to this. I'm sure you'll see the point of this one. Once when Lasus[133] found he was competing against Simonides,[134] he said: 'Ha, ha! What do I care?'

BAKING-WOMAN Did he now?

PHILOCLEON And as for you, Chaerephon, how can you act as a witness for a woman when you're as pale as Ino supplicating Euripides?[135]

[*The* BAKING-WOMAN *storms off taking* CHAEREPHON *with her. Next a* CITIZEN *with a bandaged head enters. He has brought a friend with him to act as witness.*]

BDELYCLEON Here comes somebody else to summon you, by the looks of it. He's brought a witness too, I see.

CITIZEN I'm bringing an action against you for assault and battery.

BDELYCLEON Not assault and battery,[136] for heaven's sake! I'll gladly pay you whatever you want as compensation.

PHILOCLEON No, no, I'll be happy to settle this myself. I admit I hit him, and threw the odd thing. [*To the* CITIZEN] Come here a minute. Will you leave it to me to decide how much to pay you, so that we can be friends in future? Or would you rather name a sum yourself?

CITIZEN Let's hear your offer. I don't really want the fuss of going to court.

PHILOCLEON This reminds me of the story of the man from Sybaris who fell out of a chariot, and managed to injure his head pretty badly – he wasn't a very good driver. A friend of his came along and said, 'A man should stick to his own trade.' So why don't you go to Pittalus[137] and get yourself seen to?

BDELYCLEON I might have known you'd do this.

CITIZEN [*to his* FRIEND] Take note of what he said.

[*The* CITIZEN *and* FRIEND *prepare to go.*]

PHILOCLEON Listen, don't go. Do you know the one about the woman from Sybaris who broke a jug?

CITIZEN [*to his* FRIEND] I call you to witness.

PHILOCLEON That's exactly what the jug did. It called a friend to witness, and the woman said, 'If you spent less time calling people to witness and went out and bought a rivet, you'd show more sense.'

CITIZEN Go on, insult me – until your case comes up in court!

[*The* CITIZEN *and his* FRIEND *depart in great indignation.*]

BDELYCLEON I'm not letting you stay here a moment longer, do you understand? I'm going to heave you over my shoulder [*he does so*] and carry you inside. Otherwise there won't be any people left to act as witnesses for all these complainants.

PHILOCLEON [*struggling against him*] When the . . . Delphians accused . . . Aesop . . .

BDELYCLEON Never mind Aesop.

PHILOCLEON . . . of stealing a sacred cup, he told them the story of the dung-beetle[138] that . . .

BDELYCLEON [*stopping him from speaking*] You'll be the death of me with those dung-beetles . . . [*He carries* PHILOCLEON *indoors.*]

CHORUS

At last he has fallen on happier days,
I envy his lot beyond measure:
He's going to exchange his abstemious ways
For a life of refinement and pleasure.
It may not be easy at first, I dare say,

A lifetime's opinions to smother;
Yet many men find that they can change their minds
When truly convinced by another.

His son, as all right-thinking men will agree,
Has shown both good sense and devotion;
His kindness and charm are so touching to see
That I'm quite overcome with emotion.
In grooming his sire for a life that is higher
He has countered each single objection;
The success that he's had in defeating his dad
Is a mark of his filial affection![139]

[XANTHIAS *comes out of the house and sits down, exhausted.*]

XANTHIAS Holy Dionysus! You've no idea the chaos that's erupted in this house. The old man just isn't used to drinking and listening to music like this. He's in such high spirits, we can't do anything to stop him. It looks as if he'll go on dancing all night, at this rate. He's been giving us 'Scenes from Thespis'[140] no less. He says that all the modern dancers are old fogies, and he's threatening to come out and prove it by competing with them.

[*Shouting, banging and flute-playing are heard within.*]

PHILOCLEON
What ho! Who sitteth at the outer gate?

XANTHIAS
Oh, no, a thing of evil this way comes . . .

PHILOCLEON
Fling wide the portals![141]

[XANTHIAS *opens the door and* PHILOCLEON *leaps out and stands, in the ludicrous costume of a tragic dancer, waiting to begin a dance.*]

Let the dance begin!

XANTHIAS
The madness, more like.

PHILOCLEON
Now stiffen the sinews . . .

And stretch the nostril wide – oh, how I wheeze!
Bend up the backbone – my god, how it cracks!

XANTHIAS
What you need is a dose of hellebore.[142]

PHILOCLEON
Phrynichus cowers like a strutting cock . . .[143]

XANTHIAS
They'll stone you.

PHILOCLEON
. . . leg thrown high into the air!
See how rectum gapes!

XANTHIAS Be careful there!

PHILOCLEON
For now the hip rolls smoothly in its socket.
Not bad, eh?

XANTHIAS
On the contrary, quite mad.

PHILOCLEON And now for my challenge. If there's any tragic dancer present who claims to dance well, let him step forward and dance against me. No takers?

XANTHIAS Only one: that fellow over there.

[*A* DANCER *costumed as a crab presents himself.*]

PHILOCLEON That forlorn creature – who is he?

XANTHIAS One of the sons of Carcinus the Crab.[144] The middle one.

PHILOCLEON I'll swallow him alive. I'll soon dispatch him with a knuckle dance. [*He beats out a rhythm on the crab-dancer's 'shell' with his fist. The* DANCER *sidles off.*] He's got no rhythm whatsoever!

XANTHIAS Here comes another crab-tragedian – his brother.[145]

[*A larger* 'CRAB' *enters.*]

PHILOCLEON I'll have myself a sizeable meal.

XANTHIAS Crabs, crabs, and yet more crabs – here comes another one of the family.

[*A smaller* 'CRAB' *enters.*]

PHILOCLEON What is this creeping creature? A shrimp? A spider?

XANTHIAS It's the tiniest of them all: the Little Nipper.[146] He also writes tragedies.

PHILOCLEON Ah, Carcinus, I congratulate you on a fine brood of twitterers. Well, I must go down and take them on. And, Xanthias, you'd better start preparing a dressing in case I win.

CHORUS

Make way, make way! The human tops are all wound up
to spin.
Stand back and make a space for them, and let the show
begin!

[*The* CHORUS *withdraw to the rear of the dancing area. While the* SONS OF CARCINUS *perform the 'Dance of the Crabs',* PHILOCLEON *executes a solo burlesque and the* CHORUS *sing the final lyric.*]

CHORUS

Ye sons of him who rules the waves
And brothers of the prawn,
Come where the barren sea still laves
The sands where you were born.

Oh whirl and twist upon the beach,
Rotate with supple ease;
Then stand upright and try to reach
Your stomachs with your knees.

Now kick straight upwards from the hips
As Phrynichus might try,
And draw from each spectator's lips
A complimentary sigh.

But crawling from the ocean deep
Its Lord, their father, scuttles
To watch his offspring gambol, leap
And whirl like spinning shuttles.[147]

The time has come to end our play;
But you dance off before us;
And this at least it's safe to say –
No comic poet till today
Has hit on such a clever way
Of leading off his Chorus.[148]

[*The* CHORUS *march out, preceded by the* SONS OF CARCINUS, *leaving* PHILOCLEON *to finish his dance and receive applause from the audience.*]

WOMEN AT THE THESMOPHORIA

PREFACE TO *WOMEN AT THE THESMOPHORIA*

The *Women at the Thesmophoria* ('Thesmophoriazusae') was produced in 411 BC, probably at the Dionysia. At the time Athens was still reeling from the disastrous Sicilian expedition, in which almost its entire fleet was destroyed. The city was short of money to rebuild its navy and men to man it; moreover, many of Athens' allies were threatening revolt. Most Athenians probably felt a Spartan victory looming. In the summer, dissatisfaction with the way the war was being conducted had led to a revolution in which democracy was replaced by an oligarchic regime of four hundred men. This was soon modified to a more moderate rule by five thousand, but it was not until 410 that democracy was restored.

Despite being written during this period of upheaval and mistrust, *Women* is the least political of Aristophanes' surviving plays. This need not surprise us. While *Lysistrata* (produced at the Lenaea of 411) is on the face of it an anti-war play, its far-fetched plot culminating in a fanciful peace is in fact a prime piece of Old Comic escapism. Both the avoidance of Athens' political situation in *Women* and its wishful transformation in *Lysistrata* suggest that Aristophanes chose to avoid the polemically political stance of many of his earlier plays. Perhaps it was simply too dangerous to be strongly critical at a time when democracy had been abandoned.

Aristophanes' preoccupation with Euripides and his controversial, innovative brand of tragedy date back to his early plays. He had presented Euripides on the stage twice (that we know of) before, first in *Acharnians* and then in (the lost) *Preview*, and he did so again later in *Frogs* after the tragedian's death.

While in other plays Euripides is presented solely as a public figure, *Women* focuses on a personal predicament. The women of Athens, offended by Euripides' presentation of female characters in his plays, plan to do away with him. This premise is, of course, preposterous: the women of Athens could not, in reality, decide on Euripides' fate; in addition, their particular grievance with Euripides in the play is undermined in the formal debate, where their indignation is caused as much by his having revealed the truth about them as having maligned them. In any case, while some of Euripides' earlier plays, such as *Medea* and *Hippolytus*, present heroines under the influence of dangerous passions, his recent plays, two of which are parodied extensively in the second half of this comedy, actually present conspicuously virtuous heroines.

Aristophanes' presentation of female characters in *Women* shows similarities with his two other surviving plays centred around women, *Lysistrata* and *Assemblywomen*. All three are full of jokes at women's expense, mainly concerning their alleged weakness for drink and extramarital escapades. Such are jokes written from a male perspective for a predominantly, if not entirely, male audience. (It is worth noting that the purportedly misogynistic Euripides presents his tragic women far more favourably than Aristophanes does his comic women.) Much of the play's humour also derives from cross-dressing. Most male characters in the play – not only Mnesilochus (whose dressing up by Euripides and dressing down by the women comprise two of the play's funniest scenes) but also Agathon, Cleisthenes and Euripides – either dress or disguise themselves as women. An additional layer of playful humour arises from the fact that the female characters were played by male actors.

While the play begins with the implausible premise that the women control Euripides' fate, its subsequent action is not as strongly fantastic as other plays (e.g., *Birds*, where an ordinary Athenian travels to Cloudcuckooland, gulls the birds, and then, with Prometheus' help, seizes supreme power from Zeus). Euripides' attempts to resolve his predicament, and his various ploys to rescue Mnesilochus, involve a development of action that is unusually consistent for Aristophanic comedy; moreover, the outcome of events hangs in the balance until the very end. In these respects *Women* seems to emulate Euripidean tragedy. The action of the first half of the play also imitates an early Euripidean play, *Telephus* (produced in 438), with Mnesilochus adopting the title role, seemingly inadvertently. The second half of the play involves elaborate set-piece parodies of two Euripidean tragedies produced in 412, *Helen* and *Andromeda*. Both plays involve tragic heroines whose plights mirror Mnesilochus' situation in the comedy. They may also have been chosen because their title heroines are actually presented as models of virtue – in Euripides' play Helen is removed by the gods to Egypt while a phantom Helen is sent to Troy – further undermining the women's main charge against Euripides.

The Thesmophoria was a festival for women in honour of the goddesses Demeter (entitled Thesmophoros, 'Bringer of Law') and her daughter Persephone (or Kore). It was held at sowing time, its primary purpose being to ensure the fertility of the earth and the city's women. Men were strictly excluded and details of the rites were guarded carefully. Consequently, little is known about them.

In Athens the festival took place over three days around October–November. While the characters in the play speak of a precinct called the Thesmophorion, no such site has been identified. Most likely there was a shrine within the Eleusinion, a large sanctuary on the north slope of the Acropolis. This location would tally with a reference in the play to 'going up' to the Thesmophoria (585). It would also explain the name of the first day of the festival, the 'Ascent'. In Aristophanes' day there was probably already a priestess of the Thesmophoroi who presided over proceedings. There were, in addition, two women chosen from each deme (probably by lot) to take a leading role in the celebrations. The Chorus in the play refer to themselves as 'freeborn women of Athens' (329), implying that the festival was restricted to citizens' wives. There is also evidence to suggest that only married women were permitted; all the female characters in the play either have or claim to have children, including the disguised Mnesilochus.

The second day (called the 'Middle' Day), on which the play is set, was a day of fasting, probably commemorating Demeter's refusal to eat or drink after the abduction of Persephone by Hades. Other related rites included the sacrifice of piglets and the utterance of ritual obscenities. There would also have been singing of various hymns and dancing. What makes the festival a suitable setting for the play is that the rites were kept secret from men. The women may have discussed certain issues which were of concern to them, but their imitation of the formal procedure used in the assembly is an Aristophanic invention which, besides being humorous in itself, accords with the play's premise that the women can decide on Euripides' fate.

In *Women* we find a fuller and more sympathetic portrayal of Euripides than elsewhere in Aristophanes. He is also presented more positively than Socrates in *Clouds* (the other main avant-garde intellectual to appear as a major character in Aristophanes' surviving plays). Euripides begins the play as the comic hero in a predicament and ends it saving his relative, who takes over the role of comic hero by proxy, and coming to an amicable resolution with the women. His erudite air at the start of the play and his ingenious attempts to rescue Mnesilochus are not so much caustically mocked as endearingly sent up, in marked contrast with his depiction as a shifty, sophistic pedant in *Frogs*. The willing Mnesilochus, who selflessly puts himself in mortal danger for Euripides' sake, is also one of Aristophanes' most likeable and mischievous creations.

Women abounds both in verbal and visual humour. It seamlessly blends highbrow parody of tragedy and reflexive theatrical games with decidedly lowbrow slapstick and transvestitism. While it may lack the political bite and urgency of many of his other comedies, it is nonetheless – without doubt – one of his most entertaining plays.

CHARACTERS

EURIPIDES, *the tragedian*
MNESILOCHUS, *an old man, related by marriage to Euripides*
AGATHON, *the tragedian, a younger contemporary of Euripides*
CLEISTHENES, *a notorious effeminate*
SERVANT *to Agathon, a slave*
A MAGISTRATE
A SCYTHIAN CONSTABLE
MICA, *an Athenian woman*
SECOND WOMAN, *a seller of garlands*
CRITYLLA, *a friend of Mica*
ECHO, *a character from a play of Euripides*

CHORUS OF ATHENIAN WOMEN

Silent Characters

MANIA, *nursemaid of Mica* } *slaves*
PHILISTA, *another maid of Mica's* } *slaves*
ARTEMISIA, *a dancing-girl*

ACT ONE

Scene I: *A street in Athens.*

[*Enter* EURIPIDES. *He has been walking for some time and is looking for a house. He stops to wait for his companion* MNESILOCHUS.[1] The latter is an elderly relative of EURIPIDES, *who is accompanying him but lagging behind, clearly resentful of the length of their journey.*]

MNESILOCHUS They say the swallow brings fresh hope: I wish I could see one. This man'll be the death of me, lugging me around since dawn. Listen, Euripides, before I'm out of breath entirely, I'd like to hear where you're taking me.

EURIPIDES You need not *hear* the things that you will soon be *seeing*.

MNESILOCHUS What's that? I needn't hear . . . ?

EURIPIDES What you're about to see.

MNESILOCHUS And what mustn't I see?

EURIPIDES What you're about to hear.

MNESILOCHUS I don't follow. It's too clever for me. You mean I mustn't hear *or* see?

EURIPIDES The two concepts are, in their respective natures, sharply differentiated.

MNESILOCHUS You mean *not* hearing and *not* seeing?

EURIPIDES Precisely.

MNESILOCHUS How do you mean 'differentiated'?

EURIPIDES Let me explain how all these things are arranged.[2] When Ether was first separated, and creatures capable of movement came into being under her, for the purpose of vision she devised the eye – modelled on the orb of the sun. For hearing, however, she provided a funnel, known as the ear.

MNESILOCHUS And I mustn't hear or see, because of this funnel? I'm so glad to have learnt that. What joy it is to talk with men of wisdom![3]

EURIPIDES Oh, I can teach you many things of this sort.

MNESILOCHUS Perhaps you could teach me how to avoid becoming lame after all this exertion.[4]

EURIPIDES Come over here and pay attention.

MNESILOCHUS Well?

EURIPIDES Do you see that door?

MNESILOCHUS I think so.

EURIPIDES Keep quiet.

MNESILOCHUS Keep quiet about the door?

EURIPIDES Sh! Listen.

MNESILOCHUS I'm listening – and keeping quiet about the door.

EURIPIDES This is where the famous tragedian Agathon[5] lives.

MNESILOCHUS Which Agathon is that, now?

EURIPIDES The Agathon who . . .

MNESILOCHUS Not that big, strong, dark fellow?

EURIPIDES No, a different one. You must have seen him.

MNESILOCHUS Not that chap with a bushy beard?

EURIPIDES No! You must have seen him.

MNESILOCHUS I'm sure I haven't. Not that I can remember, anyway.

EURIPIDES And yet you've buggered him – though perhaps without knowing it![6] [*The door opens.*] Quick, get down, out of sight! There's a servant coming out with a brazier and myrtle twigs. He must be about to offer up a prayer for inspiration.

[*The* SERVANT *comes out of* AGATHON*'s house and sets up his paraphernalia. He begins to speak in pompous, elevated tones.*[7]]

SERVANT

Let all men keep silence, and be you closed,

O mouths! Inasmuch as the Muses in
Mellifluous concourse do grace these lordly
Halls with their presence! Let the windless air
Be free from breezes; and the sea's blue wave,
Let it not roar.

MNESILOCHUS Drivel!

EURIPIDES Sh! What's he saying?

SERVANT
Be still, ye tribes of birds, and do not stir;
Neither let any foot of beast be heard
Within the forest.

MNESILOCHUS Complete drivel!

SERVANT
For Agathon our champion, Agathon
The fair of speech is about to . . .

MNESILOCHUS Not be buggered, surely?

SERVANT Who said that?

MNESILOCHUS The 'windless air'.

SERVANT
. . . is about to set down
The frame of a new drama, yes, with mighty
Crossbeams shall it be built, and with new arches
Of words shall it be erected. For look,
He rotates his verses upon the lathe
And fastens them together. For both maxim
And metaphor does he hammer out, yes,
In molten wax does he mould his creation.
He rolls it till it be round; he whittles it . . .

MNESILOCHUS And fellates it!

SERVANT What lout is lurking near our corniced walls?

MNESILOCHUS One who'll take you and your precious poet and probe your cornices with his protuberance.

[*The* SERVANT *now stops his chanting tone and speaks in his normal voice.*]

SERVANT You must have been a wayward youth, old man.

EURIPIDES [*to the* SERVANT] Listen, my friend, never mind about him. Could you call Agathon for me? You must get him out here at all costs.

SERVANT No need to ask. He's coming out any minute now, to do some composing. It's this wintry weather. Not easy to bend the stanzas into shape. He has to bring them out into the sun. [*He goes into the house.*]

MNESILOCHUS What about me, what am I supposed to do?

EURIPIDES Stay where you are, he's coming out. O Zeus, what will you do to me this day?[8]

MNESILOCHUS [*to himself*] I must say, I'd like to know what this is all about. [*To* EURIPIDES] Why do you weep? What disconcerts you so? You must not hide the truth from me; I am your kin.[9]

EURIPIDES There's serious trouble brewing for me today.

MNESILOCHUS What kind of trouble?

EURIPIDES This day decides if Euripides lives or dies.

MNESILOCHUS How can it? The juries aren't sitting today. Nor is the council – it's the middle day of the Thesmophoria.[10]

EURIPIDES That's just it. And I fear it'll be my last. The women have been plotting against me. And today, at the Thesmophoria, they're going to debate my downfall.

MNESILOCHUS But why?

EURIPIDES They say I denigrate them in my tragedies.

MNESILOCHUS And so you do. It would serve you right if they did get you. But what's your plan of escape?

EURIPIDES I thought of persuading Agathon to go to the Thesmophoria.

MNESILOCHUS To do what? Tell me.

EURIPIDES He could sit in the assembly with all the women and, if necessary, speak in my defence.

MNESILOCHUS What, openly? Or in disguise?

EURIPIDES Disguised, assuming feminine attire.[11]

MNESILOCHUS A brilliant idea! And very much your style. I must say, for sheer cunning we really take the biscuit.

EURIPIDES Sh!

MNESILOCHUS What is it?

EURIPIDES Agathon's coming out.

[*The front of the house swings open, revealing* AGATHON,

clean shaven and in a wig, wearing female clothing and a white ('female') mask, seated at a dressing-table.]

MNESILOCHUS Where? I can't see him.

EURIPIDES There, coming round on the revolving platform.[12]

MNESILOCHUS I must be going blind. I can't see a man there at all – only Cyrene.[13]

EURIPIDES Be quiet, he's getting ready to sing.

[AGATHON *rises and utters a few practice trills in falsetto.*]

MNESILOCHUS He's got ants in his larynx.

[AGATHON *sings,*[14] *taking the parts of* CHORUS-LEADER *and* CHORUS OF MAIDENS *alternately.*]

AGATHON

[*As Leader*] Come, you maids, receive the torches
Sacred to the infernal twain![15]
Dance, your voices freely raising
In the fashion of your homeland.

[*As Chorus*] Which god shall we celebrate, then?
We are only too delighted
Any of the gods to worship
At the slightest provocation.

[*As Leader*] Sing, for lo, the archer Phoebus
With his bow of gold appears,
By his presence sanctifying
All the glades of fair Simoïs.[16]

[*As Chorus*] With our fairest songs we greet you,
Phoebus, on your throne of glory
O'er all graceful arts presiding
And the sacred prize bestowing.

[*As Leader*] Praise you now the virgin huntress,
Ranger of the tree-clad mountains.

[*As Chorus*] Child of Leto,[17] maid untainted,
Artemis, we glorify you.

[*As Leader*] Now let us give praise to Leto
And the lyre that sets us dancing
To the spry Phrygian rhythm[18]
When the strings go twingle twangle.

[*As Chorus*] We have not forgotten Leto
Or the twanging harp of Asia,

Mother of our songs and dances:
Loudly let us sing their praises!
[*As Leader*] Now with eyes divinely flashing,
Voices raised in sudden outcry,
Sing the praise of lordly Phoebus.
[*As Chorus*] Hail to you, O son of Leto!

MNESILOCHUS Ah, what soft seductive strains! How feminine, how deliciously arousing! Like French-kissing, all tongues! Oh, how it makes me tingle. And as for you, my young friend, I can only ask, in the words of Aeschylus: 'Whence art thou, girlish man? What's thine attire, And what thy country?'[19] Why this disruption of nature? Why a lute with a saffron gown? A lyre with a hairnet? A woman's girdle and a wrestler's oil flask? Why this union of sword and hand-mirror? It makes no sense. What are you – a man? Then where's your cloak? And your shoes? And where's your prick? If you're a woman, where are your breasts? Well, what do you say? Why are you silent? If you won't tell me, I'll have to judge by your singing.

AGATHON Old man, old man, I sense a note of envy in your reproach, yet I will not be riled. I wear my clothes to suit my inspiration. A poet has to merge his personality with what he is portraying. If he shows a woman's actions, he must participate in her experience – mind, body and soul.[20]

MNESILOCHUS So if you wrote about Phaedra would you assume the straddling position?[21]

AGATHON If one writes about a man, one already has all the bits and pieces, as it were. But what nature does not provide, art must imitate.

MNESILOCHUS Let me know if you're writing a satyr-play, and I'll come and help by ramming you from behind.

AGATHON Anyway, it's unseemly for a poet to go round looking all wild and hairy. Look at Ibycus, and Anacreon of Teos, and Alcaeus,[22] with those exquisitely tempered harmonies of theirs. They all wore the proper minstrel's sash, and their movements were graceful, like mine. And Phrynichus[23] – you went to his recitals perhaps – what a handsome man and how beautifully turned out. That's why his dramas turned out so beautifully too: what you write depends so much on what you are.

MNESILOCHUS That would explain why that graceless man Philocles[24] writes such graceless verse. And why dreadful Xenocles[25] writes so dreadfully, and lifeless Theognis[26] so lifelessly.

AGATHON It follows necessarily. And knowing this, I gave myself this treatment.

MNESILOCHUS How on earth did you manage it?

EURIPIDES Stop yapping! I was just the same myself at his age, when I first started writing.

MNESILOCHUS I don't envy you your schooling.

EURIPIDES Now, if you don't mind, I'd like to get down to business.

AGATHON What do you have in mind?

EURIPIDES A wise man, Agathon, can curb his speech, and utter many thoughts in but few words.[27] I have been struck by misfortune once more, and come to you as a suppliant.

AGATHON What can I do for you?

EURIPIDES The women are meeting at the Thesmophoria today, and . . . they're going to condemn me to death for slandering them.

AGATHON But how is it you think that *I* can help?

EURIPIDES In every way. If you would only go up there secretly and take your seat with the women, as if you were one of them, you could speak up for me and save my life. No one but you can make a speech worthy of me.

AGATHON Why don't you go yourself and make your own defence?

EURIPIDES Well, first of all I'm well known by sight. Secondly, I'm old and white-haired and bearded. You, on the other hand, are good-looking, fair-complexioned and clean-shaven. You have a woman's voice and a dainty manner – you're pretty to look at.

AGATHON Euripides.

EURIPIDES Yes?

AGATHON Did you not write the line, 'You love your life; your father loves his too'?[28]

EURIPIDES I did.

AGATHON Then why do you expect me to bear your misfortunes? I would be insane to do so. Your troubles are your own, and you must cope with them yourself. Misfortunes are not meant to be averted through cunning ruses; one must submit oneself to them.[29]

MNESILOCHUS You mean just as you, you filthy catamite, have a slack passage not from clever words but through submissive acts?

EURIPIDES Come, tell me honestly why you're afraid to go.

AGATHON It would be even worse for me than you.

EURIPIDES Why?

AGATHON They think I snatch away their female sexual rights by poaching their nocturnal business.

MNESILOCHUS Poaching indeed! Letting yourself be buggered, more like! Still, it's a fair excuse.

EURIPIDES Well, will you do it?

AGATHON Not on your life!

EURIPIDES O three times luckless me! Euripides is done for!

MNESILOCHUS O dearest friend, my kinsman, don't give up like this!

EURIPIDES But what can I do?

MNESILOCHUS Tell him to bugger off, and use me instead. I'll do anything.

EURIPIDES [*with new hope*] Well, in that case, off with that cloak!

MNESILOCHUS [*taking it off*] There! What are you going to do to me?

EURIPIDES [*indicating* MNESILOCHUS' *beard*] Shave all this off. [*He peers under* MNESILOCHUS' *tunic.*] The rest we'll have to singe.

MNESILOCHUS [*reluctantly*] All right, if you have to. It's my fault for offering.

EURIPIDES Agathon, you've always got a razor handy. Could you lend us one?

AGATHON Take one out of that razor case.

EURIPIDES That's kind of you. [*To* MNESILOCHUS] Now, sit down. Puff out your right cheek. [*He starts to shave him.*]

MNESILOCHUS Hey, that hurts! [*He continues groaning and objecting.*]

EURIPIDES Stop making such a fuss. I'll have to gag you if you don't settle down.

[MNESILOCHUS *utters a wild howl and makes off.*]

EURIPIDES Hey, where are you going?

MNESILOCHUS To the holy altar.[30] I'm not going to stay here, so help me Demeter, to be hacked to pieces.

EURIPIDES Won't you look a little odd with one shaved cheek?

MNESILOCHUS I don't care.

EURIPIDES Now don't let me down, I beg you. Come back here.

MNESILOCHUS [*returning reluctantly*] Oh dear, oh dear!

EURIPIDES [*resuming the operation*] Sit still, will you, and keep your chin up. And stop fidgeting! [*He takes hold of* MNESILOCHUS' *nose, so as to shave his moustache.*]

MNESILOCHUS Mh, mh!

EURIPIDES Stop whingeing, it's all over now.

MNESILOCHUS I feel like a shaven recruit.[31]

EURIPIDES Don't worry, you look rather attractive. [*He picks up one of* AGATHON*'s mirrors.*] Want to take a look at yourself?

MNESILOCHUS All right. [*He takes one look at himself and thrusts the mirror away in horror.*]

EURIPIDES Well?

MNESILOCHUS It's not me, it's . . . Cleisthenes![32]

EURIPIDES Now stand up and bend over, I have to singe you.

MNESILOCHUS Oh no, I'll be scorched like a suckling pig!

EURIPIDES [*calling into the house*] Will someone bring me out a torch or lamp? [*A slave comes out with a blazing torch.*] Bend over! [*He takes the torch and begins the singeing operation.*] Keep your todger out of the way!

MNESILOCHUS I'm trying to, but I'm on fire. Help! Water, water, quickly, before my backside catches fire too!

EURIPIDES Cheer up, it's all over now.

MNESILOCHUS Cheer up? When I'm burnt to a frazzle?

EURIPIDES Nothing more to worry about. The worst is over.

MNESILOCHUS Phew! What a stink of soot. You've char-grilled my crotch!

EURIPIDES Don't worry, someone will sponge it for you.

MNESILOCHUS Anyone who tries to wipe my arse will rue the day.

EURIPIDES Agathon, if you're not prepared to help in person, could you at least lend me a dress and a headband for my friend here? You can't pretend you don't possess such things.

AGATHON Yes, help yourself, use anything you like.

MNESILOCHUS Hm, which one shall I take?

EURIPIDES Here, put on this yellow gown.

MNESILOCHUS [*burying his face in it*] Ah, what a delicate scent of . . . cheesy pudendum!

EURIPIDES Come on, get it on.

MNESILOCHUS Pass me the girdle.

EURIPIDES Here you are.

MNESILOCHUS Help me will you, I can't get this bit round the legs right.

[*Between them they make a mess of things but eventually achieve an acceptable result.*]

EURIPIDES Now we need a hairnet and a headdress.

AGATHON You can borrow this wig, if you like. I wear it at night.

EURIPIDES Oh yes, that's exactly what we need.

[MNESILOCHUS *puts the wig on.*]

MNESILOCHUS Does it suit me?

EURIPIDES You look fabulous. Now you want a shawl.

AGATHON You can have that one on the couch there.

EURIPIDES And shoes?

AGATHON Here you are, take these.

MNESILOCHUS Will they fit me, I wonder – you like a slack fit yourself.

AGATHON Only you can tell. Well, you've got everything you need, so would someone kindly wheel me in again.[33]

[*He is wheeled in and* EURIPIDES *and* MNESILOCHUS *are left alone.*]

EURIPIDES Well, you certainly look like a woman now. Just make sure you put on a feminine voice when you speak.

MNESILOCHUS [*in a camp voice*] I'll do my best.

EURIPIDES Right, off you go.

MNESILOCHUS Wait! Not until you swear a solemn oath.

EURIPIDES To do what?

MNESILOCHUS To come to the rescue, if anything happens to me – without fail.

EURIPIDES I swear by Ether, dwelling place of Zeus.[34]

MNESILOCHUS No, that won't do. You might as well swear by a block of flats.[35]

EURIPIDES All right, I swear by all the blessèd gods.

MNESILOCHUS And remember: it was your heart that swore, not just your tongue. And I didn't force you.[36]

[*A babble of female voices is heard.*]

EURIPIDES Hurry up, I can see the flag for the assembly going up over the temple. I'd better clear off.

[EURIPIDES *departs as the women begin to arrive. The next scene follows without a break.*]

Scene 2: *The forecourt of the Temple of Demeter Thesmophoros.*

[*Women pour into the forecourt (the orchestra) and gather round the altar to deposit their offerings. Besides the* CHORUS, *the crowd includes* MICA,[37] *a formidable woman and a* SECOND WOMAN *of anxious disposition.* MICA *is accompanied by two maids, one of whom carries a baby.* MNESILOCHUS, *conspicuous in his dubious disguise, mingles with the chattering throng and addresses an imaginary slave of his own.*]

MNESILOCHUS Come along, Thratta,[38] this way. Oh look, Thratta, look at all the smoke! What a lot of torches. [*He approaches the altar, where numerous women are uttering prayers.*] O beauteous Twain, receive me now, and may I be blessed with good fortune – both coming here and getting home. [*He suddenly realizes that the women are placing offerings before the altar.*] Oh, yes, Thratta, just put the basket down and take out the sacrificial cake so that I can offer it to the two goddesses. Beloved mistress Demeter, divine Persephone, grant that I may sacrifice to you often – or at least get away with it this once. Show favour to my little ones. May my sweet little daughter, Fanny, find a rich-but-dim husband; and may my dear son, Willy,[39] have brains and good sense, amen! Now I wonder where's best to sit so that I can hear the speakers? You can go now, Thratta; slaves aren't supposed to listen to the speeches.

[*The* CHORUS *and the other women take their seats, and* MNESILOCHUS *places himself among them.*]

CHORUS-LEADER[40] Silence, silence! Pray you to Demeter and the Divine Maiden,[41] the Holy Twain. Pray you to Pluto, and to the mother of all beauty, the fruitful nourishing Earth. Pray you to Hermes and the Graces, that this assembled congregation may in fair and seemly debate bring blessings to the city of Athens and haply to ourselves as well. And she who in act and speech best serves the people of Athens and the interests of women, may her words prevail. Pray you for these things, and for blessing upon yourselves. Sing the paean, sing the paean, and lift up your hearts!

CHORUS

And may the gods rejoice also,
Appearing gladly among us,
And sanctify our prayers.
Come, mighty Zeus:
For great is your name.
Come, Apollo, Lord of holy Delos,
Bearing the golden lyre.
Come, bright-eyed Pallas, invincible maid,
For your spear is of gold
And your city was contested by the gods.[42]
Come, child of Leto, huntress of beasts:
Many are your names.
Come, dread Poseidon, ruler of the briny waves:
Forsake your deep hiding places

In the fish-filled, whirling sea.
Come from your streams and rivers, O Nereids;
And descend, you roaming Nymphs of the mountains.
May the strings of the golden lyre echo our prayers,
And may we the freeborn women of Athens
Delight the gods with our assembly.

CHORUS-LEADER

Now raise your voices and invoke the great Olympian gods
And goddesses, and call upon the mighty Delian gods
And goddesses, and supplicate the noble Pythian gods
And goddesses, and pray to all the other, lesser gods
And goddesses, that they will take this opportunity
To punish those who threaten this female community.
A curse upon the man who plans our enemies to please,
Or puts his lot in with the Persians or Euripides,[43]
Aspires to be a tyrant or to set one on the throne,
Or tells a woman's husband that the baby's not his own;
The maid who knows the very man when Mistress wants some fun,
But spills the beans to Master when a good night's work is done;
The messenger who bears false tales; the lover who seduces
With talk of all the gifts he'll bring, and then no gift produces;
The girl who takes his presents when he goes to her instead,
The hag who presses gifts on him to lure him to her bed;
And last of all the characters who meet with our displeasure,
The barman or the barmaid who serves us a short measure.
On these and on their houses may the wrath of heaven fall.
But otherwise we pray the gods will guard and bless us all.

CHORUS

We pray now for blessing
On people and state,
And on all that is said
In our solemn debate:
That she who speaks wisely
May carry the day,
And none play us false
Or our secrets betray.
On all who from motives
Of malice and greed
Dishonour the City,
Connive with the Mede,
Or basely endeavour
The laws to reverse,
We hereby pronounce
An appropriate curse;
And to Zeus our most humble
Petition we tender,
That our prayers may be valid
In spite of our gender.

CHORUS-LEADER All hear! [*Reading*] 'At a meeting of the Women's Council, held under the chairwomanship of Timoclea, with Lysilla as secretary, it was proposed by Sostrate that an assembly be held on the morning of the second day of the Thesmophoria, this being the least busy time, to decide what steps should be taken for punishing Euripides, who is unanimously agreed to be guilty.' Who wishes to speak?

MICA [*rising*] I do.

CHORUS-LEADER [*handing her the speaker's garland*] Put this on first. Silence, attention everyone. She's clearing her throat just like orators do. I can see we're in for a long speech.

MICA I assure you, ladies, my getting up to speak like this is not from any personal ambition, it's just that I can no longer bear to sit by and see us women dragged through the mire by this cabbage-woman's son[44] Euripides. The things he says about us! Is there any crime he has not accused us of? Wherever there's a stage[45] and a theatre full of punters, there he is, coming out with his slanders, calling us double-dealers, strumpets, boozers, cheats, gossips, bad eggs and a curse upon mankind. And naturally the men all come home after the play and give us suspicious looks, and start looking in all the cupboards for concealed lovers. A woman can't do any of the things she used to in the old days. He's filled our husbands' minds with such awful ideas. Why, if you just sit plaiting a wreath your husband thinks you must be in love with someone. And suppose you accidentally drop something about the house, he says: 'Whom did she have in mind? It cannot be but 'twas our guest from Corinth.'[46] Or perhaps a girl isn't feeling too well: in comes her brother and says, 'Whence come these guilty flushes to thy cheek?'[47] And another thing. Supposing a woman finds she can't bear her husband a child. She's got to produce one from somewhere, hasn't she? What chance has she got with her husband sitting watching her the whole time? And what's happened to all the rich old men who used to marry young girls? Euripides has put them off completely with his 'An old man weds a tyrant not a wife'.[48] It's because of him that they've started putting bolts and seals on the doors of the women's quarters, and keeping those great Molossian dogs[49] to scare off lovers. One might forgive him all this, but now we're not even allowed a free hand on our own side of the house any more. We can't get at the flour or the oil or the wine. Our husbands carry the keys around with them – nasty complicated Laconian ones with triple teeth.[50] In the old days you could get a ring made for three obols that would reseal any larder door in Athens, but now this home-wrecker Euripides has got them all wearing seals that look like pieces of worm-eaten wood. In conclusion, ladies, I feel that somehow or other we have got to devise a sticky end for him: perhaps by poison or some other way.[51] At any rate, he must die. That's all I have to say in public. I'll draw up a more detailed indictment with the secretary.

[*She returns the garland to the* CHORUS-LEADER *and sits down, amid applause.*]

CHORUS

I've never heard a woman speak
With such assurance and technique:
Such fine felicity of phrase
Is worthy of the highest praise.
It was no negligible feat
To think of arguments so neat;
She said exactly what was needed,
With each and every aspect heeded.
If, after wingèd words like these,
We had a speech by Xenocles,
Even this audience, I am sure,
Would find the man a dreadful bore.

[SECOND WOMAN *rises to speak and is handed the garland.*]

SECOND WOMAN I don't want to say more than a few words. This lady seems to have covered everything very well. I would just like to tell you what I've been through myself. My husband died in Cyprus and left me with five young children to look after; it was as much as I could do to keep them alive by selling myrtle chaplets in the market. Then this man comes along and starts writing his tragedies, saying that there aren't any gods.[52] Now my trade's gone down to half what it was. I tell you ladies one and all, that man ought to be punished for all he's done; he's so harsh to us. I suppose it comes of being brought up on his mother's bitter potherbs. Well, I must be getting back to the market myself; I've got some gentlemen waiting for a special order of twenty wreaths.[53]

[*She returns the garland and departs amid applause.*]

CHORUS

Bravo! Did you ever
Hear phrases so clever,
A style so polished and neat?
Every word that she said
Hit the nail on the head:
A real oratorical treat!
In sensible terms

She broadly confirms
What we've hinted several times;
And now that his guilt
Is proved to the hilt,
The man must pay for his crimes.

[MNESILOCHUS *now rises and assumes the garland.*]

MNESILOCHUS Well, I'm not surprised, ladies, that you're all feeling very annoyed with Euripides, after hearing all this about him. I expect you're seething with indignation. Personally I can't stand the man – I swear on my children's lives. Still, let us all be frank with one another. For we're alone, with no outsider present. Why is it that we blame him for these things,[54] getting so worked up, when all he's done is mention two or three of our little tricks? There are thousands of other things he *doesn't* know about. Take me, for instance, not to mention anyone else, I've done so many terrible things. I think the worst was when I'd been married just three days. My husband was sound asleep beside me, when an old friend – you know, seduced me when I was little – came tapping ever so lightly on the door because he was feeling frisky. I knew who it was straightaway. So I started creeping downstairs, and suddenly my husband called out, 'Where are you going?' 'It's my tummy,' I said, 'it really hurts – it's churning inside. I'm just going out to the toilet.' 'All right,' he said, and started pounding up some dill and sage and juniper to cure my indigestion. Meanwhile I got some water to stop the door creaking, and went out to lover boy. And, boy, was he good! He did me from behind as I held on to a laurel bush by the altar of Apollo.[55] Now Euripides has never said anything about that! Nor about how we let ourselves be rogered by slaves and mule-drivers when there's no one better. And what about that trick of chewing a bit of garlic in the morning, when you've had a bit of fun? The man of the house comes home from Wall Duty, takes one sniff and says, 'Well, she can't have been up to any mischief this time.'[56] Euripides has never mentioned that either. If he wants to rail about Phaedra, let him, I say. He's never said a word about the woman who spread her skirt out wide to show her husband how nice it looked in the sunlight, while smuggling her boyfriend out underneath it. I know another woman who claimed to be in labour for ten days because she couldn't get hold of a baby. Her husband went all round town buying medicines to speed things up. In the end the old midwife managed to find a baby and brought it home in a jar, with its mouth bunged up with beeswax to stop it yelling; and when the old woman gives her the nod, the wife calls out to her husband, 'Go away, go away, it's starting!' He trots off delighted; they pull out the baby, unbung its mouth and the baby cries. The sly old midwife runs off to the husband, beaming, and says, 'It's a boy, a real lion of a boy, the image of his father, even down to his little winkle – the same bend halfway along.'[57] I ask you, ladies, do we do these things? Of course we do. Why be so angry with Euripides? We suffer nothing worse than we deserve.[58]

[*A murmur of indignation breaks out.*]

CHORUS

Where did this creature come from?
I'm shocked, amazed, distressed.
I didn't think I'd ever hear
Such sentiments expressed.

To say such things in public –
I don't know how she dared!
Well, there it is – it goes to show
One has to be prepared.

What says the ancient proverb?
'Be careful when you tread;
Wherever you walk an *orator*
May rear his ugly head.'[59]

CHORUS-LEADER There's nothing quite so loathsome as a shameless woman – except, of course, the rest of womankind.

[*There is an awkward silence. Everybody looks at* MNESILOCHUS. *Eventually* MICA *springs to her feet.*]

MICA Women, women, are you thinking straight? What has come over you, are you bewitched? Are you going to let this outrageous woman stand here and insult us all? All right, if no one else will help, my maids and I will deal with her ourselves. Let's pluck her bush and singe her so that she learns that a woman doesn't criticize her fellow women.

MNESILOCHUS Not my bush, I beg you, please! Listen to me, ladies: every woman here has the right to free speech. Just because I tell you the truth about Euripides, do I have to be plucked and singed?

MICA Do you expect to get away with this, when you have the nerve to stand up for that man? A man who goes out of his way to choose plots with bad women in them? It's always Melanippe or Phaedra – he never writes a play about a virtuous woman like Penelope.[60]

MNESILOCHUS And I know why. There aren't any women like Penelope these days, they're Phaedras to a woman.

MICA There she goes again, the bitch! Do you hear what she's saying about us all?

MNESILOCHUS I haven't finished yet, not by a long chalk. Shall I tell you what else I know?

MICA You've spilt all the beans already. There can't be anything left to tell.

MNESILOCHUS Oh yes there is! You haven't heard the thousandth part of it yet. Did Euripides ever mention our latest scheme for tapping the wine jar? You know, with those long-handled things you have in the bath, to scratch your back with.

MICA This is scandalous!

MNESILOCHUS Or how we give the meat from the Apaturia[61] to our pimps, and then blame the cat?

MICA Outrageous!

MNESILOCHUS He never let on about the woman who killed her husband with an axe; or the one who gave her husband a drug that sent him mad;[62] or the woman from Acharnae who buried her father –

MICA Shame on you!

MNESILOCHUS – under the hot-water tank in the kitchen.

MICA This is insufferable!

MNESILOCHUS [*pointing to* MICA] And he never let on about *you*, did he? How you had a girl and your maid had a boy, and you changed them round and passed the boy off as yours?

MICA You won't get away with saying such things! I'll tear your hairs out!

MNESILOCHUS Keep you hands off me!

MICA Come on, then!

MNESILOCHUS Come on, then!

MICA Hold this, Philista.

MNESILOCHUS Just you lay a finger on me and, by Artemis, I'll . . .

MICA You'll what?

MNESILOCHUS I'll make you shit out that seedcake I saw you eat.[63]

CHORUS-LEADER Stop squabbling! A woman has just turned up. In a great hurry by the look of it. If everyone settles down before she gets here, we can receive her in an orderly fashion and find out what she has to say.

[*The newcomer is not a woman but* CLEISTHENES *dressed in women's clothing. He hurries in breathless with excitement.*[64]]

CLEISTHENES Dear ladies, kindred souls to my persuasion. That I am a friend to you my hairless cheeks attest. I adore you all, and always try to protect your interests. Just now I've heard a vitally important piece of news. They were all talking about it in the marketplace. I've come straight here to warn you: you must stay on full alert, be on your guard, or else a grievous situation may befall you.

CHORUS-LEADER What is it, child? It's fair to call you 'child', especially as you have such smooth cheeks.

CLEISTHENES They say Euripides has sent an old man up here today, a relative of his.

CHORUS-LEADER But what exactly does he have in mind?

CLEISTHENES To listen secretly to what you say and find out what it is you mean to do.

CHORUS-LEADER You really think a man could hide amid us women?

CLEISTHENES Euripides has plucked the man and singed his hairs, and dressed him up as a woman.

MNESILOCHUS Do you believe such a preposterous story? I ask you – what man would be so stupid as to let himself be singed? I don't believe a word of it, by the Holy Twain.

CLEISTHENES You're mistaken. Do you think I'd have come here, unless I had it on the best authority?

CHORUS-LEADER This is a most disturbing piece of news. Ladies, there's not a moment to be lost. He must have been amongst us all this time; we must find out at once where he's been hiding. If you, kind patron, help us to expose him, we'll be indebted to you all the more.

CLEISTHENES Well, let me see now. [*Picking on* MICA] Who are you?

MNESILOCHUS [*aside*] What shall I do?

CLEISTHENES [*still to* MICA] You'll all have to be questioned.

MNESILOCHUS [*aside*] Oh no, I'm doomed!

MICA I'm the wife of Cleonymus,[65] if you must know.

CLEISTHENES [*to the* CHORUS] Do you know this woman?

CHORUS-LEADER Yes, yes, we know her. Go on to the others.

CLEISTHENES Who's this woman with the baby?

MICA She's my nursemaid.

[*It is now the turn of* MNESILOCHUS.]

MNESILOCHUS [*aside*] I'm done for! [*He starts to slope off.*]

CLEISTHENES You there, where are you off to? Stop! What's the matter?

MNESILOCHUS I need to pee.

[CLEISTHENES *starts to accompany him.*]

You shameless man!

CLEISTHENES All right, go on. I'll wait here.

CHORUS-LEADER Yes, wait there, and make sure she comes back. She's the only one we don't really know.

CLEISTHENES You're passing rather a lot of water, aren't you?

MNESILOCHUS [*offstage*] It's that cress I had yesterday – makes you terribly retentive.

CLEISTHENES Stop gibbering about cress, and come back here!

MNESILOCHUS [*returning*] Don't maul me. Can't you see I'm not well?

CLEISTHENES So, who's your husband?

MNESILOCHUS My husband? Yes, ahem. He's – you know, old What's-his-Name, up at Cothocidae.[66]

CLEISTHENES Old What's-his-Name? Which one?

MNESILOCHUS Oh, old What's-his-Name, son of What's-his-Face!

CLEISTHENES What absolute twaddle! Have you been here before?

MNESILOCHUS I've been coming for years.

CLEISTHENES Who's your tent-partner?

MNESILOCHUS Oh, er – What's-her-Name, you know. [*Aside*] Oh dear!

CLEISTHENES You're talking nonsense.

MICA Leave her to me. I'll question her in detail about the rites we performed last year. If you could stand aside, as you're a man – of sorts. [*To* MNESILOCHUS] Now, tell me, what sacred rite came first?

MNESILOCHUS Let me see now, what did we do first? [*Suddenly inspired*] Why, we drank.

MICA All right. And what did we do after that?

MNESILOCHUS [*pausing for thought*] We drank again.

MICA Someone's been telling you! What happened after that?

MNESILOCHUS Xenylla asked for a basin because there wasn't a piss-pot.

MICA Wrong! Cleisthenes, come here, I've found our man!

[CLEISTHENES *returns.*]

CLEISTHENES What shall I do with him?

MICA Strip him. He's been saying the most dreadful things.

MNESILOCHUS Surely, you wouldn't strip a mother of nine!

CLEISTHENES Off with that girdle, quick!

[MNESILOCHUS' *girdle is removed and the upper half of his robe falls, but he continues to clutch the lower half.* CLEISTHENES *and* MICA *inspect his torso.*]

MICA She's very strong and muscular for a woman. And, look – she doesn't have breasts like ours.

MNESILOCHUS That's because I'm barren – I've never had a baby.

MICA A moment ago you were a mother of nine.

[CLEISTHENES *now manages to remove the lower part of* MNESILOCHUS' *clothing.* MNESILOCHUS *bends over in a bid to conceal his manhood.*]

CLEISTHENES Stand up straight!

[MNESILOCHUS *stands up with legs slightly crossed in a mincing pose.* CLEISTHENES *and* MICA *look for proof of his gender.*]

Where's his . . . thing? He's hidden it!

MICA [*lifting the robe at the rear*] Ooh! He's pushed it through to the back. A nice one too!

CLEISTHENES Where? I can't see it.

MICA It's back at the front again.

CLEISTHENES [*lifting the robe at the front*] No, it isn't.

MICA Oh no, it's here again.

CLEISTHENES What is this? He's sending his old chap back and forth like a shuttle service across the Isthmus?[67]

MICA The filthy devil! To think he was abusing us and defending Euripides!

MNESILOCHUS [*aside*] This is a fine mess I've got myself into!

MICA What shall we do with him?

CLEISTHENES Keep him guarded, and see that he doesn't escape. I'll go and inform the Council right away.

[CLEISTHENES *departs.* MICA *and her maids stand guard over* MNESILOCHUS *as the* CHORUS *prepare for the Torch Dance.*]

CHORUS-LEADER

Come and light your torches,
 Quickly don't delay!
Hitch your skirts up boldly,
 Cast your cloaks away.
Run and search the hillside!
 Flit without a sound

Through the tents and gangways,
In between and round.
Prying, peeping, peering
Everywhere you can:
Any nook or cranny
May conceal a man!

Hurry now, and form a circle: cover every inch of ground;
If another male is lurking, track him down, he must be found!

[*The* CHORUS, *having lit their torches at the altar, form a circle, and the dance begins.*]

CHORUS

If any other man has dared
To desecrate our Mysteries,
His punishment, once he is found,
Will be the worst in history.
The story of his gruesome fate
Will serve to teach society
The perils that attend upon
The practice of impiety.
The man who fails to lead a life
Of strict religiosity,
Neglects his pious duties or
Commits some grave atrocity,
Is apt to find himself held up
Before the whole community
To prove that gods are gods and none
Can slight them with impunity.

CHORUS-LEADER

Now, I think, we have examined every corner carefully.
And we haven't seen another man amongst us secretly.

[MNESILOCHUS *suddenly snatches* MICA*'s 'baby'*[68] *and runs to the altar.*]

MICA Hey, where are you going? Hey, you, stop! Oh! He's taken my baby! Snatched it from my very breast!

MNESILOCHUS Scream away! You'll never feed this child again, unless you let me go. [*He picks up the sacrificial knife from the altar.*] I shall engrave its limbs with this my knife, and stain the altar with its bleeding veins.[69]

MICA Oh, no, for pity's sake! You women, help me! Raise the alarm, set up a trophy – do something! Don't stand by and see me robbed of my only child!

CHORUS Help us, help us, what an outrage!
Holy Fates, what's this I see?
Friends, I ask you, have you ever
Witnessed such audacity?
Evil deeds could go no further.

MNESILOCHUS I'll soon stop your stubborn game.

MICA He has snatched my precious baby.

CHORUS Has the man no sense of shame?

MNESILOCHUS Even so I'll stop at nothing.

MICA But you will not get away!
You'll not live to tell the story
Of the wrongs you did this day.

MNESILOCHUS There I hope you are mistaken.

CHORUS Foolish man, you hope in vain.
Do you think the gods will aid you?
Give the infant back again.

MNESILOCHUS No, I never will release her.

CHORUS We shall have our vengeance soon:
For your wrongs we shall repay you,
Then, perhaps, you'll change your tune.
Raise your torches, build a bonfire,
Pile the brushwood round his feet!
Let him be incinerated!
Then revenge will be complete.

MICA [*to the* NURSEMAID] Come on, Mania, let's fetch some kindling. [*To* MNESILOCHUS] I'm going to have you burnt to a cinder.

[MICA *and her* NURSEMAID *go off.*]

MNESILOCHUS [*calling after them*] That's right, roast me alive, barbecue me! [*To the 'baby'.*] As for you, little one, let's take off these Cretan clothes and have a look at you. [*He starts to unwrap the 'baby'.*] You must die, but it's all your mother's fault – what's this? It isn't a baby at all – it's a full skin of wine, complete with Persian booties![70]

Oh women, women, ever thirsting after booze!
Forever plotting to find more through some new ruse.
To all mankind, and all his worldly goods, a curse –
A blessing only to the tavern-keeper's purse.

[MICA *and the* NURSEMAID *return with their arms full of brushwood.* MNESILOCHUS *partially rewraps the 'baby'.*]

MICA [*dumping her load*] Pile up the kindling, Mania, we need lots and lots.

MNESILOCHUS Yes, pile it up. But tell me something. You say this is your child?

MICA I should know, I carried it nine months.

MNESILOCHUS You carried *this*?

MICA Yes, by Artemis.

MNESILOCHUS How big is it, a pint?

MICA What have you done? You shameful man, you've undressed my baby! The poor little thing!

MNESILOCHUS Little!

MICA She's tiny.

MNESILOCHUS Why, she must be getting on for three or four festival years![71]

MICA Four, last Dionysia. Give her back to me!

MNESILOCHUS Never!

MICA Then you must burn.

MNESILOCHUS All right, burn me. But meanwhile I shall slaughter the victim.

MICA No, no, I beg you! Do what you like to me instead.

MNESILOCHUS Could a mother's love go any further? All the same, I'm going to slay the victim.[72] [*He plunges the knife into the skin.*]

MICA My child, my child! Quick, Mania, give me the bowl so that I can at least catch my baby's blood.

MNESILOCHUS Hold it out, then, I won't begrudge you that.

[MICA *holds out the bowl but he drinks the lot without spilling any.*]

MICA You mean, selfish, spiteful man!

MNESILOCHUS This skin is for the priestess.

[*Enter* CRITYLLA.]

CRITYLLA What's for the priestess?

MNESILOCHUS This. Catch! [*He tosses her the empty wine-skin.*]

CRITYLLA Oh, my poor Mica, you've lost your precious daughter. She is utterly drained. Who did this?

MICA This criminal here. But since you're here, would you stay and keep an eye on him while I go and catch Cleisthenes: the Council must be informed of this.

[MICA *and her maids go off.*]

MNESILOCHUS [*soliloquizing*] What path to safety is there left to me? What stratagem, what exit? Oh, it was my kinsman who first put me in these straits! But where is he? How can I send him word? I know! A trick from one of his own plays – *Palamedes*![73] I'll write a message on oar-blades. [*He looks round hopefully.*] Damn, there don't seem to be any oar-blades. Now where, oh where, can I find oar-blades . . . I've got it! These votive tablets are made of wood – they're perfect! [*He takes a number of tablets from the temple wall and starts carving letters on them with the sacrificial knife, singing as he works.*]

O hands assist me if you can
To bring about this daring plan:
Upon these wooden plaques we'll send
An urgent message to our friend.

Sweet tablets, on your backs allow
My knife its furrowed track to plough.
'E', 'U', then 'R' – just one last hack –
Quite easy, once you've got the knack.

And now, dear tablets, if you please
Fly quickly to Euripides:
Fly you, and you! Fly left and right!
Apprise him of my hopeless plight.[74]

[*Having scattered his tablets* MNESILOCHUS *sits down forlornly to await the arrival of Euripides.* CRITYLLA *settles down to guard him. The* CHORUS-LEADER *now steps forward and addresses the audience.*]

CHORUS-LEADER

It's time we women stood up for ourselves,
and glorified the name
Which graces a gender that none much praise
and all and sundry blame.
According to you we're a plague and a curse,
the source of trouble and strife
And grief and war and sorrow and pain –
everything dire in life!
That's all very well, but tell me this:
if what you say is right,
Why do you marry us, when we're so bad,
and earn yourselves a blight?
You will not allow us to leave the house,
or even peep out the door,
And if ever you find your wife has gone out,
you bellow and rage and roar.
But what you should do, if your taunts are true,
and women are what you say,
Is give thanks to the gods on bended knee
for taking your troubles away.
She may have been paying a friendly call
on someone who's just had a son,
And sleeping it off quite innocently
when the games and dancing are done.
But what do you do? Do you leave it be?
Of course not, you moan and complain,
Then gather your strife, your 'source of all friction',
and drag her back home again.

If a wife is spied when she happens to lean
from her window to take in the view,
Do you shrink from the sight of this fearful blight,
as you might be expected to do?
No, you peep and you peer, you snigger and leer,
and when she recoils in disdain
You don't disappear, you just wait there all day
till she comes to the window again.
I think I have shown by these cases alone,
that the female sex is the best;
But if you're not sure, it can still be proved,
by this comparative test.
Just mention a man – think hard as you can –
we'll better him, despite his fame.
I swear we can find a woman to surpass
any man you're willing to name.

[*Members of the* CHORUS *impersonate the various characters as they are mentioned.*[75]]

Charminus, you say? Why, his fleet ran away!
We don't have to look very far:
Here's Nausimache, 'Pugnacious at Sea',
to show you what cowards you are.
Oh, here's Salabaccho, the queen of the drabs:
can anyone viler be found?
Why, yes, she's a model of virtue and grace,
if Cleophon's knocking around!
Stratonice, my dear, come, stand over her!
Her name means 'Unbeaten in War'.
I'd like to see any man taking *her* on:
your Marathon days are no more.
And as for Euboule, 'Good council', well, truly –
can any ex-councillor claim,
When handing his job to another last year,
to have earned such a glorious name?
Have you heard of a woman who'd steal from the State
to the tune of a million or so,
Then ride in a coach with pockets distended,
Like one politician we know?

You won't catch a woman behaving like that;
it's not good and it isn't right.
Her spoils from the larder when her husband's away,
she pays back the very same night.

CHORUS

Well, you must admit it's true
That it's chiefly among you
That gluttons, thieves and criminals abound.
Have you heard of banditresses,
Let alone hijackeresses?
Are there many female pirates to be found?

And then there's your omission
To keep up your old tradition
As the women of our race have always done:
We maintain our ancient craft
With the shuttle and the shaft
And the parasol – our shield against the sun.

But the shafts of war are dusty,
And the points have all gone rusty,
And though, like us, you ought to have a shield,
It's all too often better not to
Ask a soldier where it's got to –
In case it's been abandoned on the field!

If ever it came to be tried in court,
we'd have charges by the score
To bring against men, but I'll tell you the thing
that really makes us sore:
If one of us women should bear a son
who does fine things for the State,
An admiral, or a general, say –
anyone brave or great –
She ought to be treated with greater respect
and seated in the front row
At all of the games and festivals
where women are wont to go;

But as for the mother whose son is a coward,
no good for the army or fleet,
She should have to come with her hair cropped short
and sit in a commoner's seat.
When Lamachus' mother attends the games,
do you citizens think it right
That Hyperbolus' mother[76] should sit there too,
in a robe of spotless white,
Lending out money? One thing I know –
if she tried to make *me* pay
At the rate of whatever per cent per month,
I'd grab the money and say:
'We endured your son, do you want us to bear
your rates of interest too?
Be gone, be gone! We've borne enough –
and so, by heaven, have you!'

ACT TWO

Scene I: *The same. There is no break in the action.*

[MNESILOCHUS *is seated on the steps of the altar.* CRITYLLA *is guarding him.*]

MNESILOCHUS I'm going cross-eyed with all this watching and waiting. And still no sign of him. I wonder what's holding him up. Perhaps he's embarrassed because his *Palamedes* is lifeless. Now which of his plays can I lure him with? I know! I'll use his brand-new *Helen*.[77] I'm certainly dressed for the part.

CRITYLLA Now what mischief are you up to? What's the matter with you, rolling your eyes like that? You'll find yourself 'between Hell an' high water'[78] if you're not careful. Just sit there quietly till the magistrate comes.

MNESILOCHUS [*as Helen*]
Here flows the Naiad-haunted Nile, whose streams
In place of rain refresh the plains, and bring
Relief to Egypt's dark-clogged citizens.[79]

CRITYLLA You're up to no good, I can see that, by Hecate.[80]

MNESILOCHUS
Great Sparta was my home, and great the fame
My father Tyndareus had.

CRITYLLA Was he your father? I thought it was Phrynondas.[81]

MNESILOCHUS
My name
Is Helen.

CRITYLLA At it again – pretending to be a woman! Before you've even been punished for your first time.

MNESILOCHUS And so many lost their lives
On grim Scamander's banks[82] because of me.

CRITYLLA It's a pity you didn't lose yours.

MNESILOCHUS
Now I sit here; but of my dearest spouse,
The wretched Menelaus, there is no sign.
Why do I go on living?

CRITYLLA Don't ask me, ask the crows.

MNESILOCHUS
And yet, and yet, there flickers in my heart
A spark of hope! O Zeus, deceive me not!

[*Enter* EURIPIDES, *dressed for the part of the shipwrecked Menelaus.*]

EURIPIDES
What lord within these rugged halls resides?[83]
Will he give shelter to a shipwrecked crew
That lately grappled with the stormy seas?

MNESILOCHUS
These are the halls of Proteus.

EURIPIDES Who is he?

CRITYLLA [*to* EURIPIDES] Take no notice, he's having you on. It's ten years, at least, since old Proteas[84] died.

EURIPIDES
Unto what country have we steered our ship?

MNESILOCHUS
Egypt.

EURIPIDES
Alas, so many miles from home!

CRITYLLA You mustn't believe a word he says – he's talking nonsense. You're at the Thesmophorion in Athens.

EURIPIDES
Is Proteus here at home, or is he out?

CRITYLLA You must still be suffering from seasickness. I'm telling you, Proteas is *dead*. At home, indeed!

EURIPIDES
What, dead? How sad! But where is he interred?

MNESILOCHUS
His tomb is here, where I am sitting now.

CRITYLLA You'll come to a bad end, truly you will, calling the sacred altar a tomb!

EURIPIDES
What makes you sit all day upon a tomb?
Shrouded from head to foot?

MNESILOCHUS
I am to wed –
Not of my own accord – the son of Proteus.

CRITYLLA Why do you keep telling the gentleman such lies? [*To* EURIPIDES] I tell you, sir, this man is up to no good. He just sneaked in among the women to steal their jewellery.

MNESILOCHUS
Yes, scold away! Pile insults on my head!

EURIPIDES
Who is this shrew that does abuse you so?

MNESILOCHUS
Why, she is Proteus' daughter, Theonoë.[85]

CRITYLLA I beg your pardon, but I'm nothing of the kind. My name is Critylla, daughter of Antitheos, from Gargettos. The cheek of the man!

MNESILOCHUS Say what you will, I'll pay no heed:
For I will never wed your brother, or be
Untrue to Menelaus, who's in Troy.

EURIPIDES What did you say? Come, let me see your face.[86]

MNESILOCHUS I blush to do so, with such cheeks as these!

EURIPIDES Alas, what ails me? I can hardly speak.
O gods, what do I see? Who are you, woman?

MNESILOCHUS Who are you, sir? What strange coincidence –
You took the very words out of my mouth!

EURIPIDES Are you Hellenic, or Egyptian born?

MNESILOCHUS I? Hellenic. But tell me, what are you?

EURIPIDES You're so like Helen – why, you must be she!

MNESILOCHUS You're Menelaus – from your rags I see.[87]

EURIPIDES You have me right: I am that wretched man.

MNESILOCHUS Oh, take me, take me in your arms at last!
How long you took to reach your loving wife!
Let me embrace you! Lift me in your arms!
(And now, for god's sake, get me out of here!)

CRITYLLA Anyone who tries to take you out of here, will feel the hot end of this torch.

EURIPIDES
Alas, my wife, child of Tyndareus!
Will you not let me take her home to Sparta?

CRITYLLA I think you're both in this together. You can't fool me by talking Egyptian. Well, this one's going to be punished, at any rate: here comes the magistrate with an officer.

EURIPIDES This doesn't look good. I'd better disappear.

MNESILOCHUS [*aside to* EURIPIDES] What about me? What am I to do?

EURIPIDES [*aside to* MNESILOCHUS] Don't worry. I won't let you down, so long as I live and breathe. I've got hundreds of tricks left. [*He hurries off.*]

CRITYLLA He didn't have much luck with that bit of bait.

[*Enter a* MAGISTRATE *and a* SCYTHIAN 'ARCHER' *or officer.*]

MAGISTRATE We've had a report from Cleisthenes. Is this the culprit? [*To* MNESILOCHUS] Stand up straight there! [*To the* SCYTHIAN] Take him off and tie him to the plank.[88] Then stand him up out here so you can keep your eye on him. Don't let anyone come near him: if anyone tries to, use your whip.

CRITYLLA That's right, there was a fellow here just now, spinning some yarn, who nearly whisked him off.

MNESILOCHUS Oh, sir, I beg you, by your right hand – the one you hold out so readily – grant me one small favour before I die.

MAGISTRATE What is it?

MNESILOCHUS Tell the officer to strip me before he ties me to the plank. I'm an old man; please don't leave me dressed up in women's clothes. I don't want to give the crows a good laugh as well as a good dinner.

MAGISTRATE The Council's decision is that you are to be exposed with all this on, so that the passers-by can see what a bad egg you are.

MNESILOCHUS O saffron dress, what have you done to me? There is no hope of rescue any more.[89]

[MNESILOCHUS *is led into the temple by the* SCYTHIAN. *The* MAGISTRATE *and* CRITYLLA *also depart, leaving only the* CHORUS *onstage.*]

CHORUS

The day of the dancing has come round again,
The day when we fast for the Goddesses Twain
And pray them to free us from sorrow and pain
  And crown us with joy everlasting.
And Pauson[90] is with us in spirit today:
For year after year he joins in when we pray
For many returns of the wonderful day
  When he isn't the only one fasting.

[*The tune of the round-dance is struck up. At the* CHORUS-LEADER*'s summons the* CHORUS *form a circle.*]

CHORUS-LEADER

Come forward with a tripping step and listen as I sing:
Take hands as quickly as you can and get into a ring.
Pick up the rhythm as you go, and cast a circling glance
To check on your position for the merry whirling dance.

[*The round-dance proper begins.*]

CHORUS

And as we dance in ecstasy, let each one raise her voice
In praise of the Olympian gods! We praise them and rejoice!

[*As the dance proceeds, they utter ecstatic cries. During*

the last repetition of the tune, however, their words are addressed to the audience.[91]]

If any of you gentlemen expect us to abuse
The audience, take it from us, it's not the time to
choose.
A woman in a temple court should never soil her lips
With satire or buffoonery, coarse jokes or dirty quips.

CHORUS-LEADER

But now the measure must be changed, the merry whirl
must end:
Step forward now, and pray the gods our revels to
attend.

[*The* CHORUS *take up positions for the second dance.*]

CHORUS

Let us praise the Far-Shooter, Lord of the Lyre;[92]
And Artemis, Queen of the Bow;
And pray that Apollo will grant to our choir
The prize that is his to bestow.
Be with us, sweet Hera, great goddess and queen,
Take part in our dancing today;
Defender of marriage, protectress serene,
Lend grace to our revels and play.
On the gods of the countryside, Hermes and Pan,
And the nymphs of the woodland we call:
We have fasted all day, let us do what we can
With our dances to gladden them all.

[*The* CHORUS *now partake of the ceremonial wine. The final dance, to Dionysus, is wild and maenadic in character.*]

Come, leap and bound
With rhythmic sound
In Bacchic frenzy prancing!
The god of joy,
The madcap boy,
Shall lead us in our dancing!
Euoi, euoi!

The god of joy
Shall lead us in our dancing.
He loves to leap
On hillsides steep
And dance across the mountains,
While nymphs in praise
Do sing their lays
Beside Cithaeron's fountains.[93]
Euoi, euoi!
The madcap boy,
Who loves the wooded mountains!
The hills around,
In joy resound
Whenever the god advances;
The ivy weaves
Its pretty leaves
About him as he prances.
Euoi, euoi!
The god of joy
Has come to lead our dances!

[*Shouts and screams are heard from within the temple. The* SCYTHIAN *emerges carrying* MNESILOCHUS, *whom he has now bound to a plank. He props the plank up against one of the columns of the temple portico.*]

SCYTHIAN You wanna shout, shout in da sky.[94]

MNESILOCHUS Oh, officer, officer, I beg you . . .

SCYTHIAN Iz no good begging me.

MNESILOCHUS Please, loosen the peg a bit!

SCYTHIAN Like dis?

MNESILOCHUS Aghh, you're making it tighter!

SCYTHIAN You wan I screw harder?

MNESILOCHUS Aghh! Damn you!

SCYTHIAN You keep mouth shut! I fetch da mat. Den I guard you.

[*The* SCYTHIAN *goes off to fetch a mat.*]

MNESILOCHUS This is a fine mess Euripides has got me into.

[*At this moment* EURIPIDES *appears*[95] *dressed as Perseus from his play* Andromeda. *He just has time to make a sign to* MNESILOCHUS.]

MNESILOCHUS But wait! Thank god! There's still hope! He won't let me down after all. He just signalled to me as Perseus. He wants me to play Andromeda. Well, I'm tied up all right, so I should look the part. He must be coming to save me. Why else would he have passed by?

[*As Andromeda*[96]]

Say, ye gentle virgins, say,
How am I to get away?
How can I to safety flee
With that Scythian watching me?
Echo, in your rocky grot,
Do you hear, or do you not?
Hush your voice and save my life:
I must get back to my wife.
  Pitiless, ah me,
  Was the hand that bound me.
Bad enough to be alone
With that dreadful toothless crone:
Now my state is worse by far –
Lord, how rough these Scythians are!
Here my mournful moan I make,
Tied to this confounded stake,
Waiting till I end my woes
As some titbit for the crows.
  Was ever a maiden
  So forlorn, so forlorn?
Not for me the merry dance,
While the young men round me prance;
Nor for me the bridal choir,
Joyful chords of lute and lyre.
Cords I have, but far from sweet:
How they hurt my hands and feet!
And my tender limbs shall please
None but whales – or Glaucetes.[97]
Ah, bewail my dreadful fate,
Weep and groan as I relate

How a kinsman stern and harsh
Shaved my whiskers and moustache:
Dressed me up in frills and lace,
Sent me to this awful place,
Full of women fierce and grim,
Keen to tear me limb from limb.
O cruel demon of Fate,
Accursed, accursed am I.
Who can look upon my plight
And not shudder at the sight?
Thunder-god, your lightning send,
Bring my anguish to an end!
(Smite the Scythian, not me!)
It profits little now to gaze
On the sun's immortal rays:
It would suit me just as well
Down among the shades to dwell.

[ECHO,[98] *in the form of a woman, speaks from offstage.*]

ECHO
Hail, dearest child! I pray the gods destroy
Your father Cepheus, who exposed you thus!

MNESILOCHUS
Who are you, that take pity on my plight?

ECHO
Echo, the mocking singer-back of words.
Last year I was here in the festival.
I worked together with Euripides.[99]
But now, my child, you must fulfil your role
And utter lamentations pitifully.

MNESILOCHUS
I see, and then you'll lament after me.

ECHO Yes, leave all that to me.

[ECHO *conceals herself behind a column of the temple portico.*]

Now you can start.

MNESILOCHUS O holy night,
Long, long is the journey

You take in your chariot,
Crossing the ridges of the starry sky
Over proud Olympus.

ECHO Proud Olympus.

MNESILOCHUS
Why should I, Andromeda,
Of all maidens, have so great
A share of woe?

ECHO Share of woe.

MNESILOCHUS
Ah, wretched me!

ECHO Ah, wretched me!

MNESILOCHUS Stop interrupting!

ECHO Stop interrupting!

MNESILOCHUS You're coming in too often.

ECHO In too often.

MNESILOCHUS I'd really be obliged if you would let me soliloquize. So shut up!

ECHO So shut up!

MNESILOCHUS To hell with you!

ECHO To hell with you!

MNESILOCHUS What's wrong with you?

ECHO What's wrong with you?

MNESILOCHUS Just you wait!

ECHO Just you wait!

MNESILOCHUS You'll regret this.

ECHO You'll regret this.

[*The* SCYTHIAN *returns with a mat.*]

SCYTHIAN [*to* MNESILOCHUS] Wat you say?

ECHO Wat you say?

SCYTHIAN I call da magistrate.

ECHO I call da magistrate.

SCYTHIAN Waz dis?

ECHO Waz dis?

SCYTHIAN Where dis voice?

ECHO Where dis voice?

SCYTHIAN Wat you say?

ECHO Wat you say?

SCYTHIAN [*still to* MNESILOCHUS] You wan I punch you?

ECHO You wan I punch you?

SCYTHIAN You make fun-a me?

ECHO You make fun-a me?

MNESILOCHUS Not me, it's this woman here.

ECHO [*from somewhere else*] This woman here.

SCYTHIAN [*looking for the source of the voice*] Chiky beetch! Where she go?

ECHO Where she go?

SCYTHIAN I give you pain!

ECHO I give you pain!

SCYTHIAN You still make fun?

ECHO You still make fun?

SCYTHIAN [*trying to grab* ECHO] I catch you now!

ECHO [*from elsewhere*] Catch you now! [*She makes her escape.*]

SCYTHIAN Dat bloody woman, she talk too much.

[*Enter* EURIPIDES, *aerially on the stage-crane. He is disguised as Perseus, complete with winged sandals and Gorgon's head. He lands by* MNESILOCHUS *and the* SCYTHIAN.]

EURIPIDES

Gods, to what barbarous country have I come
On my swift sandal, cleaving through the sky
My wingèd path? For Argos I am bound,
And in my hand the Gorgon's head I bear.[100]

SCYTHIAN Wat you say? Gorgas da writer?[101] You got his head?

EURIPIDES I said 'the Gorgon's head'.

SCYTHIAN Da Gorgas' head, aha!

EURIPIDES

But wait, what rock is here? And what is this?
A divine maiden tied up like a ship?

MNESILOCHUS

Have pity, stranger, on my wretched fate,
And loose me from my bonds!

SCYTHIAN You shuddup! You soon die, still you no keep-a ya mouth shut?

EURIPIDES

Fair virgin, how my heart with pity fills

To see you hanging there.

SCYTHIAN No, no, he no maid. This dirty ol' man.

EURIPIDES

Oh, Scythian, you are wrong:
This is Andromeda, the child of Cepheus.

SCYTHIAN You no believe me? I show you his pi-pi. [*He lifts* MNESILOCHUS' *dress.*] Is big, no?

EURIPIDES

Lend me your hand, that I may reach the maid.
Come, Scythian, help me up! For men are prone
To every kind of ill, and in my case
Love for this maid has struck me to the core.

SCYTHIAN You got very strange taste. If he other way round, den I understand.

EURIPIDES

O Scythian, let me release her bonds,
And I will bear her to the bridal bed.

SCYTHIAN You want very much make love to ol' man? Den you go round da back and make hole in wood.

EURIPIDES Nay, I will free her!

SCYTHIAN Den I beat you.

EURIPIDES I will, I insist!

SCYTHIAN I cut off your head wid my knife.

EURIPIDES [*aside*]

Alas, what can I do? What can I say?
His barbarous mind – it will not understand.
'To use new schemes upon a witless fool'[102]
Is just a waste of time. I must devise
A stratagem more suited to this man.

[EURIPIDES *takes off again.*]

SCYTHIAN Dirty fox, he make-a da monkey out-a me!

MNESILOCHUS

Farewell then, Perseus, but forget me not:
No maid was ever in a tighter spot.

SCYTHIAN You wan I whip you?

[*After glaring at* MNESILOCHUS, *the* SCYTHIAN *settles down to sleep.*]

CHORUS [*Hymn to Pallas Athene*]

Who but we should call her,
Who but we, the dancers?
Pallas, maid and goddess,
Pallas, the unwedded!
Pallas of Athens!
For she takes delight
In song and in the dance,
And the keys in her hand
Are the keys of our city.
Hers is the power,
And she is our goddess.
Who but we should call her?
Who but we, the Chorus?
Come to us, Pallas,
Enemy of tyranny!
Come to the call
Of the women of Athens!
Come, and bring peace,
For then we shall have feasting!

[*Hymn to Demeter and Persephone*]
And you, Immortal Pair,
Come, come joyfully
To your sacred grove,
To the rites no man may look upon.
Show us the holy vision
In the dazzle of the torches.
Hear us, O hear!
If ever you have come at our call,
Come to us now!
Come to us, O come!

[*The* SCYTHIAN *is still asleep. Enter* EURIPIDES, *carrying a lyre and the mask and costume of an old woman. He approaches the* CHORUS *conspiratorially.*]

EURIPIDES Ladies, if you would like to come to terms from now on, this is your chance. I promise solemnly never to say anything bad about you again. This is a serious offer.[103]

CHORUS-LEADER And what do you want in return for this proposal?

EURIPIDES The man on the plank there is a relative of mine. If I can get him out of here, you'll never hear another bad word from me. But if you refuse to help, when your husbands get back from war I'll tell them everything that's been going on at home.

CHORUS-LEADER As far as we are concerned, we accept your terms. But you yourself must tackle the barbarian.

EURIPIDES Leave that to me. [*He puts on the disguise, and calls out in an old woman's voice.*] Come on, Twinkletoes!

[*Enter a young* DANCING-GIRL.]

Now remember what I told you on the way here. We'll just run through it – and don't forget to hitch your skirt up. [*To a* PIPER *in the orchestra*] Give us a Persian dance, will you, piper?

[*The* PIPER *begins to play, and the* SCYTHIAN *wakes up.*]

SCYTHIAN Wat dat noise? Ah, da music wake me up.

EURIPIDES She just wants to practise her dance, officer. She has to go and dance for some gentlemen.

SCYTHIAN Oho, da practise dancing! Very nice! I no stop her.

[*The* GIRL *begins her dance.*]

Girlie very light! Like flea on back of sheep.

EURIPIDES [*as the dance ends*] Now put your cloak down here, dear, and sit down a moment – here you are, on the Scythian gentleman's knee – and give me your foot so I can undo your shoes.

SCYTHIAN Thas right, girlie, sit down here. Hmm, she have nice titties – like lid'l turnips.

EURIPIDES [*to the* PIPER] Liven it up, now. [*To the* GIRL] You're not afraid of the nice Scythian any more, are you?

[*The* GIRL *dances again, with fewer clothes on.*]

SCYTHIAN Hmm, she have nice bottom. [*To* MNESILOCHUS] You stay inside dem clothes,[104] ol' man. [*To* EURIPIDES] She nice down here in front also.

EURIPIDES You're quite right. [*To the* GIRL] Well, put your cloak on again: it's time we were off.

SCYTHIAN You no let me kiss her first?

EURIPIDES Give the gentleman a kiss.

[*The* GIRL *does so.*]

SCYTHIAN Ooh! Hmm! She have sweet tongue, like honey. You sleep wid me, yes?

EURIPIDES Now, officer, really! She's not supposed to do that.

SCYTHIAN Please, please, old lady! You fix for me?

EURIPIDES Will you pay one drachma?

SCYTHIAN Yes, yes, I give drachma.

EURIPIDES Hand it over, then.

SCYTHIAN But I no have drachma. I know: I give quiver, you give girlie, yes? [*He hands the quiver to* EURIPIDES.] You come-a dis way, lid'l girlie. [*To* EURIPIDES] You watch ol' man for me. [*To the* GIRL] Wat your name?

EURIPIDES Her name's Artemisia.

SCYTHIAN I no forget her name: Am-nesia.

[*The* GIRL *runs off and disappears.*]

EURIPIDES Oh, Hermes, god of trickery, how neat your work! [*To the* SCYTHIAN, *who has already set off in pursuit*] Run after her, quickly, and catch her! [*The* SCYTHIAN *is soon out of sight.*] And now to free the prisoner. [*To* MNESILOCHUS] As soon as you are free, escape immediately, and make sure you go straight home to your wife and children.

MNESILOCHUS Trust me, I will – as soon as I get out of this.

[EURIPIDES *releases him as quickly as possible.*]

EURIPIDES There, you're free. Now, off with you, quickly, before you-know-who comes back and finds you.

MNESILOCHUS I'm off, don't worry.

[MNESILOCHUS *hurries off, followed by* EURIPIDES. *The* DANCING-GIRL *and the* SCYTHIAN *return.*]

SCYTHIAN Ol' woman, your daughter she so nice! She no complain, very willing – hey! Where ol' woman go? Oh no! Dis not good. Ol' man gone too. Hey! Ol' woman, ol' woman! I no like you. De ol' woman trick me. [*To the* GIRL] Go after dem! [*She runs off.*] I give her one in quiver, and now me is done for! Ol' woman! Amnesia!

CHORUS-LEADER Are you by any chance looking for the old woman with the harp?

SCYTHIAN Yes, yes. You see her?

CHORUS-LEADER [*pointing the wrong way*][105] She went that way – there was an old man following.

SCYTHIAN Ol' man in yellow dress, yes?

CHORUS That's right. You can still catch them, if you go that way.

SCYTHIAN Bad ol' woman! Which way she go? [*Shouting*] Amnesia!

CHORUS [*severally*] Straight up there. No, where are you going? Not back! This way! That's right! No, you're going the wrong way!

[*The* SCYTHIAN *runs wildly about, trying to follow their instructions, and eventually runs offstage.*]

SCYTHIAN [*as he disappears*] Amnesia! Amnesia! I lose Amnesia!

CHORUS

Run along, run along; you can run straight to Hell
  For all we care, and good riddance, I say.
But it's time we were all moving off, truth to tell;
  We've had our measure of fun for one day.
May the goddesses bless us, and praise us as well,
  If they're pleased with our work – and with our play.

FROGS

PREFACE TO *FROGS*

Frogs was first performed at the Lenaea of 405 BC, about a year after the death of Euripides in the winter of 407/6. The political situation in Athens in 405 was fraught with danger and uncertainty. A Spartan army was permanently encamped at Deceleia in Attica. This confined the Athenians to the city, the harbour at Piraeus and the walled strip of land connecting them. The Athenian navy, meanwhile, was struggling to maintain superiority, while Sparta's fleet was boosted by new allies including the Persian king Cyrus. Athens' grip over her allies was also very insecure. Admittedly, the Athenians had won a major naval battle at Arginusae (off Lesbos) in the summer of 406, but the victory was Pyrrhic; twenty-five Athenian ships and up to five thousand men were lost. There was heated debate about the responsibility for such heavy casualties. In an atmosphere of intimidation and scant regard for law, most of the victorious commanders were sentenced to death. Afterwards, many Athenians felt they had been coerced into acting wrongly by certain radical democrat leaders (including Theramenes and Cleophon, whom Aristophanes criticizes in *Frogs*). Such leaders had increased their influence by freeing, and granting citizenship to, the large contingent of slaves who fought at Arginusae. They also rejected an offer of peace by Sparta that was extremely generous considering Athens' various predicaments.

One man who might have turned Athenian fortunes was Alcibiades, an ambivalent figure who was still in exile, but had been exiled before only to be readmitted. While he had spent some time as a defector in Sparta, he was still widely recognized as Athens' most capable general and statesman. Dionysus' questioning of Aeschylus and Euripides about Alcibiades towards the end of the play is not merely capricious, it was a burning issue of the day. It is, however, difficult to extricate Aristophanes' own viewpoint from the play itself. What is said about Alcibiades – while it appears, taken as a whole, to commend his recall – nonetheless seems to be left deliberately ambivalent.

Frogs offers clearer advice about the treatment of those who took part in the oligarchy and were disenfranchised after the return to democracy in 410. According to one ancient source, it was on the strength of Aristophanes' advice in the parabasis, namely to restore the rights of such men, that the play received the unique accolade of a second performance at a city festival (in 404). One consequence of *Frogs* being granted a second performance is that the text as we have it seems, in one or two places, to amalgamate the original and revised scripts. This is most acutely evident in the last phase of the contest for tragedy, where Dionysus asks both tragedians what should be done about Alcibiades and how the city might be saved. Still, such differences as there may be between the original and revised scripts do not significantly affect the overall action of the play or the treatment of Aeschylus and Euripides.

A second issue that has some bearing on our text of *Frogs* is the death of Sophocles. It is generally supposed that Sophocles, who died later in 406, was alive while much of the play was being written, but that his death entailed some hasty rewriting. While he does not appear as a character, there are two passages of dialogue – the first is between Dionysus and Heracles, the second between Xanthias and a fellow slave – that pointedly explain his non-participation in the contest for the throne of tragedy. Both passages have an air of improvisation. The same is true of the final mention of Sophocles at the end of the play, where Aeschylus says that he has asked Sophocles to guard the throne of tragedy in his absence.

There are many reasons for presenting a contest between Aeschylus and Euripides rather than Aeschylus and Sophocles or Sophocles and Euripides. Aeschylus' plays were already a mainstay of the tragic canon; he was the only playwright known to have been granted the privilege of having his plays produced posthumously (his character alludes to this in the play, 866–9). It is therefore only to be expected, if there were a throne of tragedy in the underworld, that Aeschylus should be its incumbent. The choice of Aeschylus and Euripides as characters may be explained partly in terms of the play's prominent thematic interest in the contrast between Old and New. It requires a two-man contest between divergent factions. The only way to oppose Old and New Tragedy – among Aeschylus, Sophocles and Euripides – is to pit the revered past master Aeschylus against the tirelessly innovative maverick Euripides. It is unsurprising that Sophocles should side with Aeschylus. While he was only a few years older than Euripides, and was capable of equally breathtaking innovation in his plays, he had never been associated with radicalism or the avant-garde; moreover, as someone who had served as a general and a politician, unlike Euripides, he also embodied more traditional, 'Aeschylean' values. In addition, Aeschylus and Sophocles had actually competed in 468 when Sophocles defeated Aeschylus with his first performed play. This may have disinclined Aristophanes from presenting another contest between the two. While Euripides may have competed against posthumously produced Aeschylus plays, he never competed against him in person, since Aeschylus died in 456, a year before Euripides' first performed play. Thus *Frogs* presents us with the only contest, among these three tragedians, that never actually took place.

The action of *Frogs*, put simply, is as follows. Dionysus attempts a descent to Hades (the underworld) to fetch Euripides from the dead. His motives are twofold: first, he simply adores Euripidean tragedy; secondly, he means to save tragedy. There are, he complains, no good tragedians left. Later in the play Dionysus' grounds for choosing a poet changes, as he declares that he needs a poet to save the city. It is on this basis that we are given some indication that Dionysus will choose Aeschylus. The play is divided into two halves. The second half is taken up entirely with the contest for the throne of tragedy in Hades. The first half loosely imitates a type of mythological story known as *katabasis*, in which a journey is taken by a hero down to the underworld to rescue, or steal, something or someone. The best-known examples are Orpheus' unsuccessful rescue of Eurydice, Heracles' descent to fetch Cerberus and the (failed) attempt by Theseus and Pirithous to abduct Persephone; *Frogs* contains allusions to both of these myths. Dionysus' journey to Hades also incorporates a series of stock comic routines – these include the disguise as Heracles; the opening porter scene; the double act with dim-witted master and clever slave; the competitive scene between Dionysus and the Frog-Chorus; the costume swapping scene between Dionysus and Xanthias; the scene with Dionysus and Xanthias being beaten onstage – that collectively comprise a retrospective assessment of Old Comedy itself.

Frogs is the earliest sizeable work of ancient Greek literary criticism. It is, however, difficult to gauge its critical intent, partly because it is comedy first and foremost, and partly because, as a dramatic text, the author's own voice remains elusive. But while Aeschylus and Euripides make numerous specific criticisms of one another's work, these do not alter the fact that the fictional situation, with Aeschylus and Euripides competing for the throne of tragedy, implies a positive judgement, on Aristophanes' part, upon both tragedians.

If we were to hypothesize some kind of overall artistic purpose behind *Frogs*, reductive as such an idea undoubtedly is, it might be twofold. First, the play seems to canonize Aeschylus, Euripides and Sophocles as the greatest exponents of tragedy. While Aeschylus wins the contest, it is Euripides whom Dionysus quotes with greater familiarity and relish; Sophocles, meanwhile, whenever he is mentioned, is also shown as eminently worthy of competing for the throne of tragedy. Secondly, *Frogs* both analyses and exemplifies what is best about Old Comedy (to Aristophanes' mind, at any rate). And the fact that Aristophanes' play is able to encompass within its own action a tragic contest between Aeschylus and Euripides seems to imply mischievously that Old Comedy is superior to its more 'serious' generic rival.

CHARACTERS

DIONYSUS, *patron god of drama*
XANTHIAS, *his slave*
HERACLES
A CORPSE
CHARON, *aged ferryman of the dead*
AEACUS, *doorkeeper of Hades*
MAID *to Persephone (queen of the underworld)*
TWO LANDLADIES
SLAVE, *elderly servant to Pluto*
EURIPIDES, *the tragedian*
AESCHYLUS, *the tragedian*
PLUTO, *god of the underworld*

MAIN CHORUS OF INITIATES
SUBSIDIARY CHORUS OF FROGS

Silent Characters

A CASTANET-GIRL
CORPSE BEARERS, SLAVES, DANCING-GIRLS, THE DISTINGUISHED DEAD, *etc.*

ACT ONE

Scene I: *The action begins at ground level before the house of* HERACLES *but then moves to the underworld (Hades), ending up before the palace of* PLUTO.

[*Enter* DIONYSUS *and his slave* XANTHIAS. DIONYSUS, *though a god, is presented as a paunchy middle-aged man. He wears a yellow robe, which is appropriate for the Dionysiac festival but feminine in appearance, and buskins.*[1] *The overall look is effeminate but he also wears a lion-skin over the robe and carries a large club. All of this amounts to a readily recognizable attempt by* DIONYSUS *to disguise himself as* HERACLES. *He is on foot but his slave is riding a donkey. The slave is laden with various pieces of luggage, some of which are suspended from a pole across his shoulders.*]

XANTHIAS How about one of the old gags, sir? I can always get a laugh with those.

DIONYSUS All right, only don't say 'God, what a heavy load!' I've had enough of that sort of thing already.

XANTHIAS Something a bit wittier then?

DIONYSUS Yes, but don't start off with 'Oh, my poor neck!'

XANTHIAS What *can* I give them, then? Shall I say something *really* funny?

DIONYSUS By all means. Just don't shift that pole about and say . . .

XANTHIAS What?

DIONYSUS . . . that you need a crap.

XANTHIAS

How about this then:
'If nobody will take away my pack,
I'll fart so hard it'll blow off my back.'

DIONYSUS Save that one till I need to throw up.

XANTHIAS Do you mean to say that I've been lugging these props around but I'm not allowed to use them to get a laugh? That's what usually happens. Phrynichus, Lycis, Ameipsias[2] – all the popular playwrights do it. The comic porter scene. There's one in every comedy.[3]

DIONYSUS Not in this one. Every time I go to a show and have to sit through one of those scintillating routines, I come away more than a year older.

XANTHIAS Oh, my poor neck! And all for nothing.

DIONYSUS Anyway, it's an absolute outrage that I, Dionysus, son of Juice,[4] have to struggle along on foot while this spoilt brat is allowed to ride so that he won't tire himself out with the luggage.

XANTHIAS That's rich. I am carrying the luggage, aren't I?

DIONYSUS Of course you're not, you're riding.

XANTHIAS I'm carrying luggage all the same.

DIONYSUS I don't get it.

XANTHIAS That's because I've got it. And, believe me, it weighs a ton.

DIONYSUS But the donkey's carrying everything.

XANTHIAS Oh, is he? You tell my shoulders that!

DIONYSUS If the donkey's so little use to you, why don't you change places with him?

XANTHIAS Oh, for god's sake! If only I'd been in that sea-battle, I'd be a free man now.[5] And if I got my hands on you . . .

DIONYSUS Come on, get down off that beast. Here we are, if I'm not mistaken. This is our first port of call. You see, I've walked the whole way.

[*While* XANTHIAS *extricates himself and the luggage from the donkey,* DIONYSUS *approaches the front door and knocks tentatively. There is no response.*]

Hullo there! Slave! Open up!

[*Still no response.* DIONYSUS *strikes the door loudly with his club.*]

HERACLES [*within*] Who strikes my door? Some centaur, no doubt!

[*The door opens and* HERACLES *appears. He stares at* DIONYSUS *in amazement.*]

What . . . who . . . ?

[*Laughing hysterically, he collapses to the floor.*]

DIONYSUS Slave!

XANTHIAS What?

DIONYSUS Did you notice?

XANTHIAS Notice what?

DIONYSUS How I frightened him.

XANTHIAS Mistook you for a lunatic, I expect.

HERACLES Oh, by Demeter, I can't stop laughing. [*He struggles to his feet and starts to head back into the house.*]

DIONYSUS Come back a minute, my good man, there's something I want to ask you.

HERACLES [*returning*] Sorry, friend, I couldn't help it. A lion-skin over a yellow negligee! What's going on? Why the high-heel boots? Why the club? What's your regiment?[6]

DIONYSUS Well, it's like this. I climbed aboard Cleisthenes'[7] vessel . . .

HERACLES Saw a bit of action, I expect, one way or another.

DIONYSUS We sank twelve enemy ships. Or was it thirteen?

HERACLES Just the two of you?

DIONYSUS Of course.

XANTHIAS Then I woke up.

DIONYSUS As I was saying, I was on the ship one day – I was reading the *Andromeda*[8] at the time – when I felt this sudden urge, you wouldn't believe how strong . . .

HERACLES A big urge?

DIONYSUS Yes, Molon's size.[9]

HERACLES For a woman?

DIONYSUS No, no.

HERACLES A boy?

DIONYSUS Certainly not!

HERACLES A man, then?

DIONYSUS *Please!*[10]

HERACLES You did say Cleisthenes was a friend of yours.

DIONYSUS Don't tease me, this is serious. I'm in a terrible way. I'm *consumed* with desire.

HERACLES What sort of desire, little brother?[11]

DIONYSUS You wouldn't understand. Let me put it this way. Have you ever felt a sudden craving for . . . pea soup?

HERACLES Are you serious? When do I *not* have a craving for pea soup?

DIONYSUS Are you with me, or should I give another example?

HERACLES Pea soup will do nicely. I understand perfectly.

DIONYSUS Well, that's the kind of desire I have for . . . Euripides.

HERACLES *Euripides!* But he's . . . dead!

DIONYSUS Even so. No one on earth can stop me from going to find him.

HERACLES What, down to Hades?

DIONYSUS Deeper still, if need be.

HERACLES To what end?

DIONYSUS I need a poet who can really *write*. Nowadays it seems like 'many are gone, and those that live are bad'.[12]

HERACLES What about Sophocles' son, Iophon?[13]

DIONYSUS He's the only decent one left, and I'm not even sure how good he is.

HERACLES Why not bring back Sophocles rather than Euripides, if you must fetch one of them?

DIONYSUS Not until I've seen how Iophon manages without his father's help. Besides, Euripides will be readier to sneak away with me; he's a much more slippery customer.[14] Sophocles, on the other hand – well, he always took life in his stride,[15] and he's probably taking death the same way.

HERACLES What about Agathon?[16]

DIONYSUS He's gone! He too has left me! A good poet, much missed by all his friends.

HERACLES Gone where?

DIONYSUS To the banquets of the Blest – specially laid on by the king of Macedon.[17]

HERACLES Well, what about Xenocles?

DIONYSUS To hell with Xenocles!

HERACLES Pythangelus?[18]

XANTHIAS Never a word about me. Look at my poor shoulder, it'll never be the same again.

HERACLES Surely there are dozens of young tragedians these days churning out plays by the thousand. If it's verbiage you're after, they leave Euripides for dust.

DIONYSUS Small fry, I assure you – insignificant squeakers, twittering like a choir of swallows.[19] A disgrace to their calling. If they're ever actually granted a chorus, they piss all over the art of tragedy, and then you never hear of them again. I defy you to find a genuine poet among the whole lot of them: one who can coin a memorable line.

HERACLES What do you mean, genuine?

DIONYSUS One who can produce something truly original, like 'Ether, bedsit of Zeus',[20] or 'the tread of Time',[21] or that bit about the tongue being allowed to perjure itself when the heart is not committed.[22]

HERACLES You actually like that sort of thing?

DIONYSUS I love it!

HERACLES But that stuff's all drivel, you must see that.

DIONYSUS 'Seek not within my mind to dwell', as the poet says, 'you have your own.'[23]

HERACLES What's more, it's positively harmful.

DIONYSUS When I want advice about food, I'll come to you. Meanwhile . . .

XANTHIAS Never a word about me.

DIONYSUS To get to the point – I see you're looking at my lion-skin. I took the liberty, seeing as you travelled in those parts when you went to fetch Cerberus – well, I was wondering if you could give me a few tips, you know, any useful contacts down there: where you get the boat, how to find the best restaurants, bakeries, boozers, knocking shops . . . and which places have the fewest creepy-crawlies.

XANTHIAS I might as well not exist.

HERACLES You're not seriously planning to go down there, are you? You're mad!

DIONYSUS Never mind that, just give me a simple answer:

what's the quickest way to Hades? I want a route that's not too warm and not too cold.

HERACLES Let me see now. You could go via rope and scaffold, if you don't mind hanging around for a bit.

DIONYSUS It would be a pain in the neck.

HERACLES Well, there's the 'executive route' via pestle and mortar.

DIONYSUS You mean hemlock?

HERACLES That's right.

DIONYSUS Now you're giving me cold feet![24]

HERACLES You want a way that just goes straight down?

DIONYSUS Exactly. I'm not much of a walker.

HERACLES A runner, eh? Well, you know the tower in the Potter's Quarter?

DIONYSUS Yes.

HERACLES Just go and wait on top of that.

DIONYSUS Then what?

HERACLES Watch the start of the torch race,[25] and when they shout 'One, two, three, *go*!' – well, off you go.

DIONYSUS Where to?

HERACLES The bottom.

DIONYSUS No, no! Just think – all that brain pudding. Not that way.

HERACLES Which way then?

DIONYSUS The way *you* went.

HERACLES That's a long trip. First you come to a great bottomless lake.

DIONYSUS How do I get across?

HERACLES There's an old ferryman who'll take you across in a tiny boat, about so big, for two obols.[26]

DIONYSUS Amazing what you can do with two obols! How did they make their way down there?

HERACLES Theseus introduced the idea.[27] Anyway, after that you come to the snakes and the wild beasts – thousands of them, all terrifying.

DIONYSUS It's no good trying to scare me off.

HERACLES Then you come to the Great Mire of Filth and the Eternal Stream of Dung. You'll find some pretty unsavoury characters wallowing in there: people who have wronged a guest, or had a pretty boy and failed to pay him, or knocked their mothers about, or punched their fathers on the jaw, or committed perjury, or copied out a speech by Morsimus[28] –

DIONYSUS Not to mention anyone who's learnt that war-dance by Cinesias.[29]

HERACLES After that you'll hear the sound of flute-playing and you'll come out into brilliant daylight, just like up here. Further on you'll see plantations of myrtle, and happy bands of revellers, men and women, dancing and clapping their hands and so on.

DIONYSUS And who are they?

HERACLES People initiated into the rites of the Mysteries[30] –

XANTHIAS Well, I'm going to stand up for *my* mystic rights, and have a sit down. [*He starts to lay down his various burdens.*]

HERACLES They'll tell you anything you need to know; they're right on the road to Pluto's palace. Well, goodbye, brother, and the best of luck.

DIONYSUS And to you too.

[*Exit* HERACLES.]

[*To* XANTHIAS] Now, pick up that baggage, and let's get going.

XANTHIAS But I haven't even put it all down yet! [*He looks for the donkey but it has gone.*]

DIONYSUS Look sharp!

XANTHIAS Come on, have a heart! Why not hire a corpse on his way to the grave to take your things down with him.

DIONYSUS Supposing he won't?

XANTHIAS Then I'll do it.

DIONYSUS All right.

[*A* CORPSE *appears being carried in slow procession across the stage.*]

Look, here's one now. I'll ask him. Er – hello, excuse me! Yes, you there! Corpse!

[*The* BEARERS *come to a halt. The* CORPSE *sits up with a jerk.*]

How would you like to take my baggage to hell?

CORPSE How many pieces?

DIONYSUS Just these.

CORPSE That'll be two drachmas.[31]

DIONYSUS What? That's far too much!

CORPSE Bearers, proceed!

DIONYSUS Hey, wait a minute! Can't we come to some arrangement?

CORPSE Two drachmas up front, or no deal.

DIONYSUS [*counting his change*] I've got . . . nine obols. What do you say?

CORPSE I'd sooner live again! [*He lies down again with a jerk.*]

XANTHIAS Well, of all the stuck-up people. I hope he comes to a bad end. All right, sir, load me up again.

[DIONYSUS *helps him with his bags, and they move on.*]

DIONYSUS You're a good lad. Now, where's this ferryboat?

CHARON [*offstage*] Heave, ho! Heave, ho!

[*The stage grows darker and eerier.*]

XANTHIAS Where are we?

DIONYSUS This must be the lake he was talking about, and – look, here comes the boat.

[CHARON *comes into view propelling a small boat on wheels.*]

XANTHIAS That must be Charon.

DIONYSUS Charon! [*No response.*] Charon! Charon!! [*No response.*] It seems that *Char*on couldn't *care* less.[32]

CHARON Who wants respite from toil and trouble? Anyone for Lethe, Oblivion, Perdition or the Dogs?

DIONYSUS Yes, me.

CHARON Get aboard, quickly.

DIONYSUS Where do you stop? Can I really go to Hell?

CHARON You can as far as I'm concerned. Get in!

DIONYSUS [*to* XANTHIAS] Come on, then!

CHARON I don't take slaves. Not unless they fought in the sea-battle.

XANTHIAS I was exempted on medical grounds: eye trouble.

CHARON You'll have to walk round the marsh.

XANTHIAS Where will I find you?

CHARON There's a resting place just past the Withering Stone.

DIONYSUS Got that?

XANTHIAS The creeps is what I've got. It's not my lucky day.
[*He tiptoes nervously off into the dark.*]

CHARON Sit at the oar. Any other passengers, get a move on. Here, what are you doing?

DIONYSUS Sitting on the oar, like you said.

CHARON I didn't say *on* the oar, fatso! This is where you sit, on the cross-bench.

DIONYSUS Like this?

CHARON Yes. Now stretch your arms forward and take hold of the oar.

DIONYSUS Like this?

CHARON Don't talk so much. Just push us off!

[CHARON *settles down comfortably in the stern, while* DIONYSUS *makes clumsy efforts to get the boat moving.*]

DIONYSUS How do you expect me to move this thing? I'm not the seafaring type.

CHARON It's easy. Come on, you'll soon have the singing to help you.

DIONYSUS What singing?

CHARON The Frog-Swans. They're quite something.

DIONYSUS Right, you start me off then.

CHARON I-i-i-n, out! I-i-i-n, out!

[*As soon as* DIONYSUS *has got his stroke adjusted to the tempo set by* CHARON, *the voices of the* FROG-CHORUS[33] *are heard offstage, singing in an entirely different rhythm.*]

FROGS

Brekekekex, koax, koax,
Brekekekex, koax, koax!
Oh we are the musical Frogs!
We live in the marshes and bogs!
Sweet, sweet is the hymn
We sing as we swim,
And our voices are known
For their beautiful tone
When on festival days[34]
We sing out in praise
Of the genial god –

And we don't think it odd
When the worshipping throng,
To the sound of our song,
Rolls home through the marshes and bogs;
Brekekekex!
Rolls home through the marshes and bogs.

DIONYSUS
I don't want to row any more,

FROGS
koax!

DIONYSUS
My bottom is getting too sore,

FROGS
koax!

DIONYSUS
But what do you care?
You're nothing but air,
And your 'koax' is really a bore –

FROGS
Brekekekex, koax, koax!
Your remarks are offensive in tone,
So we'd like to make some of our own.
Our plantation of reeds
For all musical needs
In the very best circles is known.
Should Apollo require
A new bridge for his lyre,
He comes to the frogs
Of the marshes and bogs;
We've exactly the type
Pan needs for his pipe
When he plays for our chorus;
The Muses adore us!
We're the rage on Parnassus,
For none can surpass us
In harmony, sweetness and tone.

DIONYSUS

What a sweat! I'm all wet! What a bore!
I'm so raw! I'm so sore! And what's more,
There are blisters here –
All over my rear –
Where I've never had blisters before.

FROGS

Brekekekex, koax, koax!

DIONYSUS

Give over, my musical friends!

FROGS

What, silence our chorus? Oh, no!
Let us sing as we sang long ago,
When we splashed in the sun –
Oh, wasn't it fun? –
'Mid the weeds and the sedge
At the pond's muddy edge.
If it happened to rain
We'd dive under again
To avoid getting soaked –
Still harder we croaked
Till from under the slime
Our sub-aqueous rhyme
Bubbled out loud and clear
For all men to hear,
And burst with a plop at the top,
Plepepeplep!
And burst with a plop at the top.

DIONYSUS

Brekekekex koax koax!
It's all this exertion, no doubt,
But I fancy that I'm about
To take over from you!

FROGS

We'll be sunk if you do!

DIONYSUS

I'll burst if I don't, so look out!

FROGS
Brekekekex koax koax!

DIONYSUS
Now listen, you lyrical twerps,
I don't give a damn for your burps!

FROGS
Then we'll burp all the more,
Twice as loud as before,
Till our cavernous throats
Cannot hold all the notes
Of our ear-splitting song
That we chant all day long:

DIONYSUS
Brekekex! Brekekex! Brekekex!
It's hopeless, you see:
You'll never beat me

FROGS
We'll see about that.

DIONYSUS
You won't, and that's that:
I'll go on till I'm bust,
All day if I must;
But I know I shall win in the end,
Brekekekex koax koax!

[*He pauses. The* FROG-CHORUS *remains silent.*]
Yes, I *knew* I would win in the end.

CHARON Whoa there, land ahoy! Bring her alongside with your oars! [*The boat docks.*] Well, here we are. Don't forget to pay.

DIONYSUS Ah, yes, those two obols. [*He pays the fare, and the boat moves off.*] Xanthias! Xanthias! Where are you? Xanthias!

[*It is now quite dark. Ghostly shadows flit across the stage.*]

XANTHIAS Coo-ee!

DIONYSUS Come here!

XANTHIAS [*emerging from the shadows*] Greetings, master!

DIONYSUS What's it like over here?

XANTHIAS Very dark. And very muddy.

DIONYSUS Any sign of those murderers and perjurers he told us about?

XANTHIAS Use your eyes, sir.

DIONYSUS [*looking towards the audience*] Oh, yes, I see them now. Well, what are we going to do?

XANTHIAS We'd better push on. The place is full of horrible monsters according to what's-his-name.

DIONYSUS That old rogue! He was just exaggerating to scare me off. He knew I was a services man with a thirst for glory. He's very sensitive about his exploits, old Heracles. In fact, I'm rather hoping we do meet something. One ought to slay a beast or two on a trip like this, wouldn't you say?

XANTHIAS Shush! What's that noise?

DIONYSUS [*panicking*] Where's it coming from?

XANTHIAS It's somewhere behind us.

DIONYSUS Here, let me go in front.

XANTHIAS No, it's in front of us!

DIONYSUS Actually, why don't you go first?

XANTHIAS There it is! Oh, what a horrible creature!

DIONYSUS W-w-what sort of creature?

XANTHIAS Terrifying – it keeps on changing. It's sort of like a bull – no, now it's a mule! Wait a minute, it's turned into a woman, a very nice one too!

DIONYSUS Here, let me past!

XANTHIAS Oh, what a shame – it's become a dog.

DIONYSUS [*with a shudder*] It must be Empusa.[35]

XANTHIAS Her face is certainly all lit up.

DIONYSUS Has she got a copper leg?

XANTHIAS Yes, I do believe she has. The other one's made of cow dung.

DIONYSUS Ugh, where can I turn?

XANTHIAS Where can I, come to that?

DIONYSUS [*appealing to the priest of Dionysus, who is sitting in the front row*][36] Oh, Mister Priest, protect me! Remember that drink we're going to have after the show!

XANTHIAS Lord Heracles, we're done for!

DIONYSUS Sh! Don't call me that, for god's sake: don't even breathe my name.[37]

XANTHIAS Dionysus, then.

DIONYSUS No, that's even worse.

XANTHIAS [*to the spectral creature*] Be gone to whence you came! [*To* DIONYSUS, *who has taken refuge somewhere*] Come back here!

DIONYSUS [*returning*] What is it?

XANTHIAS Don't worry. It's all right now. We've weathered the storm. Or, as Hegelochus would say, 'the pillows heave no more'.[38] Which is to say, Empusa's gone.

DIONYSUS Do you promise?

XANTHIAS I swear.

DIONYSUS Swear again.

XANTHIAS Cross my heart.

DIONYSUS You're quite sure?

XANTHIAS She's gone, I'm telling you.

DIONYSUS My god, I turned quite white when I saw her!

XANTHIAS [*pointing to the back of his robe*] This, on the other hand, has turned brown with fear.

DIONYSUS Oh dear, how did such misfortune befall me? Which of the gods was it that brought me down?[39]

XANTHIAS 'Ether, bedsit of Zeus'? Or 'the tread of Time', perhaps?

[*Flute music is heard from offstage.*]

Sh!

DIONYSUS [*nervously*] What is it?

XANTHIAS Listen, can't you hear it?

DIONYSUS What?

XANTHIAS Music. Flute-playing.

DIONYSUS So it is. And a most mystical whiff of torches. Keep quiet, let's crouch down here and listen.

[*They conceal themselves. The sound of music comes nearer, and the* CHORUS *is heard chanting 'Iacchus, Iacchus!'*]

XANTHIAS These must be the happy bands of Initiates Heracles told us about. They're singing the hymn to Iacchus by that fellow Diagoras.[40]

DIONYSUS I think you're right. Let's keep quiet and make sure.

[*Enter, by torchlight, the* CHORUS OF INITIATES, *the men and women in separate groups.*]

CHORUS[41]

Come, Iacchus, leave your temple,
  Join your pious acolytes!
Come and dance across the meadows,
  Lead us in your mystic rites!

Toss your head and swing the berries
  On your myrtle crown so gay;
Stamp and prance with feet delirious,
  Whirling all our qualms away.

Here with dancing, songs and laughter –
  All the best of all the arts –
We your worshippers await you:
  Come, oh come! The revel starts!

[*They dance with abandon as the sacrificial meal is prepared and the wine cups are filled.*]

XANTHIAS Oh, Persephone, paragon of perfection. Oh, divine daughter of Demeter[42] – what a wonderful smell of pork![43]

DIONYSUS You'd better keep quiet, or you won't get a sausage.

[*The* CHORUS *resume their hymn. At the cue in the second line, torches are raised and light up the stage.*]

CHORUS

Call upon him, call Iacchus!
  Raise the torches, wake the flame!
See at once the darkness scatter
  As we shout his sacred name.

See, the meadows blaze! Iacchus,
  Lodestar of our secret rite,
Comes to wake the mystic knowledge
  Born in us at dead of night,

Turning all to dance and movement,
   Setting souls and bodies free;
Aged knees shake off their stiffness
   In the rhythmic ecstasy.

Shine for us, and we will follow!
   Lead us on, our strength renew:
Young and old shall dance together
   'Mid the flowers, moist with dew.

[*They dance again, and then sit down to partake of the sacrificial meat and wine. Meanwhile the* CHORUS-LEADER *pronounces the traditional warning to the uninitiated.*]

CHORUS-LEADER

Now all you bystanders, keep silent, we pray!
The holy procession proceeds on its way.
And all you outsiders who know not our rite,
Stay clear of our revels and keep out of sight.
We've no use for heathens who don't understand
Conventions of Comedy, noble and grand;[44]
Who snigger and leer till the festival's ended,
And find double-entendres where none are intended.
We don't want the leaders who stoke party strife
When what we all need is a nice quiet life;
Or customs inspectors from somewhere nearby
Who smuggle out naval supplies on the sly.[45]
We don't want the traitor who sides with the foe,
We don't want the soldier who lets the fort go;
The greedy official who'd even be willing
To sell his own city just to make a killing.
Some people there are who, when mocked in a play,
Vent spleen on the poet by cutting his pay.[46]
We've no use for them, nor for poets who bore us
And persons caught short in the middle of the chorus.[47]
Stand aside, stand aside, to all these I say:
You're banned from our dances so just keep away!

Now stir up your voices, and let's hear the song.
May our revels begin and go on all night long.

[*The feasting over, the* CHORUS *group themselves for the ceremony, which consists of songs and dances in honour of Persephone, Demeter and Iacchus.*]

CHORUS

Now we're well fortified,
Let's get into our stride;
To the sweet flowery meadow let's march off with pride.
At distinguished bystanders
We'll jest and we'll jeer;
It's the feast of the Goddess, we've nothing to fear.

The praises we'll sing
Of the Princess of Spring,[48]
Who returns at this season salvation to bring;
Though traitors endeavour
Her plans to frustrate,
We know she will save us before it's too late.

CHORUS-LEADER And now, in a different strain, let us honour our queen and goddess Demeter, bringer of plenty, with a holy hymn.

CHORUS

Queen Demeter, stand before us,
Smile upon your favourite chorus!
Grant that when we dance and play,
As befits your holy day,
Part in earnest, part in jest,
We may shine above the rest,
And our play in all men's eyes
Favour find, and win the prize.

CHORUS-LEADER Now with your songs call forth the youthful god, to join us in our dancing.

CHORUS

[*Men*] Iacchus, Iacchus, lead on to the shrine![49]

Our hearts are on fire with your music divine!
Come, teach us to dance over hedgerows and stiles,
And keep up the tempo for several miles.

[*All*] Iacchus, Iacchus, dance on and we'll follow.

[*Women*] Last night as we revelled from twilight till dawn
My clothes and my sandals were utterly torn –
The fault of the god, but perhaps his defence is
It raises a laugh and cuts down on expenses.[50]

[*All*] Iacchus, Iacchus, dance on and we'll follow.

[*Men*] A girl did I spy as we sported and played:
She certainly was an attractive young maid.
She winked and she giggled, but what I liked best
Was the way that her titty peeped out through her vest.

[*All*] Iacchus, Iacchus, dance on and we'll follow.

DIONYSUS Tell you what, being a sociable sort, I wouldn't mind sporting with her myself.

XANTHIAS Me too. What are we waiting for?

[*They join the ensuing dance, after which the* CHORUS *halt, facing the audience, and proceed to 'jeer' at notable members of the audience, as promised in the Hymn to Persephone.*]

CHORUS

You've heard of Archedemus?[51] Well, he's not renowned for looks;
His parentage is doubtful, and he isn't on the books;
Yet down among the dead-folk he's the prince of all the crooks.

But what's come over Cleisthenes? He looks so full of care;
He's lost his precious lover boy, his sad cries rend the air,
As he takes a pair of tweezers to his last superfluous hair.[52]

Now Callias,[53] the naval man, is at his best ashore,
Where he can show his seamanship in actions by the score,
And when they see his lion-skin the girls cry out for more.

DIONYSUS

Excuse me interrupting, but we're strangers here in Hell:
Can some kind person tell us, where does Master Pluto dwell?

CHORUS

You haven't got too far to go, his house is very near.
No need to ask me more than once, it's pretty much right here.

DIONYSUS

Pick up the luggage, Xanthias, pick up the bags once more!

XANTHIAS

This portering, it really is becoming quite a bore!

[DIONYSUS *and* XANTHIAS *return to their luggage as the* CHORUS *prepare for the procession.*]

CHORUS-LEADER Dance on merrily through the flowery grove; let all who take part in our festival tread the sacred precinct of the Goddess. And I will bear the holy torch for the girls and women; let them dance to the glory of the Goddess, the whole night long.

[*The* MEN *and* WOMEN *move to opposite sides of the stage, singing as they go off.*]

CHORUS

Let us hasten to the meadow,
Where the roses are so sweet,
And the little flowers grow
In profusion at our feet;

With the blessèd Fates to lead us
We will laugh and sing and play,
And perform the choral dances
In our own traditional way.

Now to us alone is given,
When our earthly days are done,
To look out upon the splendour
Of a never-setting sun;
For we saw the holy Mysteries,
Yes, we heard the god's behest,
And were mindful of our duty
Both to kinsmen and to guest.

Scene 2: DIONYSUS *and* XANTHIAS *stand before the palace of* PLUTO.

[*The* CHORUS *are present, but stand apart from the action.*]

DIONYSUS [*approaching the door*] What sort of a knock should one give, I wonder? [*He raises his hand to knock, but thinks better of it.*] One ought to conform to the local customs.

XANTHIAS Come on, don't dither. Remember you're supposed to be Heracles!

DIONYSUS [*knocking tentatively*] Hello there! Slave!

[*The door is opened by* AEACUS, *the doorkeeper of Hades,*[54] *a formidable figure.*]

AEACUS Who's there?

DIONYSUS Heracles the b-b-bold.

AEACUS [*coming out*] So it's you, you foul, shameless, desperate, good-for-nothing criminal! You ought to be ashamed of yourself! Coming down here and taking away our poor mutt Cerberus, throttling him in the process! I was responsible for him. Well, we've got you now! I'll have you flung over the cliff, down to the dark Stygian rocks, where you'll be chased by the prowling hounds of Hell, and the hundred-headed viper will tear your guts out, and the Tartessian lamprey will devour your lungs, and the Tithrasian Gorgons will pluck out your kidneys and – just wait there while I fetch them.

[AEACUS *goes back into the palace.* DIONYSUS *collapses to the ground in terror.*]

XANTHIAS What are doing down there?

DIONYSUS Oh no! My bowel is empty.[55] Call on the god!

XANTHIAS Stand up! Somebody might see you.

DIONYSUS I feel faint. Give me a sponge.

[XANTHIAS *extracts a sponge from one of the bags.*]

Press it on my heart, there's a good chap.

XANTHIAS There you go.

DIONYSUS No, here. That's it.

XANTHIAS The heart's slipped a bit, hasn't it?

DIONYSUS What? Oh, yes – the sudden shock. It's taken refuge in my . . . lower intestine.

XANTHIAS [*realizing what has happened within* DIONYSUS' *clothing*] O most cowardly of men and gods!

DIONYSUS How can you say that? When I had the courage to ask for a sponge. A coward wouldn't have done that.

XANTHIAS What would he have done?

DIONYSUS Wallowed in his own filth. At least I got up and cleaned myself.

XANTHIAS How very brave of you.

DIONYSUS Yes, I rather think it was. Most people would have been terrified by all those threats and long words. Confess, now, weren't you a tiny bit scared yourself?

XANTHIAS Not a bit.

DIONYSUS Well, if you're feeling so brave and heroic, how about taking my place? Here you are, you take the club and lion-skin – a chance to show your courage – and I'll carry the luggage for you.

XANTHIAS Anything you say. You're the boss.

[*They exchange roles.*]

There, how do I look? Xanthias as Heracles! I reckon the part suits me better than it does you, you old coward!

DIONYSUS It's a very good imitation of a slave dressed up as Heracles. Come on, let me have those bundles.

[*Persephone's* MAID *comes out of the palace.*]

MAID TO XANTHIAS Oh, Heracles, darling, how sweet of you

to come and see us again! As soon as our mistress heard you were coming she started baking. There's several cauldrons full of pea soup, and we're roasting a whole ox for you, and she's been making cakes and biscuits. So come on in!

XANTHIAS Well, thank you very much, but I –

MAID I won't take no for an answer. The birds are done to a turn, and you should see the dessert! Mistress has mixed the wine herself, it's delicious. Come along!

XANTHIAS As a matter of fact I've eaten already.

MAID Don't be silly. I'm not going to let you get away that easily. There's such a pretty flute-girl waiting for you inside, and some other girls to dance for you.

XANTHIAS Dancing-girls, eh?

MAID Hand-plucked, and ripened to perfection. Come in and see for yourself. The cook's just ready with the fish and the table's laid.

XANTHIAS Tell those dancing-girls I'll be with them shortly. [*To* DIONYSUS] Boy, bring in the luggage.

[*The* MAID *goes in.*]

DIONYSUS Here, wait a minute! Can it be that you're taking my little joke seriously? Give me back my things and get back to your luggage!

XANTHIAS Can it be that you're thinking of taking back this beautiful lion-skin, after you gave it to me and all?

DIONYSUS I'm not *thinking* of doing so, I *am* doing so. Give it here!

XANTHIAS Well, I'll be – as god is my witness . . .

DIONYSUS What god? I *am* a god. You didn't really expect to pass yourself off as Heracles, did you? You, a puny mortal!

XANTHIAS All right, all right. Take them. But if you ever need my help again . . .

CHORUS

The moral is plain as plain can be;
As everyone knows who has served at sea,
If you want to be comfy just roll with the ship!
Don't stand like a fool with a stiff upper lip,
But learn from Theramenes,[56] shrewd politician,
To move with the times and improve your position.

DIONYSUS

You can hardly expect me to watch my own man
Hard at it with dancing-girls on the divan,
And giving me orders, as likely as not:
'Boy, straighten these covers and bring me the pot!
And take that lascivious grin off your face –
I'll teach you that slaves should remember their place!'

[*No sooner has* DIONYSUS *resumed the lion-skin than two* LANDLADIES *enter.*]

FIRST LANDLADY Come here quick, here's that rogue who came to our inn that time and wolfed down sixteen loaves.

SECOND LANDLADY So it is.

XANTHIAS This isn't going to be fun for somebody.

FIRST LANDLADY And twenty portions of meat stew at half an obol each.

XANTHIAS Who's going to get it in the neck now?

SECOND LANDLADY And all that garlic.

DIONYSUS Nonsense, madam, you don't know what you're talking about.

FIRST LANDLADY Thought I wouldn't recognize him in his kinky boots! And what about all that salt-cod you had?

SECOND LANDLADY And cheese – fresh that day it was. He scoffed the lot, rind and all.

FIRST LANDLADY And when I asked him for the money, oh, you should have seen the look he gave me. He started roaring like a lion.

XANTHIAS That's him all right. He's always doing that.

FIRST LANDLADY And then he waved his sword round like a lunatic.

SECOND LANDLADY You poor dear.

FIRST LANDLADY Oh, he gave us such a fright. We had to run upstairs and lock ourselves in. And he went flying off, taking the doormat with him.

XANTHIAS He never could resist a nice doormat.

FIRST LANDLADY Well, we must do something. I know, what about calling Cleon?[57]

SECOND LANDLADY Yes, and Hyperbolus[58] – he's down here too.

FIRST LANDLADY We'll fix him. Look at that greedy gob of his. I'd like to knock his teeth down his throat for him, eating us out of house and home!

SECOND LANDLADY Over the cliff with him!

FIRST LANDLADY Slit his throat with a sickle!

SECOND LANDLADY I'll go and find Cleon: he'll have him up in court before the day's out.[59]

[*The* LANDLADIES *go back in.*]

DIONYSUS You know, Xanthias, I've come to grow very fond of you.

XANTHIAS Oh no you don't! I know your game. I'm not playing Heracles again.

DIONYSUS Dearest Xanthias! Sweet Xanthias!

XANTHIAS How could I possibly get away with passing myself off as Heracles? Me, a puny mortal.

DIONYSUS Yes, yes, I know I've offended you. You've every right to be angry. Look, take this lovely lion-skin, it really suits you. And if I ever ask for it back, may I rot in hell. My wife and children too – even bleary old Archedemus.

XANTHIAS All right! On those terms, I'll do it. [*He takes the lion-skin and club, and loads* DIONYSUS *with the baggage once again.*]

CHORUS

Well now you're dressed up just the same as before,
A sight to make anyone tremble,
You must roll your eyes and swagger and roar
Like the god you're supposed to resemble.

If you flinch or waver or fluff your role
And forget to speak bravely and brag, man,
You'll be putting those suitcases back on that pole
And going back to your job as a bagman.

XANTHIAS

I'm sure you are right: I've been thinking a lot –
I know my own master, and if he
Considers there's anything good to be got
He'd have these things back in a jiffy.

Meanwhile I must practise my sourest glare
And puff out my chest and stand steady.
How's this for a truly horrific stare?
But wait – someone's coming already!

[AEACUS *returns, with numerous* SLAVES *carrying whips, ropes and chains.*]

AEACUS Quick, tie-up this dog-stealer and I'll give him what he deserves. Get cracking!

[*Two* SLAVES *bear down on* XANTHIAS.]

DIONYSUS This isn't going to be fun for somebody!

XANTHIAS [*as Heracles*] To hell with the lot of you! Don't you dare come near me!

AEACUS Oh, so you're a tough guy, eh? Ditylas! Skobylas! Pardokas! Come here! The man wants a fight.

[*Three more* SLAVES *come forward.*]

DIONYSUS He ought to be ashamed of himself. Taking other people's things and then resisting arrest!

AEACUS The cheek of the man!

DIONYSUS He's a hardened criminal.

XANTHIAS Listen, I've never been here before and I've not stolen so much as a bean off of you, I swear on my life. I'll tell you what I'll do: I'll let you torture this slave of mine. And if I'm proven guilty, take me off and execute me.

AEACUS Hm. What kind of torture do you suggest?

XANTHIAS Give him the full works. Rack, thumbscrew, gallows, cat-o'-nine-tails. Pour vinegar up his nose, pile bricks on his chest – anything you fancy. Only don't hit him with leeks or spring onions – it'd bring tears to my eyes.

AEACUS Fair enough. And if he gets damaged in the process, I suppose you'll want compensation.

XANTHIAS No, no. Don't worry about that. Just take him away and do your worst.

AEACUS We might as well do it here, under his master's eye. [*To* DIONYSUS] Come on, put down those bags, and mind you tell the truth.

DIONYSUS You can't torture *me* – I'm an immortal. If you do, I'll . . . hold you responsible!

AEACUS You'll *what*?

DIONYSUS Look here, I'm a god: Dionysus, son of Zeus. It's this fellow who's a slave.

AEACUS Did you hear that?

XANTHIAS I most certainly did. All the more reason to flog him: if he's a god, he won't feel a thing.

DIONYSUS Well, you're a god too, aren't you, Heracles? Why not let them flog you as well?

XANTHIAS Fair enough. Whichever of us squeals first, or even winces, isn't really a god.

AEACUS You're a good sport, sir. That's what I call fair and square. [*He takes a rope's end from one of the* SLAVES.] Right! Bend over, the pair of you.

XANTHIAS Wait a minute. How are you going to ensure it's a fair test?

AEACUS Easy. You each receive alternate strokes.

XANTHIAS Good idea. [*He bends over and* DIONYSUS *reluctantly follows suit.*]

AEACUS [*giving* XANTHIAS *a good whack*] There!

XANTHIAS I bet you I won't even feel it.

AEACUS I've hit you already.

XANTHIAS [*feigning incredulity*] No!

AEACUS Now for the other one. [*He whacks* DIONYSUS.]

DIONYSUS Well, get on with it.

AEACUS I've done it.

DIONYSUS Really? Well, what do you know? I didn't feel a thing.

AEACUS Well, I'm not sure about that. Let's try the other one again.

XANTHIAS Come on then. [AEACUS *whacks him, harder this time.*] Aagh!

AEACUS What's the matter? Did that hurt?

XANTHIAS How strange! I'd quite forgotten about the Festival of Heracles up at the Diomeia.

AEACUS A pious impulse. [*To* DIONYSUS] Your turn. [*He gives him another harder whack.*]

DIONYSUS Ow! [*He jumps up in pain.*]

AEACUS What's the matter?

DIONYSUS Men on horseback, look! [*He prances about imitating a man on horseback.*]

AEACUS Funny they should bring tears to your eyes.

DIONYSUS There's a smell of onions.

AEACUS Sure you didn't feel anything?

DIONYSUS Me? Not a thing.

AEACUS Oh, well, we'll have to try the other fellow. [*He whacks* XANTHIAS *harder still.*]

XANTHIAS God almighty!

AEACUS Gotcha!

XANTHIAS Would you mind pulling out this splinter for me?

AEACUS What's going on? Well, here we go again. [*He whacks* DIONYSUS *just as hard.*]

DIONYSUS Ahhhh-Apollo! Lord of Delos' holy isle, or was it Pytho . . .

AEACUS That hurt him. Did you hear?

DIONYSUS How does it go, again? – Wonderful poet, Hipponax.[60]

XANTHIAS You're wasting your time. There's too much padding down there. Try here, just under his ribs.

AEACUS No, I've got a better idea. [*To* DIONYSUS] Turn round this way. [*He hits him in the stomach.*]

DIONYSUS Poseidon!!

XANTHIAS Hurt by any chance?

DIONYSUS [*singing*] . . . king of the mighty deep, lord of the crags and cliffs . . .

AEACUS I'll be damned if I can tell which of you is the god. You'll have to come inside. My master and Persephone will be able to tell – they're gods themselves.

DIONYSUS I must say I wish you'd thought of that a bit sooner.

[DIONYSUS *and* XANTHIAS *go in, followed by* AEACUS *and the* SLAVES.]

CHORUS

Come, Muse of the holy dancing choir,
With wit and charm our songs inspire!
Here sit ten thousand men of sense,
A most enlightened audience,

Who expect a lot of a dancing choir
And set their hopes of honour higher
Than Cleophon – whose lips we've heard
Resounding, like a fateful bird,
An enigmatic spouting swallow,
Whose words, though difficult to follow,
Should not defy interpretation
Once they're translated from the Thracian.[61]
And this is what that human fowl,
Like plaintive nightingale, will howl:
'You always vote again, but wait –
Or else next time you're for it mate!'

[*The* CHORUS-LEADER *comes forward and addresses the audience.*]

CHORUS-LEADER

We chorus folk two privileges prize:
To amuse you, citizens, and to advise.
So, amid the fun that marks this sacred day,
We'll put on serious looks and have our say.
And first for those misguided souls I plead
Who in the past to Phrynichus[62] paid heed.
It's history now; their folly they regret.
The time has come to forgive and forget.
Oh, yes, they erred, but it does not seem right,
When slaves who helped us in a single fight
Now vote beside our allies from Plataea[63]
And put on masters' clothes, like Xanthias here.
Not that I disagree with that decision –
No, no, it shows intelligence and vision –
But if we're going to treat these men as brothers,
Let's be consistent and excuse the others.
When we have been so wise, it seems a pity
That men of our own kin, who've served the City
In many naval battles – not just one –
Should still be paying for this thing they've done.
Come, wise Athenians, come swallow your pride!
We need those loyal kinsmen on our side;

As they will be, if every man who fights
Is a full citizen with all his rights.
But if we choose to strut and put on airs
While Athens founders in a sea of cares,
In days to come, when our history is penned,
They'll say we were completely round the bend.

CHORUS

If I've any knowledge of people at all,
I'll tell you with confidence what will befall
A rascal with whom we have long been encumbered,
Whose days on this earth, I assure you, are numbered.
He's sly as a monkey, his voice might be quieter,
He does very well as a wash-house proprietor;
He's Lord of the Earth, for he sells it in pots
For cleaning your woollies and getting out spots;
He makes up detergents that won't even lather,
By mixing in cinders to make them go further.
Wee Cleigenes[64] knows that his joys will soon cease
Yet he won't be persuaded to advocate peace;
A cudgel is one thing on which he'll insist
To save him from thieves when he staggers home pissed.

CHORUS-LEADER

I'll tell you what I think about the way
This city treats her soundest men today:
By a coincidence more sad than funny,
It's very like the way we treat our money.
The noble silver drachma, which of old
We were so proud of, and the one of gold,
Coins that rang true (clean-stamped and worth their weight)
Throughout the world have ceased to circulate.
Instead the purses of Athenian shoppers
Are full of phoney silver-plated coppers.
Just so, when men are needed by the nation,
The best have been withdrawn from circulation.
Men of good birth and breeding, men of parts,
Well schooled in wrestling and the gentler arts,
These we abuse, and look instead to knaves,

Upstarts, nonentities, foreigners and slaves –
Rascals all! Honestly, what men we choose!
There was a time when you'd have scorned to use
Men so debased, so far beyond the pale,
Even as scapegoats to be dragged from jail
And flogged to death outside the city gates.
Misguided friends, change now, it's not too late!
Try the good ones again: if they succeed,
You will have shown that you have sense indeed;
And if things don't go well, if these good men
All fail, and Athens comes to grief, why, then
Discerning folk will murmur (let us hope):
'She hanged herself, but with a first-rate rope!'

ACT TWO

Scene I: *Before the palace of* PLUTO.

[XANTHIAS *and a* SLAVE *of* PLUTO*'s are engaged in menial tasks.*]

SLAVE He's a real gentleman, your master, by Zeus.

XANTHIAS Of course. Like all real gentlemen he only understands two things: swigging and frigging.

SLAVE But fancy him not flogging you for making out you were the master and he was the slave!

XANTHIAS He'd have been sorry if he tried.

SLAVE Ah, that's the way I like to hear a slave talk – I love it.

XANTHIAS Love it, eh?

SLAVE There's nothing I like more than badmouthing my master behind his back.

XANTHIAS I bet you mutter a few things under your breath when he's had a go at you.

SLAVE Oh, yes! I like a spot of muttering.

XANTHIAS And what about prying into his affairs, eh?

SLAVE There's nothing quite like prying.

XANTHIAS I can see we're going to get along fine, you and me. Have you ever tried eavesdropping when he's got company?

SLAVE Eavesdropping? Are you kidding me? That's my favourite.

XANTHIAS And then passing it all on to other people, eh?

SLAVE That's so good, it makes me shoot off on the spot!

XANTHIAS Put it there, old boy! Listen, my old mucker, my partner in crime, what's all that yelling and shouting in there? What's all the fuss about?

SLAVE That'll be Aeschylus and Euripides.

XANTHIAS What on earth are they up to?

SLAVE There's serious trouble among the dead at the moment. You might almost call it civil war.

XANTHIAS What do you mean?

SLAVE Well, there's a custom down here that applies to all the fine arts and skilled professions: whoever's the best in each discipline has the right to have his dinner in the Great Hall, with his own chair of honour,[65] up near Pluto.

XANTHIAS I see.

SLAVE But if somebody else comes along who's better in the profession, then the incumbent has to stand down.

XANTHIAS So what is it that's upset Aeschylus?

SLAVE Well, he had the chair for tragedy, being the best and all.

XANTHIAS And now?

SLAVE Well, Euripides came along and started showing off to all the other people we've got down here, you know, cut-throats, highwaymen, murderers, burglars – a right rough lot they are – and of course he soon had them all twisted round his little finger, with all his arguments and clever talking. So they've all started saying he's the best, and he's decided to lay claim to the chair instead of Aeschylus.

XANTHIAS Didn't he get a shoeing for that?

SLAVE Not at all. The people all said they had the right to judge who was the greatest.

XANTHIAS What people? All those criminals you mentioned?

SLAVE A hell of a fuss they kicked up too.

XANTHIAS Didn't anyone side with Aeschylus?

SLAVE There aren't many decent folk down here – take a look for yourself. [*He points towards the audience.*]

XANTHIAS What's Pluto going to do about it?

SLAVE He's going to do things properly, you know, hold a contest to test their skill.

XANTHIAS Just those two? Didn't Sophocles put in a claim?

SLAVE Lord, no! When he came down here, he went straight up to Aeschylus, took his hand and kissed him like a brother. He renounced any claim to the chair. And now he's sent word that if Aeschylus wins – all well and good, but if Euripides wins, he'll take him on himself.

XANTHIAS It's really about to happen?

SLAVE Any minute now – right here where we're standing. They'll even have the scales out for weighing their poetry.

XANTHIAS Weighing poetry? What, like slices of meat?

SLAVE Oh, yes, it's all got to be measured properly, with rulers, yardsticks, compasses and wedges, and god knows what else.

XANTHIAS A regular torture chamber.

SLAVE Euripides says he's going to put every line to the test.

XANTHIAS I imagine Aeschylus is boiling with rage.

SLAVE He's been looking at the ground all day, glowering like a bull.

XANTHIAS Who's going to be the judge?

SLAVE That was a tricky one. It was hard to find anyone clever enough. And then Aeschylus said he didn't see eye to eye with the Athenians.[66]

XANTHIAS All those rogues and what have you – I see his point.

SLAVE And as for the others, he says, none of them could tell a poet from the back end of a donkey. So in the end they settled on your master – after all, he's supposed to be an expert. Anyway, we'd better go in. It never pays to get in their way when they're busy.

[XANTHIAS *and the* SLAVE *withdraw. Now* DIONYSUS *and* PLUTO *emerge from the palace and take up their seats.*[67] SLAVES *also come out carrying pieces of weighing and measuring equipment, and arrange the seating for the contest. Meanwhile an altercation is heard as* EURIPIDES *and* AESCHYLUS *appear mid-argument. They come to some sort of order in the presence of* DIONYSUS, *and take up seats beside him.*]

CHORUS

Ah, how impressive the rage that burns in the heart of
the Thunderer,
Seeing the fangs of his rival exposed in a gesture of hate!
Note how superbly he raves, and with what
independence his eyeballs
In divers directions gyrate!

Words are his weapons: watch out, as the armour-clad syllables hurtle,
Helmeted, crested and plumed, from the lips of the poet most high!
Wait for the clash and din as the metaphors collide and mingle,
The sparks as the particles fly!

See the great spread of his mane, as it bristles in leonine fury:
No one can doubt for a moment those whiskers truly are his own!
Huge are the words that he wields, great compounds with rivets and bolts in,
And epithets hewn from stone.[68]

Now it's the challenger's turn to reply to this verbal bombardment:
Neatly each phrase he dissects, with intelligence subtle and keen;
Harmless around him the adjectives tumble, as he ducks for cover
And squeaks, 'It depends what you mean.'[69]

EURIPIDES [*jumping to his feet*] I see no reason why I should withdraw. I happen to be the better poet.

DIONYSUS Why silent, Aeschylus? You heard his words?

[AESCHYLUS *remains silent with rage.*]

EURIPIDES It's just like the entire Aeschylean approach. The dignified silence, the pregnant pause?

DIONYSUS That's a bit of a sweeping statement, Euripides.

EURIPIDES I saw through him years ago. All that rugged grandeur – it's all so uncultivated and unrestrained. No subtlety whatsoever. Just a torrent of verbiage, stiffened with superlatives and padded out with pretentious polysyllables.

AESCHYLUS [*apoplectic with rage*] That's about the level of criticism one might expect from you, 'son of the seed-goddess'.[70] And what are your plays but a concatenation of commonplaces, as threadbare as the ragged beggars who populate them.

DIONYSUS Come now, Aeschylus, 'Do not inflame your inward parts with baleful rage.'[71] Calm down!

AESCHYLUS Not till I've told this cripple-merchant[72] where to get off.

DIONYSUS Someone fetch me a black lamb,[73] quick! There's stormy weather blowing this way.

AESCHLYUS Not only do you clutter the stage with cripples and beggars but you make your characters sing and dance Cretan arias. What's more, you build your plots around unsavoury topics like incest[74] and –

DIONYSUS Whoa there, Aeschylus, steady on! And you, Euripides, wouldn't it be wiser if you moved back out of range? I'd hate to see you get hit on the head by a main clause and give birth to a premature tragedy. Aeschylus, try not to lose your temper. Surely two poets can criticize each other's work without screaming like fishwives, or flaring up like a forest fire.

EURIPIDES I'm ready for him. Let Aeschylus have first say if he wants to. I can handle it. Criticize whatever you like – diction, lyrics, the very sinews of tragedy. I don't care which play you take: *Peleus*, *Aeolus*, *Meleager* – why, even *Telephus*![75]

DIONYSUS Well, Aeschylus?

AESCHYLUS I had hoped to avoid having a contest here: it puts me at a considerable disadvantage.

DIONYSUS How so?

AESCHYLUS My plays have outlived me so I don't have them to hand down here.[76] His died with him. But never mind. Let's have a contest, if we must, by all means.

DIONYSUS Right. Bring the brazier and the incense! [DIONYSUS *rises, takes incense and a libation cup, and goes to the altar. He burns the incense and pours a libation.*] Before the shafts of wit begin to fly, I pray that I may judge this cultural event with the highest artistic sensibility. [*To the* CHORUS] You, meanwhile, offer up a prayer to the Muses.

CHORUS

When men of sage and subtle mind
In fierce debate their views do vent,
And strive some priceless phrase to find
To mask each specious argument,
Then Zeus's virgin daughters nine
Stand by to watch the sport divine.

Come then today, you Muses bright!
Two worse foes never took the field:
For one is armed with words of might,
And one the sword of wit does wield.
O heavenly maids, your presence lend!
The game's afoot! Descend, descend!

DIONYSUS Now you must each offer a prayer before we begin. [*He offers some incense to* AESCHYLUS.]

AESCHYLUS O Demeter, who do nourish my spirit, may I prove worthy of your mysteries![77]

DIONYSUS Euripides, take some incense.

EURIPIDES Thank you but no; I pray to other gods.

DIONYSUS What, special ones of your own? A private pantheon?

EURIPIDES Precisely.

DIONYSUS Right then. Pray to your personal gods.

EURIPIDES Hail, Ether, my sustainer! Hail, Hinge of Tongue! Hail, Mind and sentient Nostrils![78] Inspire me with successful arguments.

CHORUS

We're expecting, of course, to pick up a few tips
  From these poets so clever and wise,
As elegant utterance falls from their lips
  And their temperatures gradually rise.

Since neither is lacking in brains or in grit
  It should be a thrilling debate:
While one pins his hopes on his neatly turned wit,
  The other relies on his weight.

For shrewd dialectic he cares not a jot;
  Though traps be contrived for his fall,
He'll swoop down like thunder and quell the lot –
  Quips, quibbles, his rival and all!

[DIONYSUS *and the* TWO POETS *have resumed their seats, and the contest begins.*]

DIONYSUS Right. Let's go. And see that it's clever, original stuff – no far-fetched comparisons, or clichés! [*He invites* EURIPIDES *to begin.*]

EURIPIDES Before I deal with my own work as a creative artist, I should like to say a few words about my opponent. To put it simply, he is a charlatan and a con-artist. Look at the way he cheated his audience: although brought up on Phrynichus[79] they were pretty brainless anyway. The play would begin with a seated figure, all covered up – Niobe, for example, or Achilles. The face is veiled – dramatic tension – but not a word.[80]

DIONYSUS Yes, I remember.

EURIPIDES Then the Chorus would rattle off a string of odes – four of them, one after the other – but still not a peep from the veiled figure.

DIONYSUS I must say I rather enjoyed the old silent days. As much as all the babble we get nowadays.

EURIPIDES That's because you were stupid then.

DIONYSUS I think you're right. So what was he playing at?

EURIPIDES The whole thing was a scam. The audience sat there all keyed up, waiting for Niobe to *say* something. Meanwhile the play went on . . . and on . . . and on.

DIONYSUS The sly old dog! To think I never cottoned on! [*To* AESCHYLUS] Keep still! And stop fidgeting!

EURIPIDES He knows he's beaten. Well, eventually, after a lot more of this nonsense, about halfway through the play, we get a speech. And what a speech! A dozen bulldozing phrases, fearsome things with crests and beetling brows. Sesquipedalian stuff! But, of course, nobody knew what it meant.

[AESCHYLUS *utters a moan of rage.*]

DIONYSUS What *is* that noise?

EURIPIDES You just couldn't make sense of any of it. It was all –

DIONYSUS [*to* AESCHYLUS] Will you stop gnashing your teeth?

EURIPIDES All Scamanders, fosses, shields embossed with brazen gryphon-eagles. Words that left you utterly baffled.

DIONYSUS Yes, I once lay awake half the night trying to figure out what kind of creature a tawny Hippocock was.

AESCHYLUS It was the device painted on the ships,[81] you ignoramus!

DIONYSUS And there was I thinking it must be another name for our friend Eryxis.[82]

EURIPIDES But is a cock suitable material for a tragedy?

AESCHYLUS And you, you blasphemer, what did you put into *your* plays?

EURIPIDES No hippococks or goatstags, that's for sure – nor anything else you'd find on Persian tapestries. When I took over Tragedy from you, the poor creature was in a terrible way – all bloated with embellishment and constipated with verbiage. But I soon got her weight down with a diet of particles and a little finely chopped logic and a sprinkling of chatter-juice, freshly squeezed from books. Then I put her on to monodies –

DIONYSUS With a shot of Cephisophon.[83]

EURIPIDES At least I didn't keep rambling on about the first thing that came into my head, or plunge right into the middle of the story and leave everybody guessing. The first character that came on would immediately explain the play's background and origin.[84]

AESCHLYUS Which was invariably better than your own![85]

EURIPIDES What's more, as soon as the play began I had everyone hard at work. No one would stand idle. Women, slaves, the master, the young maiden, the old crone – they all talked.

AESCHYLUS And didn't you deserve to die for such an outrage!

EURIPIDES Certainly not. It was democracy in action.

DIONYSUS I should keep off that subject, old boy, if I were you.[86]

EURIPIDES [*indicating the audience*] And then, you see, I taught these people to talk . . .

AESCHYLUS You certainly did, by god. If only you'd been torn to pieces first!

EURIPIDES I taught them how to apply subtle rules, how to turn a phrase neatly. I taught them to observe, to discern, to interpret; to use spin, to massage the facts; to suspect the worst, to take nothing at face value . . .

AESCHYLUS You did indeed.

EURIPIDES I wrote about everyday things, things the audience knew about and could take me up on if necessary. I didn't try to bludgeon them into submission with long words, or disorient them with characters like Cycnus or Memnon, haring about with bells on their chariots and rings on their toes. You've only got to look at his disciples, and compare them with mine. He's got Phormisius and Megaenetus,[87] the beard-lance-and-trumpet, tear-'em-limb-from-limb brigade; whereas I have Cleitophon[88] and that clever Theramenes.

DIONYSUS Theramenes? He's clever all right. Whenever he runs into trouble, what happens? A lucky throw, and up pops Theramenes, well clear of the danger zone as usual.

EURIPIDES What I did was to teach the audience to use its brains, introduce a bit of logic into the drama. The public have learnt from me how to think, how to run their households, to ask, 'Why is this so? What do we mean by that?'

DIONYSUS That's right: whenever an Athenian comes home nowadays, he shouts at the servants and starts asking, 'Why is the flour jar not in its proper place? Who bit the head off this sprat? What's happened to that cup I had last year? Where is yesterday's garlic? Who's been nibbling at this olive?' Whereas before Euripides came along they just sat there staring blankly.

CHORUS

You see this, famed Achilles:[89]
  Be careful what you say!
Beware lest fury seize you
  And carry you away.

What if he dares denounce you
With taunts and rank abuse?
To fly into a passion
Will not be any use.

So leave your angry fuming,
Shorten your sail instead;
Wait till the wind blows steady
And then go straight ahead.

CHORUS-LEADER

Come, master of the towering phrase, great poet of the age,
Lord of the lofty gibberish that's spouted on the stage,
The time has come for action, flinch or falter you must not,
So open up the floodgates, and give him all you've got!

AESCHYLUS It distresses and pains me to have been drawn into an altercation with *him*. I find the whole situation extremely distasteful. But I suppose I shall have to reply, or he'll claim I'm lost for an answer. I'll start by asking him a question. [*To* EURIPIDES] What are the qualities you look for in a good poet?

EURIPIDES Technical ability. A poet should also teach people how to be better citizens.

AESCHYLUS And if you've failed to do this? If you've presented good men, noble men, as despicable wretches, what punishment do you deserve?

DIONYSUS Death! No need to ask.

AESCHYLUS Well, now, look at the characters I left him. Fine, stalwart figures, larger than life. Men who didn't shirk their duty. My heroes weren't like these marketplace loafers, delinquents and rogues they write about nowadays. They were real heroes, breathing spears and lances, white-plumed helmets, breastplates and greaves; heroes with hearts of oxhide, seven layers thick.[90]

EURIPIDES There you are! What did I tell you?

DIONYSUS I hope he's not going to start hammering helmets here.

EURIPIDES And how did you show the nobility of these characters of yours?

DIONYSUS Come on, Aeschylus, don't be priggish or difficult.

AESCHYLUS By putting them into works imbued with martial spirit.

EURIPIDES Such as?

AESCHYLUS Well, my *Seven Against Thebes*,[91] for example. No one could see that play without wanting to go off at once and slaughter their enemies.

DIONYSUS Well, it was very unwise of you. You made the Thebans brave beyond recognition!

AESCHYLUS The Athenians could have done likewise, only they couldn't be bothered. I also put on my *Persians*:[92] a telling lesson on the will to win. A truly great achievement.

DIONYSUS I did like that bit where they sang about the days of the great Darius, and the Chorus went like this with their hands, crying 'Wah! Wah!'

AESCHYLUS [*ignoring him*] That's the kind of thing a poet should be doing. You see, from the very first, the truly great artist has always had a useful lesson to teach. Orpheus[93] gave us the Mysteries and taught people that murder was wrong; Musaeus[94] showed us how to cure diseases and to prophesy; Hesiod explained about agriculture and the seasons for ploughing and harvesting.[95] And why is Homer held up as a paragon, if not for the valuable military instruction embodied in his work? Organization, training, equipment[96] – it's all there.

DIONYSUS He doesn't seem to have taught Pantacles[97] much. Of all the clumsy, cack-handed . . . Do you know, I saw him holding a parade the other day, and he had put his helmet on without a crest. There he was, on parade, trying to attach his ponytail without taking his helmet off – you should have seen it!

AESCHYLUS [*annoyed*] But a lot of excellent men did learn. Look at Lamachus.[98] And you can see the stamp of Homer on my own work clearly enough. I depicted men of valour – lion-hearted characters like Patroclus[99] and Teucer[100] – encouraging the audience to identify with these heroes when the call to battle came. I didn't clutter the stage with whores like Phaedra and Stheneboea.[101] No one can say I ever put a lustful woman into a play.

EURIPIDES How could you? You've never even met one.

AESCHYLUS And thank heaven for that. You, on the other hand, have had ample experience of Aphrodite. If I remember rightly, she proved too much for you in the end![102]

DIONYSUS He's got you there, Euripides. You were afflicted in your own home by what you showed other men's wives doing onstage!

EURIPIDES [*irritated*] Look, you pain in the neck, what harm did my Stheneboeas do to the public?

AESCHYLUS Why, every decent woman, or decent man's wife, was so shocked by plays like your *Bellerophon* that she went off and took poison straightaway.[103]

EURIPIDES Did I invent the story of Phaedra?

AESCHYLUS Of course not, but the poet should keep quiet about them, not put them onstage as an example to everyone. Schoolboys have a master to teach them, adults have poets. We have a duty to see that what we teach them is right and proper.[104]

EURIPIDES And you think the proper way to teach them is to write your high-flown, Olympian idiom instead of the language of ordinary men?

AESCHYLUS Look, you fool, noble themes and sentiments need to be couched in suitably dignified language. If your characters are demigods, they should sound like demigods – what's more, they should *dress* like them. I set an example in this respect, which you totally perverted.

EURIPIDES How?

AESCHYLUS By dressing your kings in rags so that they appear as objects of pity.

EURIPIDES What harm is there in that?

AESCHYLUS Well, these days you can't get the wealthy to pay their ship levy.[105] They dress up in rags and claim exemption on the grounds of poverty.

DIONYSUS While wearing nice warm underwear. And the next

day you see them splashing out at the most expensive fish stall in the market.

AESCHYLUS And look how you've encouraged people to babble. The wrestling schools are empty. And where have all the young men gone? Off to these notorious establishments where they practise the art of debating – and that's not all they practise either! These days even the sailors argue with their officers; in my day the only words they knew were 'slops' and 'heave-ho'!

DIONYSUS Whereas now they refuse to row, and the ships drift all over the place.

AESCHYLUS Think of all the other harm he's done showing us women playing bawds,[106] giving birth in temples,[107] sleeping with their brothers[108] and claiming that 'life is not life'.[109] Isn't that why the city's so full of lawyers' clerks and scrounging officials, swindling the community left, right and centre? And there's not a decent athlete left in the whole city – everyone's unfit!

DIONYSUS How right you are! I nearly died laughing during the torch race at the Panathenaic Games. There was a little fat, pale fellow waddling along miles behind everyone else, making a right meal of it. And when he got to the Potter's Gate, and they all ran out and slapped him, the way they do, you know, with the flat of the hand – well, talk about second wind! This fellow produced enough of a draught to keep his torch alight till the end of the race!

CHORUS

Fiercely the fight goes on,
  Doubtful the ending;
Well matched these duellers are,
  Grim their contending.
When one's in full career,
The other's quick to veer
And sneak up in the rear
  To catch him bending.

Although you think your gains
  Are quite extensive,

Time spent on digging in
 May prove expensive.
Show us what wit can do,
Vary your tactics too;
Bring out old tricks and new
 For an offensive.

As for the audience,
 You're quite mistaken
If you think subtle points
 Will not be taken.
Such fears are vain, I vow –
They've all got textbooks now –
However high your brow,
 They'll not be shaken.

No talking down to these:
 That's all outdated!
In terms of native wit
 They're highly rated;
But now they've learnt to read,
It's cultured stuff they need;
They don't want chicken-feed –
 They're educated!

EURIPIDES Well now, first things first. Let's turn to your prologues. I maintain that they fail to give a clear outline of the opening situation.

AESCHYLUS Which prologues do you propose to criticize?

EURIPIDES Quite a few. But let's start with the one from the *Oresteia*.

DIONYSUS Silence for Aeschylus.

AESCHYLUS [*reciting*]
'Netherworld Hermes, watching the paternal realm,
Hear now my prayer, and be my ally and my saviour!
For I have come back to this land and do return.'[110]

DIONYSUS Do you find anything to criticize in that?

EURIPIDES A dozen things at least.

DIONYSUS But he's only given us three lines.

EURIPIDES With several mistakes in each.

DIONYSUS You'd better not recite any more, Aeschylus – it seems you're three lines down already.

AESCHYLUS What, stop for *him*?

DIONYSUS It might be wise.

EURIPIDES You see, he starts off straightaway with a howling blunder.

AESCHYLUS Nonsense!

EURIPIDES Well, if that's how you feel – it couldn't matter less to me.

AESCHYLUS What is this blunder?

EURIPIDES Give me those lines again.

AESCHYLUS [*reciting*]

'Netherworld Hermes, watching the paternal realm . . .'

EURIPIDES And Orestes says this over the tomb of his dead father?

AESCHYLUS That's correct.

EURIPIDES So is he saying that when his father was brutally murdered by his own wife through a treacherous ambush, this all happened under the approving eye of Hermes?

AESCHYLUS Of course not! He is addressing himself to Hermes the Helper, 'Netherworld Hermes', not to Hermes as the god of deceit. This is made quite clear by what follows: 'watching the paternal realm'. His subterranean function[111] is a perquisite from his father Zeus.

EURIPIDES That makes it even worse than I thought.

DIONYSUS Subterranean perks? Sounds like he takes a cut from the tomb offerings.

AESCHYLUS A remark in the worst taste, Dionysus.

DIONYSUS [*to* AESCHYLUS] Give him a bit more. [*To* EURIPIDES] And you watch out for mistakes.

AESCHYLUS [*reciting*]

'Hear now my prayer, and be my ally and my saviour!
For I have come back to this land and do return.'

EURIPIDES The great Aeschylus tells us the same thing twice.

AESCHYLUS What do you mean, the same thing twice?

EURIPIDES Listen. I'll repeat the line. 'For I have come back to this land', he says, 'and *do return*'. Surely 'coming back' and 'returning' are the same thing.

DIONYSUS So they are: like saying to a neighbour, 'Lend me a mirror – or a looking glass will do.'

AESCHYLUS The two things are not the same, you rambling pedant! The line is a particularly good one.

EURIPIDES How so? Do explain.

AESCHYLUS Anyone can 'come back' to his native country, if he belongs there still; nothing need have happened to him at all. But when an exile comes home he 'returns'.

DIONYSUS Very good! What do you say to that, Euripides?

EURIPIDES I say that Orestes didn't 'return' home in that sense: he had to come secretly because he didn't trust those in power.[112]

DIONYSUS Ingenious! Though I'm not sure what you mean.

EURIPIDES Come on, let's hear some more.

DIONYSUS Yes, get on with it, Aeschylus. [*To* EURIPIDES] And you, look out for howlers.

AESCHYLUS [*reciting*]
'Beside this burial mound I call on my dead father
To hear me and to hearken.'

EURIPIDES There he goes again, the same thing twice: 'to hear me and to hearken'.

DIONYSUS He's calling on the dead, you fool! Even three times wouldn't be enough.

AESCHYLUS And how did you construct *your* prologues?

EURIPIDES I'll show you. And if I say the same thing twice, or if you find anything that's extraneous to the plot, you can spit on me for being a liar.

DIONYSUS Go on, then. I simply must hear the verbal precision of your prologues.

EURIPIDES [*reciting*]
'A happy man was Oedipus initially . . .'

AESCHYLUS No he wasn't! Even before he was born Apollo had decreed that he would kill his own father. I'd hardly call that being 'a happy man'.

EURIPIDES [*reciting*]
'. . . But then became the most wretched of mortal men.'[113]

AESCHYLUS He didn't become so, he *was* so all along. Look at his story. First of all, as a newborn baby he's exposed during winter in a pot to prevent him from growing up and murdering his father; next he's brought to Corinth with swollen feet; then he marries a woman old enough to be his mother. And then, as if that wasn't bad enough, it turns out she *is* his mother! Finally he blinds himself.

DIONYSUS Better to have been an Athenian commander at Arginusae!

EURIPIDES I still maintain my prologues are good.

AESCHYLUS Look, I don't want to split hairs over every word. I assure you I can demolish any prologue of yours with a little flask of oil.

EURIPIDES My prologues, with a flask of oil?

AESCHYLUS Just one. You see, the way your iambics are written, you can fit in anything: a flask of oil; tufts of wool; a purse of rags. I'll show you what I mean.[114]

EURIPIDES All right, show me.

DIONYSUS You recite one.

EURIPIDES [*reciting*]

'Aegyptus, as the story is most often told,
Crossing the sea together with his fifty sons,
On reaching Argos . . .'[115]

AESCHYLUS

'. . . lost his little flask of oil.'

EURIPIDES What do you mean, lost his little flask of oil? You'll regret this.

DIONYSUS Recite another prologue so we can see it again.

EURIPIDES [*reciting*]

'Dionysus, sporting his fennel wands and fawnskins,
Amid the pine trees on the slopes of Mount Parnassus,
Leapt to the dance and . . .'[116]

AESCHYLUS

'. . . lost his little flask of oil.'

DIONYSUS That's two flasks.

EURIPIDES He can't keep it up. I've got one here that's sure to be flaskproof. [*Reciting*]

'No man was ever fortunate in everything.

He may have been noble and lost his wealth;
He may have been lowborn and . . .'[117]

AESCHYLUS

'. . . lost his little flask of oil.'

DIONYSUS Euripides!

EURIPIDES What?

DIONYSUS Trim your sails. This is turning out to be a storm in an oil-flask!

EURIPIDES Don't you believe it, by Demeter! This one'll knock it right out of his hand.

DIONYSUS All right, let's have it. But beware the flask!

EURIPIDES [*reciting*]
'Cadmus, the son of Agenor, departing from
The town of Sidon, . . .'[118]

AESCHYLUS

'. . . lost his little flask of oil.'

DIONYSUS If I were you, I'd try and buy the flask off him; otherwise you won't have any prologues left.

EURIPIDES Me buy from *him*!

DIONYSUS If you want my advice.

EURIPIDES I've got lots of prologues he *can't* fit it into. [*Reciting*]
'Pelops, the son of Tantalus, approaching Pisa
On speedy horses, . . .'[119]

AESCHYLUS

'. . . lost his little flask of oil.'

DIONYSUS You see, he's done it again. Sell it to him, Aeschylus, for god's sake. You can get a nice new one for an obol.

EURIPIDES No, no, I've got plenty of prologues yet. [*Reciting*]
' 'Tis said that Oeneus . . .'

AESCHYLUS

'. . . lost his little flask of oil.'

EURIPIDES At least let me finish the line!
' 'Tis said that Oeneus, while offering the first fruits
From a full harvest . . .'[120]

AESCHYLUS

'. . . lost his little flask of oil.'

DIONYSUS What, in the middle of a sacrifice? How very awkward for him. Who took it, I wonder?

EURIPIDES Don't encourage him. See what he can do with this one:
'Almighty Zeus, as is avowed by Truth herself . . .'

DIONYSUS You're beaten, and you know it. That flask of oil keeps turning up like a stye on the eye. It's time you turned your attention to his lyrics.

EURIPIDES Why, yes, I'm going to show that he's a bad composer of lyrics. They're all the same.

CHORUS[121]

What, Aeschylus not write good lyrics?
You'll have the great man in hysterics!
  I don't know that much
  About dactyls and such,
Though I know a good song when I hear it;
  And I had an idea
  That this gentleman here
Was faultless, or pretty damn near it.
Old Aeschylus not write good lyrics?
My goodness, what will he say next?
  It seems a bit hard
  On the venerable bard –
No wonder he's looking so vexed!

EURIPIDES They're certainly remarkable lyrics, as we'll soon see, when I conflate all his songs into one medley.

DIONYSUS I'll keep score with these pebbles.

EURIPIDES [*singing*]

Achilles, do you not hear how the battle rages?
Ai, *ai*, I'm struck! Come quickly to the rescue!
We who dwell by the marsh, honour our forebear
    Hermes.
Ai, *ai*, we're struck! Come quickly to the rescue!

DIONYSUS That's two strikes for you, Aeschylus.

EURIPIDES [*singing*]

Lord Agamemnon, noblest of the Greeks, now hear my
    words.

Ai, *ai*, I'm struck! Come quickly to the rescue!

DIONYSUS That's three.

EURIPIDES [*singing*]

Silence! The priestesses of Artemis are opening the temple doors.
Ai, *ai*, I'm struck! Come quickly to the rescue!
I am empowered to give the lucky sign for travellers.
Ai, *ai*, I'm struck! Come quickly to the rescue![122]

DIONYSUS Zeus almighty! What a salvo of strikes! Which way is the bathroom? I can't hold out any longer. My bladder's bursting.

EURIPIDES You can't go till you've heard the next part. It has a wonderful lyre accompaniment.

DIONYSUS All right, get on with it. Only no more strikes this time.

EURIPIDES [*singing*]

Of how the twin-throned kings, the flower of Hellas' manhood
Phlatto-thratto-phlatto-thrat,
Did send the Sphinx, the bitch who brought in baleful days,
Phlatto-thratto-phlatto-thrat,
With spear and vengeful hand, a warlike bird of omen,
Phlatto-thratto-phlatto-thrat,
To be the prey of vicious sky-patrolling hounds,
Phlatto-thratto-phlatto-thrat,
And those who fought with Ajax,
Phlatto-thratto-phlatto-thrat.[123]

DIONYSUS What *is* all that *phlatto-thrat* stuff? A bit of Persian from Marathon?[124] It sounds like it comes from a rope-makers' shanty.

AESCHYLUS I may use traditional elements in my lyrics, but at least I take them from respectable sources and make them serve an artistic purpose. I didn't want it to be thought that I picked from the same 'garden of the Muses' as Phrynichus. But *he* throws in bits and pieces from all over the place: prostitutes, drinking songs by Meletus,[125] pipers, wailers, dancers from Caria.[126] I'll show you what I mean. Bring me a lyre – no, a lyre's too good for this sort of thing. Where's that girl with the castanets?[127]

[*A* DANCING-GIRL[128] *comes forward.*]

Ah, the Muse of Euripides! Come along, my dear, stand over here. Just the right accompaniment for this kind of lyric.

DIONYSUS Not in the Lesbian mode I take it.[129]

AESCHYLUS [*singing*]

You halcyons, twittering
By the ever-flowing waves,
Dampening the coat of your
Wings with watery droplets[130]–
And you spiders in the rafters,
Who with your dactyls spi-i-i-i-n
Your thread, tightened on the loom,
By the art of the singing shuttle –
Where the flute-loving dolphin leapt
At the prows with their dark-blue rams[131]
For the oracles and the stadium.
Gleaming delight of the vine's fruit,
The grape's analgesic tendril.
Fling your arms about me, child![132]
Did you notice that foot?

DIONYSUS I did.

AESCHYLUS What about that one?

DIONYSUS That one too.[133]

AESCHYLUS That's the sort of stuff that you compose, and you have the audacity to criticize my lyrics, you who give us the 'Twelve Positions' of Cyrene![134] So much for his choral songs. Now I want to give you an idea of what his solo arias are like.[135]

[*Sings*]

O shining gloom of Night,
What dire dream have you sent me,
Emerging from shadowy Hades?
It has life and yet no life,
It is a child of sable night,
Its face a horrific sight,
Shrouded in blackness.

How it glares at me –
Murder, murder in its eye –
And what long claws it has!

Light the lamp, O servants,
And in your little buckets
Fetch me the liquid that flows
In the mountain streams.
Heat it up, that I may
Wash away this dream
The gods have sent me.

Hearken, O mighty god of the sea –
'Tis done! O my housemates,
Witness these omens!
Glyce has stolen my cockerel
And scarpered.
You nymphs of the mountains,
And you Mania, help me!
Ah me, unhappy that I am,
I was sitting here busily
Spi-i-i-nning some flax
With my nimble fingers,
Whirling the wheel round and round.[136]
I was going to go out early
While it was still dark,
And sell my thread in the market,
When – ah! He flew up, my cockerel,
Flew up into the ether
On his wings, his wings.
And I was left bereft, bereft,
And from my eyes falling, falling,
Tears, the falling tears,
Shed in misery,
Fell.

O Cretans, children of Ida,
Speed to my aid,

Fetch your bows and arrows,[137]
And come over at once –
Throw a cordon round the building.
And you too fair Dictynna,
Virgin Artemis, come with your hounds
And we'll ransack the whole house.
Come now, Hecate, daughter of Zeus,
With twin torches flaming,
Light me the way to Glyce's house:
I want to catch her red-handed.

DIONYSUS I think we've had enough lyrics now.

AESCHYLUS I've had enough of them too. And now I propose that we settle this matter once and for all by a simple test on the scales to see whose poetry is the weightier, his or mine.

DIONYSUS Come over here, then, both of you, if you must make me weigh out your poetry like hunks of cheese.

CHORUS

How thorough these geniuses are!
But this thing's the cleverest by far.
  Did you ever hear
  Such a brilliant idea,
So simple and yet so bizarre?
I'd not have believed it, I swear,
If a man that I met in the square
  Had said that a friend
  Of a friend of his friend
Had known of a man who was there!

DIONYSUS Now, each of you stand by one of the two pans.

[AESCHYLUS *and* EURIPIDES *take up their positions.*]

AESCHYLUS Right.

EURIPIDES Right.

DIONYSUS Now you must each take hold of your pan, hold it steady, and recite one line. Then, when I call 'Cuckoo!', you both let go. Ready?

AESCHYLUS Ready.

EURIPIDES Ready.

DIONYSUS Right, say your lines.

EURIPIDES 'If only the Argo had never winged its way . . .'[138]

AESCHYLUS 'The watery vale of Spercheius, where cattle graze . . .'[139]

DIONYSUS Cuckoo!

AESCHYLUS *and* EURIPIDES [*letting go*] Right!

DIONYSUS Look, this side's going right down.

EURIPIDES Why is it doing that?

DIONYSUS He put in a river, like the wool merchants who wet their wool to make it weigh more; whereas you with your 'winged its way' . . .

EURIPIDES Let's try again. See what he can do this time.

DIONYSUS Right, take hold again.

AESCHYLUS *and* EURIPIDES Ready.

DIONYSUS Fire away.

EURIPIDES 'Persuasion has no temple other than the word . . .'[140]

AESCHYLUS 'Of all the gods, just Death it is that loves no gifts . . .'[141]

DIONYSUS Let go. Now, let's see – this one again. You see, he put in Death, the heaviest burden of all.

EURIPIDES What about Persuasion? Doesn't that carry any weight? So beautifully phrased too.

DIONYSUS No, Persuasion is hollow. It has no substance of its own. You'll have to think of something with real gravity to weigh your side down. Something huge and hulking.

EURIPIDES [*musing to himself*] What have I got that's huge and hulking? Hmm, let me think . . .

DIONYSUS What about that stirring line 'Achilles threw . . . a pair of singles and a four'?[142] Come on, this is the last round.

EURIPIDES [*triumphantly*] 'He lifted up his mighty cudgel ribbed with iron . . .'[143]

AESCHYLUS 'Chariot on chariot, corpse on corpse was piled . . .'[144]

DIONYSUS He's got you licked again.

EURIPIDES How come?

DIONYSUS All those chariots and corpses. A hundred Egyptians couldn't lift that lot.[145]

AESCHYLUS This line-against-line business is far too easy. Let Euripides get into the pan himself, with his children, his wife, not forgetting Cephisophon – why, even his collected works as well. I'll outweigh the whole lot with just two lines.

DIONYSUS You know, I like them both so much, I don't know how to judge between them. I don't want to make an enemy of either. One's so wise, and the other I just love.[146]

PLUTO In that case you've wasted your time by coming here.

DIONYSUS Supposing I do make a choice?

PLUTO You can take one of them back with you, whichever you prefer. That way you won't have come all this way for nothing.

DIONYSUS Bless you! Now listen, you two. I came down here for a poet. What for? To save the city, of course! Otherwise there won't be any more drama festivals – and then where would I be? Now, whoever can think of the best piece of advice to give the Athenians at this juncture, he's the one I'll take back with me. Here's my first question: what should be done about Alcibiades?[147] The city's in a tricky situation.

EURIPIDES What do the Athenians think about it?

DIONYSUS You may well ask. They long for him, but they loathe him. Then again, they want him back. But you two tell me what you think.

EURIPIDES [*after some thought*]

I loathe a citizen who acts so fast
To harm his country and yet helps her last,
Who's deft at managing his own success,
But useless when the city's in a mess.

DIONYSUS That's neat, by Poseidon! Now Aeschylus, what's your opinion?

AESCHYLUS

It is not very wise for city states
To rear a lion cub within their gates;
But if they do so, they will find it pays
To tolerate its own peculiar ways.

DIONYSUS Honestly, I can't decide between them, when one speaks so discerningly, the other so distinctly.[148] We'll try one more question. I want each of you to tell me how you think the city can be saved.

EURIPIDES I have something I'd like to tell you.

DIONYSUS Go on.

EURIPIDES

Believe the unsure safe, the safe unsure,
Mistrust what you now trust, and fear no more.

DIONYSUS What do you mean? I don't follow. Speak more clearly and not so cleverly.

EURIPIDES If we were to stop putting our trust in those we do at the moment, and put it instead in those we don't at the moment . . .

DIONYSUS Then we might be saved?

EURIPIDES Precisely. If we're faring badly with the current lot, we're bound to do better if we do the opposite.[149]

DIONYSUS [*to* AESCHYLUS] And what do you say?

AESCHYLUS Tell me, what kind of people is the city electing these days? Honest, noble sorts?

DIONYSUS Where have you been? She hates them most of all!

AESCHYLUS She prefers hypocrites and swindlers?

DIONYSUS She doesn't prefer them, but she has no choice.

AESCHYLUS Well, if the city doesn't know its own mind, I don't see how it can be saved.

DIONYSUS You'll have to think of something, if you want to come back with me.

AESCHYLUS I'll tell you there; I'd rather not down here.

DIONYSUS Oh, no, you don't. Send your advice from here.

AESCHYLUS

They must regard enemy soil
As theirs, and let their own land go.
The navy is the city's strength;
And any other wealth is woe.[150]

DIONYSUS That's good, except that these days the 'other wealth' all goes to the jurymen.

PLUTO Now please decide.

DIONYSUS I'll judge between you on this score alone: I shall select the man my soul desires.[151]

EURIPIDES Now remember the gods by whom you swore to take me home! Pick me, your friend!

DIONYSUS It was my tongue that swore[152] . . . but I choose Aeschylus.

EURIPIDES *No!!* What have you done, you utter traitor!

DIONYSUS Me? I've declared Aeschylus the winner, that's all. Any objections?

EURIPIDES How can you act so shamefully and look me in the eye?

DIONYSUS What's shameful if it seems not so to those who view it?[153]

EURIPIDES You villain, will you leave me here to . . . stay deceased?

DIONYSUS

Who knows if life is really death and death is life?[154]
Or breathing is eating, and sleep a woolly blanket.

[EURIPIDES, *struggling frantically, is removed.*]

PLUTO Dionysus and Aeschylus kindly step inside my palace.

DIONYSUS Why?

PLUTO So that I can entertain you before you head off.

DIONYSUS How kind of you. I don't mind if I do!

[*They enter the palace along with everyone else except the* CHORUS.]

CHORUS

Fortunate is the man who has
A mind with sharp intelligence.
We learn this truth from past examples,
Like this man here, who's clearly wise
And now will be returning home,
A blessing to his fellow citizens
And to his family and friends –
All on account of his good judgement.

So it's not smart to sit and chat
With Socrates, tossing aside
Artistic merit, shedding all
That's best of the tragedian's art.
To fritter away all one's time

On quibbling and pretentious talk,
And other such inane pursuits,
Is truly the mark of a fool.[155]

[PLUTO *and his guests emerge from the palace.*]

PLUTO Goodbye, then, Aeschylus. Off you go with your sound advice – and save the city for us. Educate the fools. You'll find a good many. And give this [*a knife*] to Cleophon with my compliments, and these [*nooses*] to the tax commissioners. And here's one for Myrmex and another for Nicomachus;[156] and this [*a mortar and pestle for grinding hemlock*] is for Archenomus.[157] Tell them all to get themselves down here fast. Otherwise I'll brand them and tie them together by the feet, along with Adeimantus,[158] and have them packed off underground before they can say 'knife'.

AESCHYLUS Very well, I will. And will you ask Sophocles to look after my chair while I'm away? I declare that the second place is his by right. And on no account let that evil, lying, foul-mouthed rogue sit on my chair, even by accident.

PLUTO Guide him with your sacred torches, escort him with his own songs and dances.

[*The* CHORUS *form up as an escort for* AESCHYLUS *and move off singing.*]

CHORUS

Spirits of the darkness, speed him on his way.[159]
Safely may he journey to the light of day.
To the city's counsels may he wisdom lend;[160]
Then of war and suffering shall there be an end.
If those doughty warriors, Cleophon and co.,
Want to keep on fighting they know where to go.
In their distant homeland they can do less harm;
Let them wage their warfare on their father's farm.

Notes

WASPS

1. *Corybant*: The Corybantes were minor deities who attended Cybele, the Phrygian mother-goddess. A prominent aspect of their cult was ecstatic dancing to flutes and drums, which produced a trance-like state of delirium. The cult was practised by a number of respectable fifth-century Athenians. In the Greek text, Sosias' subsequent remark, 'something Bacchic about it', refers to the Phrygian god Sabazius, sometimes identified with Bacchus (Dionysus). Little is known of Sabazius, but the slaves' exchange suggests that he was associated with wine.
2. *Cleonymus . . . dropped it*: Cleonymus was a politician regularly mocked by Aristophanes for being fat, effeminate and gluttonous, but above all for having run away during battle, dropping his shield in the process. Losing one's shield was a grave act of cowardice punishable by disenfranchisement, but despite Aristophanes' frequent mention of the incident, Cleonymus does not seem to have suffered this punishment. He probably lost his shield sometime between 425 and 423, possibly at Delium (424) where the Athenians were routed. The joke here defies translation: it turns on a pun on the Greek word *aspis*, which means 'shield' and 'asp'. Thus the same phrase in the original means both the copper-coloured asp picked up by the eagle and the bronze-plated shield dropped by Cleonymus.
3. *What creature . . . in the sky*: The standard answer to this riddle is a bear, eagle, snake or dog, each of which (in ancient Greek) is the name of a constellation, a land animal and a sea creature.
4. *equipment*: There is a double entendre in the original. The Greek word *hopla*, meaning 'arms' or 'equipment', can also be used to refer to the male genitalia (compare English 'tool').
5. *Pnyx*: The Athenian assembly met on the Pnyx, a hill just inside

the city walls to the west of the Acropolis. The Athenian men in Sosias' dream, who are gullible and beholden to Cleon (see next note), appear as sheep but are nonetheless identifiable as Athenians by their cloaks and staves. This anticipates the presentation of the Chorus as wasps, who are recognizable as gullible old Athenian men under Cleon's malign influence.

6. *tanner's yard*: A reference to Cleon, the demagogue who came to prominence in Athenian politics during the period after the death of Pericles. Cleon (or his family) seems to have had some connection with the leather trade. He is mercilessly berated by Aristophanes in *Knights* and in his (lost) first play, *Babylonians*.

7. *body politic*: The original contains a pun on the Greek word *dēmos*, which can mean 'the people' or, with a change of accent, 'fat' or 'lard'.

8. *Theorus*: Regularly attacked by Aristophanes as one of Cleon's hangers-on.

9. *Alcibiades . . . laven*: Alcibiades, the nephew of Pericles, was from the distinguished Athenian clan the Alcmaeonids. He was about thirty at this time and yet to become a major politician. He reputedly had a lisp that involved saying 'l' for 'r' (rather than 'w' for 'r', or 'th' for 's'), the term for which is 'lambdacism'. The joke here belies translation. The original relies on the word *korax* ('raven') becoming *kolax* ('flatterer').

10. *To the audience*: Direct address to the audience to explain the play's opening situation also occurs in *Knights* and *Peace*, both of which also begin with exchanges between two slaves. The Athenians traditionally disparaged all things to do with Megara (the city-state that bordered Attica to the north-west), including bad jokes, but there may also have been a rivalry between Athenian and Megarian comic playwrights; according to Aristotle (*Poetics* 1448a), the Megarians claimed to have invented comedy. Food was sometimes thrown to the audience to gain its goodwill.

11. *Heracles . . . Euripides . . . glory*: Heracles was a regular character in comedy. He appears in *Birds* and *Frogs*, both times as a glutton. Euripides features as a character in three of Aristophanes' surviving plays (*Acharnians, Women* and *Frogs*) and at least two other lost works (a second play entitled *Women at the Thesmophoria* and *Preview*, which was produced at the same festival as *Wasps*). The remark about Cleon not being targeted is disingenuous as he is criticized both directly and indirectly for

much of the play. It is not clear to what Aristophanes is referring in saying that Cleon has recently 'covered himself in glory'.

12. *on the roof*: Besides the main stage, Greek theatres had an upper level (the *theologeion*) on top of the stage-building. In tragedy, divine characters usually appeared on this level, but occasionally mortal characters did (e.g., the watchman on the palace roof in Aeschylus' *Agamemnon*). Here Bdelycleon is asleep on this level and Philocleon will later appear on it. The slave clearly states that Bdelycleon is master of the house. Sons were legally obliged to look after their fathers, and took over control of the household at some point, but the circumstances and conditions under which this took place are not known.

13. *disease*: The Greek term used to describe Philocleon's condition, *nosos* (meaning 'sickness' or 'disease'), was used in tragedy to indicate an uncontrollable urge or a delusion. Examples of such *nosos* include the irresistible erotic desire of Euripides' heroines Phaedra and Stheneboea, and the hallucinatory delusion suffered by Sophocles' hero Ajax (during which he slaughtered the Greek army's livestock, mistaking them for the Greek leaders with whom he had a serious grievance). Some of Aristophanes' audience would have known that in tragedy *nosos* usually leads to catastrophe.

14. *Amynias*: Mocked elsewhere and later in the play (see 466 and 1267) as boastful, long-haired and pro-aristocratic. While he may have served as a general in 423/2, he was nonetheless seen as keen to avoid military service. Presumably he was fond of gambling.

15. *Dercylus . . . alcoholic*: Nothing else is known of Dercylus.

16. *Nicostratus*: Athenian general who served several times between 427 and 418. He was a friend of the well-known general Nicias, after whom the peace with the Spartans in 421 was named. Little else is known about him, and it is unclear why he is singled out here.

17. *Philoxenus*: Regularly mocked by comic playwrights as a passive homosexual; there is a pun on his name, which means 'hospitable' but could be interpreted as 'one who enjoys sexual relations with guests/strangers/foreigners'.

18. *yearns . . . pines*: The language used to describe Philocleon's desire for the law courts is similar to that used by Euripides to describe lovesick heroines such as Phaedra and Stheneboea.

19. *new-moon*: The first day of the new month, or new moon, was a day for religious festivities including incense burning.

20. *O Demos . . . how I vote in you*: The joke in the original exploits the rhyme between the name Demos and the word *kēmos*, which means a 'voting urn'. Demos was well known for his good looks. The sophist Callicles is described, in Plato's *Gorgias*, as being in love with him.
21. *He scratches a long line . . . full damages*: This passage itself is our only evidence for that particular voting method. Jurors, it seems, would etch a line on a wax tablet, a long one for the prosecution's sentence or a short one for the defence's.
22. *Such is his madness . . . to court*: Adapted from Euripides' *Stheneboea* (fr. 665), where Stheneboea's passion for Bellerophon is described as increasing the more she attempts to suppress it.
23. *Temple of Asclepius*: Asclepius was the god of healing. It was thought that those afflicted by disease, insanity or disability might be cured by being brought to one of his sanctuaries.
24. *Philocleon . . . Bdelycleon*: The names mean 'lover of Cleon' and 'loather of Cleon' and are not only preposterous but anachronistic: Cleon was born long after Philocleon, and would have been unknown, if alive, when Bdelycleon was named.
25. *Figwood*: There is a pun here on the word *sūkinos* meaning 'from figwood' and *sūkophantes* meaning an unscrupulous informer (literally, 'a revealer of figs').
26. *son of Smoke*: The name Capnias, 'son of smoke', was applied to those prone to obscure utterance.
27. *Dracontides*: There are four Athenians known by this name and it is unclear which is meant here.
28. *Alas . . . drastic*: Philocleon's melodramatic expression of frustration, and Bdelycleon's subsequent reply, are tragic in style.
29. *first day of the month*: Market day.
30. *Why do you weep . . . groans*: Bdelycleon's concerns are tragic in style.
31. *Odysseus clinging to your underside*: In the *Odyssey*, Odysseus and his men escape from the Cyclops' cave by hanging on to the undersides of some of his rams.
32. *No-man*: In the *Odyssey*, Odysseus tells the Cyclops his name is *Metis*, which means 'no one' or 'no-man', but is also the Greek word for 'intelligence'. Two lines later Philocleon claims to be from Odysseus' native island of Ithaca.
33. *donkey*: The Greek word *klētēr* means a donkey and someone who assists in serving a summons.
34. *donkey's shadow*: To fight over a 'donkey's shadow' was proverbial for fighting over a trivial cause.

35. *Scione*: City on one of the Chalcidean peninsulas which had revolted from the Athenian alliance in 423. Athens was still having trouble guarding it when *Wasps* was performed.
36. *Phrynichus*: Tragedian and an older contemporary of Aeschylus and known for his melodious lyrics. Like Aeschylus, he wrote a play about the Persian wars, and is seen here as a favourite of the generation who fought in the battle of Marathon (490).
37. *sons ... small boys*: It stretches credibility that the old men of the Chorus, who must be at least eighty-six, even if they fought as mere eighteen year olds at Marathon, have young sons. By having their sons (rather than slaves) accompany them, Aristophanes indicates their poverty.
38. *quick march*: Despite this remark, the aged Chorus enter singing in slow, plodding iambic tetrameters to emphasize their sluggishness.
39. *Laches is on trial today*: Laches was a well-known soldier and politician. In Plato's dialogue named after him, he is portrayed as a good-humoured man who admires Socrates. He served in Sicily, where he seems to have been suspected, at least by Cleon, of financial irregularity. The Chorus's claim that Laches is going to be tried does not mean that such a trial actually took place.
40. *the old songs*: The song that follows is probably an imitation, in part, of Phrynichus' style.
41. *Father ... but to weep*: The Boy's lines are tragic in language and style, and are largely adapted from Euripides' *Theseus*, in which children sent from Athens to Crete, as victims for the Minotaur, lament their fate.
42. *Oh with what anguish ... votes on me*: Philocleon's song is based on a tragic model, most likely Euripidean, with humour arising largely from the incongruity between elevated style and mundane subject matter.
43. *Dictynna*: Cretan goddess of hunting, subsequently associated with Artemis. She is invoked here because her name is seen as being derived from the word *diktuon* meaning 'net', although it may equally be derived from Mount Dicte in Crete.
44. *Diopeithes*: Minor politician mocked for his fervent religiosity and his excessive dispensing of oracles. His name is also used because it means 'trusting in Zeus'.
45. *Lycus*: A hero whose shrine stood beside the courthouse that Philocleon attends. It is not clear whether there were such shrines at all courthouses or just this one.

46. *Smicythion . . . Tisiades*: Genuine names. It is not clear who they are but they may have been contemporary informers.
47. *Chremon . . . Pheredeipnos*: Meaning 'needy' and 'dinner-winning', and probably made up.
48. *Philippus . . . his trial*: Not much is known about Philippus. He is called the disciple of Gorgias in the original; Gorgias was a famous rhetorician. In *Birds*, Aristophanes describes both men as hovering around the law-courts and eking out a living from baseless accusations. The suggestion here seems to be that he found himself on trial and was hoisted on his own petard.
49. *envying tortoises for their hard shells*: Xanthias expresses precisely such envy after he has been beaten by the drunk Philocleon later in the play (1292ff.).
50. *Cecrops*: Legendary king of Athens.
51. *Aeschines*: Portrayed by Aristophanes as a man who brags a great deal, particularly about wealth that he does not possess (see 1243–7). Little else is known of him.
52. *long*: Long hair was seen as a mark of aristocratic tendencies and sympathies.
53. *long-haired . . . Brasidas*: The most dynamic of Spartan generals at this time. Spartan society was fiercely militaristic, conservative and opposed to change. Sparta was ruled by a pair of kings and its dominant class was the aristocracy, which controlled a large population of metics and slaves. Men of the Spartan aristocracy wore distinctive clothing and had long hair. The jump from accusing someone of being pro-aristocratic to pro-Spartan was not a big one.
54. *tyranny . . . fifty years*: The last tyrant in Athens, Hippias, fell from power nearly ninety years earlier (510 BC).
55. *Morychus*: Renowned for his gourmandizing, he was also wealthy, had an interest in politics and wrote – or at least endeavoured to write – tragedies. Old Comedy was fond of ludicrous-and-inordinately-elongated compounds.
56. *I shall fall upon this sword*: Philocleon's words are almost identical to those of Ajax in Sophocles' play of the same name, uttered during a speech just before his suicide (*Ajax* 828).
57. *pork*: The word for pork (*ta choiridia*, literally, 'piglets'), as always in Old Comedy, also suggests the female genitalia.
58. *Oeagrus*: Presumably a tragic actor; nothing else is known of him.
59. *Niobe*: A tragedy by Aeschylus.
60. *Suppose a man dies . . . in court*: If a man died without a male

heir, his daughter would become an heiress. She then had to marry the nearest male relative who claimed her, and he would manage her father's estate until any sons from that marriage came of age (and took over the estate). A father could, however, adopt a son, who would then have to marry his adoptive sister and thus become heir to the estate. Here Philocleon is suggesting a scenario in which other relatives are challenging a will in which such an adoptive heir has been named.

61. *Evathlus*: A contemporary prosecutor.

62. *Toady-onymous*: Cleonymus (see note 2).

63. *Euphemius*: Unknown, but no doubt of poor repute.

64. *fish out . . . with her tongue*: Some Athenians, it seems, carried loose change in their mouths (see also 786ff.). The daughter's oral contact with her father is meant as amusing rather than sexually deviant.

65. *A splendid performance . . . Isles of the Blest*: The Chorus's enthusiastic response to Philocleon's speech is very similar to that of the Chorus in *Women* (433ff. and 459ff.). The Isles of the Blest (or Elysium) were the ancient Greek equivalent of paradise.

66. *twelve million drachmas*: Seventy-two million obols (one drachma = six obols).

67. *No . . . not what to me*: Both here and when he next speaks Philocleon uses a blend of ordinary and elevated language to express his profound apprehension.

68. *victors of Marathon*: The battle of Marathon (490 BC) was a major victory against the Persians. Any mention of it would have struck a deep chord with the Athenian public, particularly those who were alive at the time, rather like the Battle of Britain today.

69. *Euboea*: A large island north-east of Attica, of strategic importance to the Athenians. Euboea had a fractious relationship with the imperial Athens.

70. *addressing* PHILOCLEON: During this exchange the Chorus-Leader uses some tragic, or elevated, language and a metre associated with tragedy (dochmiac). The scenario itself, with the Chorus pleading urgently with a stubborn hero in a vain attempt to change his mind, is one that occurs in Sophocles' *Ajax* and *Oedipus Rex*, and may have been seen as specifically Sophoclean.

71. *glowering brow*: Philocleon's stern, silent posture imitates the prolonged silences of certain tragic heroes (e.g., Niobe and Achilles, in Aeschylus' *Niobe* and *Myrmidons* respectively, and Ajax in Sophocles' *Ajax*). The Greek word *gruzein*, while not

tragic in itself, is used in *Frogs* 913 to describe the silences of Aeschylus' Niobe and Achilles. The Chorus-Leader's subsequent suggestion that Philocleon feels remorse for his earlier behaviour is similar to what the Chorus-Leader says in Sophocles' *Ajax*; both cases involve the hero being in a state of stunned silence after emerging from delusional sickness.

72. *Alas . . . would I be*: Philocleon's words are partly adapted from tragedy. The two closest passages are Euripides' *Alcestis* 867 and *Hippolytus* 732.

73. *Part . . . and let me pass*: This is a shortened, adapted quotation from Euripides' *Bellerophon*. In the tragedy, Bellerophon bids the 'shadowy folds' (perhaps foliage or clouds) part so that he can ascend to heaven on Pegasus. In the comedy, Philocleon is trying to part the 'shadowy folds' of his clothing so that he can commit suicide and make the journey down to Hades.

74. *May death . . . before I do that*: Quoted from tragedy, possibly Euripides' *Cretan Women* (fr. 465).

75. *a drachma between us . . . three fish scales*: The jurors' pay was three obols (small silver coins). Some Athenians were in the habit of carrying small change in their mouths (see note 64). Lysistratus was known for being fond of jokes and pranks. He was a man-about-town, and part of the crowd with whom Philocleon attends a symposium in the second half of the play. The idea that Lysistratus would have been an acquaintance of an ordinary old juror such as Philocleon is itself humorous.

76. *Hecate . . . on our porches*: Hecate was an Asiatic goddess associated with magic and infernal powers; she was also a deity of roads and travel. Accordingly, shrines of Hecate, like those of Apollo and Hermes, were often set up in front of houses.

77. *O hero Lycus . . . grant you that*: The joke is developed through the exchange. Philocleon remarks that he did not see the hero before now because the slave posing as Lycus has only just taken his place. Bdelycleon replies that he is as visible as Cleonymus, presumably because the slave is fat. Philocleon then mocks Cleonymus for losing his shield ('equipment') in battle, but may also be alluding to the lack of phallus ('equipment') in the slave's costume; this was usual for minor characters.

78. *Thratta*: The name, meaning 'from Thrace', was a common one for slave-girls; it is the name Mnesilochus gives his imaginary slave as he enters the festival precinct in *Women* (289ff.).

79. *Labes . . . wolfed the lot*: The name Labes means 'snatcher'. It is also recognizably similar to Laches, the man whom the Chorus

mentioned earlier as facing trial on this same day (see note 39). The trial that follows is a transparent domestic version of Laches' trial, which is itself fictional. Sicily was known for its cheeses but Labes' theft of a Sicilian cheese alludes to Laches' supposed misappropriation of public funds while in Sicily.

80. *pig-pen ... from scratch*: The pig-pen belongs to Hestia, the goddess of the hearth. Bdelycleon suggests, jokingly, that taking the goddess's property is sacrilege. Philocleon's reply is a humorous retort. To 'start from Hestia' was a proverbial remark for starting from scratch, because in prayers to several gods it was customary to begin with Hestia. So by taking the pig-pen Philocleon suggests that he is in fact paying the goddess her due respect.

81. *shrine of Apollo in the porch*: It was common to have a shrine of Apollo Aguiatos ('of the streets') in front of Athenian houses, just as it was to have pillars with busts of Hermes and shrines of Hecate.

82. *The Dog ... Aexone*: In court, the prosecutor and defendant were referred to by their names and district (deme) of origin. Cyon of Cydathenaeum and Labes of Aexone would have been readily recognizable allusions to Cleon and Laches respectively. Not only is Cleon's name (*Kleōn*) phonetically close to the word 'dog' (*kuōn*) but he had acquired the sobriquet 'The Dog', after styling himself the 'Watchdog of Athens'.

While the trial is ostensibly about Labes' theft of cheese, this does not preclude direct mention of the real characters and situation to which it clearly alludes. A little later we find references to cheese and the embezzlement of money in the same breath, and references to the defendant both as a dog and a man.

83. *figwood collar*: Given to dogs who had bitten people to stop them doing so again.

84. *siciliating*: Comic word which may mean 'eating in the (greedy) fashion of a Sicilian'. Sicily was known for its lavish banquets.

85. *gnawing plaster off the cities*: Cheeses were often encased in plaster to keep them fresh.

86. *Thucydides ... his trial*: Not Thucydides the historian but a major politician of the same name. He was the main adversary of Pericles in the 450s and 440s until he was banished by ostracism in 443 (for a decade). Sometime after his return, he was on trial for an unknown charge but was, it seems, unable to speak when required to defend himself.

87. *He is a good dog ... play the harp*: Bdelycleon's strategy satirizes

practice in court. He avoids, as far as possible, referring to the charge, emphasizing instead the defendant's positive qualities, even though they have no direct bearing on the case. He also seeks to obtain sympathy by saying that he 'never learnt to play the harp' (i.e., that he did not receive a privileged education).

88. *I feel myself softening . . . won over*: Philocleon's response resembles his earlier reaction during the debate with Bdelycleon (696–7 and 713–14), where he also finds himself being persuaded against his will.

89. *with a family of puppies*: This also satirizes the practice in court of bringing in the distressed relatives and friends of the defendant to elicit the jurors' sympathies.

90. *how did it go?*: In keeping with the surreal nature of the whole scene, Philocleon is prepared for either result, even though he is the only juror and (thinks he) has voted 'guilty'.

91. *Father . . . I am no more*: The exchange resembles a passage in Euripides' *Andromache* (1076–7), where the aged Peleus collapses, exclaiming that he is 'no more', after he hears of the death of his grandson Neoptolemus, which he believes to signify the end of his bloodline; the Chorus then urges him to lift himself up. Here, Bdelycleon bids his father get up when he collapses, exclaiming that he is 'no more', after he hears the unexpected verdict, which he believes to signify his own demise according to both the prophecy in 160 and his oath in 523.

92. *How can I bear . . . just did*: Philocleon expresses these sentiments in an unusually sober earnest style and tone.

93. *Hyperbolus*: He entered politics from an early age and was prominent in the mid 420s. He was first a prosecutor and then a demagogue, like Cleon. He was the primary target of plays by other comic playwrights but not, as far as we know, Aristophanes. While Cleon was mocked for his link with the leather trade, Hyperbolus was berated for his lamp-making business. He was ostracized in 417 and murdered on Samos in 411.

94. *in earlier days*: The start of a description of Aristophanes' early career. The remark that he initially worked 'like a ventriloquist' suggests that he wrote passages, or parts of plays, for other playwrights before his first complete play (*Banqueters* in 427). His description of himself as 'Driving a team of Muses of his own' seems to refer to the three plays written by him but produced by his friend Callistratus, namely *Banqueters*, *Babylonians* and *Acharnians*. Aristophanes 'first staged a play himself' with *Knights* in 424.

95. *greatest monster in the land*: Cleon. Aristophanes likens himself – as one who confronts Cleon – to Heracles, the mythical vanquisher of monsters par excellence. The description of Cleon as 'Jag-toothed' is based partly on descriptions in poetry of Cerberus (the three-headed dog guarding Hades, who was captured by Heracles). The comparison of Cleon with Cynna works on several levels, see following note.
96. *Cynna*: Renowned prostitute. Her name, *Kunna*, is the feminine form of *Kuōn*, 'The Dog', which was Cleon's soubriquet. *Kuōn* was also the name of the Dog-star, which was visible in the hottest part of summer and was believed to emit harmful rays.
97. *Jag-toothed . . . unwashed balls*: These lines (1030–37) abusing Cleon in no uncertain terms occur in almost identical form in *Peace* 752–9, produced a year later, shortly after Cleon's death.
98. *Polemarch*: An official (the third most important of the nine archons) who presided over lawsuits involving non-citizens.
99. *There never was a better comedy*: The play Aristophanes is referring to here is his *Clouds*, produced at the Dionysia of 423. The *Clouds* we possess is the revised version of the play. Clearly Aristophanes felt that the play, which came in third place, was not properly understood by the judges.
100. *barbarians . . . with flame*: A reference to the Persians who invaded in 490 BC and fought the allied Greeks until their conclusive defeat and withdrawal in 479.
101. *So thick with arrows . . . on the run*: Possibly an allusion to Herodotus' description of the battle of Thermopylae (480). The Spartans were warned prior to the battle that when the Persians fired arrows they were so numerous that they blocked out the sun, to which one of them replied, laconically, that it would be nice to fight in the shade (Herodotus 7.226).
102. *breeks*: Breeches or trousers.
103. *Our gallant three-tiered ships . . . hammered them at sea*: At the battle of Salamis (480), under the leadership of Themistocles.
104. *the Odeon*: A large hall built by Pericles for musical performances which lay just to the southeast of the Acropolis (east of the Theatre of Dionysus). The suggestion here is that it was also used as a lawcourt. Plays entered for the dramatic festivals were previewed at the Odeon; thus it may have been the fictional setting for *Preview*, the other play entered by Aristophanes in the Lenaea of 422 (produced by Philonides), which won first prize.

105. *Sardis*: The former capital of Lydia, the kingdom where the proverbially rich Croesus once ruled. Bdelycleon's point is that if Philocleon were wealthy or important, he may have visited Sardis on an embassy or, perhaps, as a tourist.
106. *Ecbatana*: Capital of Media and summer residence of the kings of Persia.
107. *Spartans*: Type of man's shoe with leather straps. The jokes that follow turn on Philocleon's refusal to have anything to do with shoes named after Athens' enemy Sparta.
108. *that story about Lamia farting*: Mentioned in *Assemblywomen* and elsewhere in Old Comedy. Lamia, when faced with possible capture, broke wind in the hope of repelling, and so evading, her would-be captors. The context for this story is not known. Euripides wrote a play called *Lamia*, but it may have been a satyr-play.
109. *Cardopion*: Unknown. He may, like Lamia, have belonged to one of the less dignified echelons of myth.
110. *Theogenes*: Prominent politician and merchant. He was satirized by comic playwrights as fat and boorish, personally vile, and a vain boaster. The reason for mentioning him here is unclear. Bdelycleon is perhaps making light of his insult to his father by suggesting that it is a case of the pot calling the kettle black.
111. *Androcles*: A demagogue. He came to prominence in the 430s and was quickly mocked by comic playwrights as being of low birth and poor or nouveau riche. Regarded as a vindictive prosecutor, he was accused of various kinds of immorality including having formerly been a male prostitute.
112. *Cleisthenes*: Well known for his effeminacy; he appears dressed as a woman in *Women*. He and Androcles seem to be mentioned here ironically; it would not be a good thing, in Bdelycleon's eyes, to claim to be a friend or colleague of either. Philocleon's point is that he went to Paros not as an Athenian dignitary but in the humble capacity of an oarsman, for which the pay was only two obols a day (less than jury pay).
113. *Ephudion . . . his arms*: Ephudion was a well-known exponent of *pankration*, or freestyle wrestling, an extraordinarily violent incarnation of the sport, which permitted punching (or hitting), kicking, jumping (or hurling oneself) and strangling. He won at the 79th Olympic games (in 464) and probably at others. Nothing is known of Ascondas (although his name sounds Boeotian).
114. *Phanos*: Associate of Cleon; also mentioned in *Knights*.
115. *Acestor*: Tragedian who was accused of foreign birth despite

being an Athenian citizen; elsewhere in Old Comedy he is portrayed as a flatterer and parasite who seeks dinner invitations.

116. *take up the singing . . . your turn*: The songs being sung here are examples of *scolia* or drinking songs. The custom at symposia was for one guest to sing a couple of lines from a traditional or improvised song, holding a myrtle branch which he then passed to the next guest, who had either to continue the song or reply with another song on a related theme. The scolion about Harmodius was well known (several versions survive). Harmodius and his lover Aristogeiton were honoured as heroes for killing Hipparchus, the brother of the tyrant Hippias, in 514.

117. *Take care . . . capsize*: Adapted from the poet Alcaeus (of Lesbos). The original is probably about Pittacus, a tyrant of Mytilene (the main city of Lesbos).

118. *It's wise . . . best friend*: From another well-known scolion, probably by Praxilla of Sicyon. Admetus was king of Pherae, and his 'courageous' friend was Heracles, who rescued the widowed Admetus' wife, Alcestis, from the underworld.

119. *It isn't as easy . . . hounds*: A jibe at Theorus for being an opportunist as well as a flatterer.

120. *Philoctemon's . . . get drunk*: Philoctemon (literally, 'lover of possessions') is probably a made-up name; the only evidence of real Athenians with this name is from a much later date. It was customary at symposia for guests to bring food while the host provided the wine.

121. *Sybarites*: Natives of Sybaris, an ancient Greek town in South Italy, famed for the luxurious lifestyle of its inhabitants.

122. *addressing the audience*: Barrett arbitrarily moves this passage, the second parabasis, to later in the play (lines 1450ff.), after the scenes between Philocleon and those he has abused. Here I have restored the order of the Oxford Classical Text of Hall and Geldart (1901), and of all major editions of *Wasps*, including MacDowell (1971), Sommerstein (1983) and Henderson (1998).

123. *Penestae*: A name, generally used of the poor, given specifically to the serf-class in Thessaly. The joke is that, although Amynias went on a diplomatic mission to aristocratic Thessaly, he still managed to end up where he belongs.

124. *Automenes*: Not mentioned elsewhere.

125. *Some people have been saying . . . subside*: This seems to refer to some kind of retaliatory action taken after Aristophanes' attack on Cleon in his *Knights*. There are hints that the retaliation was

legal, but no evidence of an actual trial. Possibly action was threatened but not undertaken, the most likely reason being some kind of apology on Aristophanes' part, or an undertaking to stop trouncing Cleon onstage. *Wasps* represents a breach of any such agreement, despite the suggestion in the prologue (62–3) that Cleon would be spared.

126. *O happy tortoises . . . stick*: Xanthias' opening utterance involves mock-elevation. The Chorus-Leader's subsequent query is tragic in language and style. The speech that follows, insofar as it informs the Chorus (and us) of events that have taken place offstage, resembles a tragic messenger-speech, but it differs inasmuch as the events being described, namely Philocleon's rampage, will very soon impinge on the action onstage.

127. *Hypillus . . . Phrynichus*: It is not clear who Hypillus or Thuphrastus were. Antiphon was a celebrated rhetorician and speech-writer, who had a reputation for avarice. Lycon was a politician in the 420s. He was well known partly on account of his wife, Rhodia, who seems to have been blatantly promiscuous. He had a handsome, athletic son, Autolycus, but was mocked by comic playwrights for being poor, unmanly and of foreign birth. This Phrynichus was a politician and an ardent prosecutor. He later took part in the oligarchic revolution in 411 and was assassinated in late summer of the same year. He is not to be confused with the contemporary comic playwright or the much earlier tragedian of the same name.

128. *Sthenelus*: Tragic dramatist whose writing was thought to be bland. Philocleon's remark implies that he relies heavily on 'stage props'.

129. *Come here . . . it can stand*: There is a double entendre and a visual joke here. The 'bit of rope' that Philocleon wants the flute-girl to take in her hand is the phallus that forms part of his comic costume, and it may well have been a deliberately frayed specimen.

130. *wind him up . . . Mysteries*: This may refer to a practice whereby candidates for initiation into the religious cult of the Mysteries were teased by those already initiated.

131. *Dardanis*: The name suggests that she is from the Troad, a region containing the cities of Troy and Dardanus, bound to the north-west by the Dardanelle straits.

132. *Chaerephon*: Friend and follower of Socrates. He is mentioned in the surviving, second version of *Clouds* (never performed) and may well have been a character in the first version, performed a

year before *Wasps* in 423. Here, as in *Clouds*, he is mocked for his lifeless, sallow appearance.

133. *Lasus*: Lasus of Hermione (near Argos) was a sixth-century dithyrambic poet.

134. *Simonides*: Simonides of Ceos was one of the finest Greek lyric poets. He claims, in an epigram, to have won fifty-six prizes in dithyrambic contests.

135. *Ino ... Euripides*: Ino was one of the daughters of Cadmus. Euripides wrote a play named after her, which presumably involved a scene with Ino pitifully supplicating another character; here Philocleon substitutes Euripides for the character whom Ino entreats.

136. *assault and battery*: A serious offence (*hubris* in Greek), for which the penalty would be set by a jury.

137. *Pittalus*: A doctor who seems to have been paid by the state to treat citizens for free.

138. *story of the dung-beetle*: This fable about the dung-beetle, which was wronged by an eagle but ascended to heaven to take revenge, is reworked in the plot of *Peace*, produced the year after *Wasps*.

139. *At last ... affection*: Barrett places these two stanzas earlier, at 1264ff. (see note 122).

140. *Thespis*: The traditional founder of tragedy, according to the Athenians (in 534 BC).

141. *What ho ... portals*: Philocleon's words here are tragic and may be quotations.

142. *hellebore*: Extract of hellebore was supposedly a cure for insanity.

143. *Phrynichus ... cock*: The early tragedian Phrynichus, of whom Philocleon was a devotee (see 268–9), was renowned for his dances; the phrase 'cowers like a strutting cock' is probably adapted from a well-known line of his.

144. *sons of Carcinus the Crab*: Carcinus was a tragic dramatist. His career dates back at least to the mid 440s. He was elected general in 432 and was subsequently one of three commanders of the Athenian fleet, a role which seems to have earned him the soubriquet Thalattios ('Lord of the Sea'); his name also means 'Crab'. These two things account for various puns in the present scene. Carcinus had either three or four sons (the implication here is either that there were three or that only three were generally known in 422), all of whom seem to have been dancers of small stature. The name of the middle son may have been Xenarchus.

145. *crab-tragedian – his brother*: Carcinus' eldest son, Xenotimus, served in the cavalry and was involved in trading overseas. He

probably wrote tragedies (as well as being a dancer) since his younger brother Xenocles, who appears next, is described as 'also' writing tragedies.

146. *the Little Nipper*: Carcinus' youngest son, Xenocles, is described as a bad playwright by Aristophanes (see *Women* 169 and *Frogs* 86), even though in 415 he defeated Euripides' trilogy that included *Trojan Women*.

147. *shuttles*: It is possible that a figure representing Carcinus would have entered at this point.

148. *No comic poet . . . his Chorus*: The claim is either that this is the first time a chorus has left the stage dancing or that this is the first time a troupe of dancers has come on specifically to lead the Chorus off.

WOMEN AT THE THESMOPHORIA

1. *Mnesilochus*: The character I have called Mnesilochus (in keeping with Barrett) is not actually named in the text; he is merely described as a relative of Euripides. The tradition of calling him Mnesilochus goes back to ancient scholars identifying him with a man of this name thought to be the father of Euripides' first wife.

2. *how all these things are arranged*: The ensuing explanation combines an account of vision and hearing with a rationalized version of the myth of Uranus (Sky/Heaven) and Gaia (Earth). Its language is similar to that found both in philosophical writing and in fragments of Euripides, but it especially resembles a speech by the heroine of his *Melanippe the Wise* (fr. 484). In *Frogs* (892) Euripides prays to 'Ether' before his contest with Aeschylus.

3. *What joy . . . men of wisdom*: Possibly adapted from a line of tragedy but the exact source is unclear.

4. *lame after all this exertion*: Aristophanes regularly jokes about Euripides' fondness for presenting heroes in various states of lameness, injury or distress (see, e.g., *Frogs* 846ff.).

5. *Agathon*: Well-known tragedian of the generation after Euripides. He won his first victory in 416 (Plato's *Symposium* is set during a celebration of this event). He was noted for his physical beauty, effeminacy and passive homosexuality. Aristotle says that Agathon was the first tragedian to use plots and characters that were freely devised rather than based on myth or history and that he was the first to compose odes wholly unconnected with the action of his plays (*Poetics* 1451b and 1456a). The few

surviving fragments of his work show a fondness for elaborate language and antithetical expression. In 411, when *Women at the Thesmophoria* was produced, Agathon would have been about forty.

In the exchange that follows Barrett changes line order; here the original order is restored.

6. *buggered him . . . without knowing it*: This crude remark seems out of character for the otherwise earnest and restrained Euripides, but characterization in Aristophanes accommodates such inconsistency without undermining the personality of the character in question. Thus the similarly earnest heroine of *Lysistrata* can describe the abstinent women of Athens as being 'desperate for a shag'.

7. *pompous, elevated tones*: Much of the language in the Servant's prayer and the exchange with Mnesilochus is tragic in style.

8. *O Zeus . . . this day*: Euripides' expression of apprehension is the first clear sign that he is in a dire predicament.

9. *Why do you weep . . . I am your kin*: Mnesilochus' concerned questions, and his reminder that Euripides should share his distress with those close to him, are imitative of tragedy.

10. *middle day of the Thesmophoria*: The second day, the 'middle' day (*mesē*), was a day of fasting.

11. *Disguised . . . attire*: The line may be tragic. Mnesilochus' subsequent suggestion that Euripides' plan is very much in the style of his tragedies alludes to the fact that it is modelled on the Euripidean hero Telephus in the play of the same name (produced in 438). The action of *Telephus* informs much of the action of the first half of *Women*. Telephus, a son of Heracles and king of Mysia (in Asia Minor), had successfully repelled an attack by the Greek army on its way to Troy under Agamemnon, despite sustaining an injury from Achilles. The Greeks were planning to attack again and destroy him utterly (just as the women plan to destroy Euripides). Telephus therefore tried to change their minds by disguising himself and infiltrating a meeting of the Greek leaders in Agamemnon's palace at Argos. Here Euripides intends to do likewise but using Agathon rather than going in person.

12. *revolving platform*: The *eccyclēma* was a device for showing interior scenes onstage in tragedy. It would probably have been wheeled out through the main central doors at the back of the stage. Aristophanic comedy frequently comments directly on itself as a theatrical performance. In *Acharnians*, the hero Dicaeopolis also draws attention to the revolving platform in a scene

that has close parallels with the present one; except that in *Acharnians*, Dicaeopolis takes the role played here by Euripides (i.e., the beleaguered character imploring a tragedian for help) while Euripides takes the role played here by Agathon (i.e., the tragedian at home).

13. *Cyrene*: Well-known courtesan of the day.
14. AGATHON *sings*: The song that follows almost certainly involves a parody of the linguistic, metrical and musical characteristics of Agathon's lyrics, although the lack of fragments by Agathon makes it difficult to assess.
15. *infernal twain*: Goddesses Demeter and Persephone, the main deities worshipped in the Thesmophoria festival.
16. *Simoïs*: River near Troy often mentioned by Homer in the *Iliad*.
17. *Child of Leto*: Artemis, the virgin goddess of hunting and sister of Apollo.
18. *Phrygian rhythm*: A musical mode (not to be confused with the later medieval mode of the same name) whose use in tragedy was considered innovative and controversial; Euripides, in his *Orestes* (written in 408, a few years after *Women*), made daring use of this mode in a long aria by a Phrygian slave.
19. *Whence art thou . . . what thy country*: From Aeschylus' lost play *Edonians*, in which Dionysus was dressed in similarly feminine garb (the same passage is alluded to in *Frogs* 46–7).
20. *Old man . . . soul*: Agathon's speech here is quasi-tragic in rhythm. Its language mixes poetic and technical vocabulary, and the overall tone is one of earnestness tinged with mock-hauteur (not unlike that of Euripides).
21. *Phaedra . . . straddling position*: Phaedra, who appears in Euripides' *Hippolytus* where she is struck by uncontrollable desire for her stepson, is often cited by Aristophanes as an example of Euripides' fondness for portraying immoral women (see also *Frogs* 1043). The joke here involves a play on the verb *kelētizein*, which means to 'ride', but also refers to a particular sexual position, and exploits the fact that Phaedra's love for Hippolytus is initially hinted at through her strange longing for horse-riding, one of Hippolytus' favourite pastimes. It is not known whether Agathon actually wrote a play about Phaedra.
22. *Ibycus . . . Alcaeus*: Ibycus of Rhegium (South Italy) flourished *c.* 530. Anacreon of Teos (on the coast of Asia Minor between Chios and Samos) wrote between *c.* 530–490. Alcaeus of Mytilene (Lesbos) was a contemporary of Sappho and flourished

c. 600. They were all lyric poets, and their fastidious dress is evident from vase-painting.

23. *Phrynichus*: Tragedian and older contemporary of Aeschylus. He was renowned for the sweetness of his lyrics and for his choreography (in *Wasps*, Philocleon and the Chorus are devotees of Phrynichean song). Mnesilochus would need to have been fairly old to have seen Phrynichus' plays, as he died in 472 (when Euripides was about twelve).
24. *Philocles*: Nephew of Aeschylus. We know from Aristophanes' *Birds* that he wrote a play about Tereus, and also that he won first prize ahead of Sophocles' *Oedipus Rex*. His work is criticized by Aristophanes elsewhere as bitter or harsh.
25. *Xenocles*: Son of the tragedian Carcinus. He and his brothers appear, ridiculously costumed, in the finale of *Wasps*. He defeated Euripides in 415 but is dismissed as inferior to him by Dionysus in *Frogs* 86.
26. *Theognis*: Contemporary tragedian. His work is regularly berated by Aristophanes for being *psuchros* ('cold', 'insipid').
27. *A wise man . . . few words*: A two-line quotation from Euripides' *Aeolus* (fr. 28). The name 'Agathon' replaces the original words 'my children'. Euripides' subsequent description of his plight is also tragic in style.
28. *You love your life . . . his too*: A quotation of Euripides' *Alcestis* 691. In the original, Admetus, who is told that he must die unless he can find someone to die in his place, asks his father Pheres, who refuses.
29. *Misfortunes . . . submit oneself to them*: Very likely a two-line quotation from one of Agathon's own plays. There is a pun on *tois pathēmasin*, which means 'through suffering' in its original tragic context, but is given the comic meaning 'through submissive acts' when repeated by Mnesilochus in 201.
30. *To the holy altar*: In the Greek text Mnesilochus refers to the temple of the 'Dread Goddesses' (*Semnai Theai*), often identified with the Furies (also known as the Eumenides or Erinyes). This sanctuary, which probably lay between the Acropolis and the Areopagus, was seen as an inviolable place of refuge.
31. *shaven recruit*: There is a pun on *psilos* meaning 'shaven' and 'a recruit'. For an Athenian man to be shaven was a serious indignity.
32. *Cleisthenes*: Regularly mocked by Aristophanes as being beardless, effeminate and a passive homosexual (see, e.g., *Frogs* 48–9).

He appears later in the play – beardless and dressed in women's clothing.

33. *wheel me in again*: Agathon refers openly to the revolving platform, like Euripides earlier.

34. *I swear by Ether . . . Zeus*: An adapted quotation from Euripides' *Melanippe the Wise* (fr. 487). The same phrase is misquoted by Dionysus in *Frogs* 100. Here Euripides' oath, though unconventional, makes reference to Zeus; by contrast, in *Frogs* 892ff., he swears by Ether but omits all mention of traditional deities.

35. *block of flats*: The original mentions 'Hippocrates' tenement block'. The Hippocrates in question, possibly a nephew of Pericles, was an Athenian general, who may have let rooms to sailors, traders, foreigners or other people of low-repute.

36. *heart that swore . . . I didn't force you*: Mnesilochus alludes to a famous line from Euripides' *Hippolytus* (612) in which Hippolytus reneges on an oath of secrecy claiming that it was elicited under duress and that it was 'his tongue that swore and not his heart'. Fearing Euripides may do likewise, Mnesilochus stresses that he has sworn of his own accord with both heart and tongue.

37. *MICA*: This character is referred to simply as 'First Woman' in some editions, but since she is the same character as the woman who appears in later scenes with Mnesilochus, and she is addressed there as Mica, it makes sense to call her by this name throughout.

38. *Thratta*: Meaning 'from Thrace', a common name for slave-girls.

39. *Fanny . . . Willy*: The name *Choirios* ('Fanny') is a diminutive of *choiros*, which means 'piglet' but also – invariably in comedy – the female pudenda. *Posthaliskos* ('Willy') is a diminutive of *posthē* ('penis').

40. *CHORUS-LEADER*: There is disagreement about who speaks the lines given to the Chorus-Leader in this scene. In most texts they are given (as here) to the Chorus-Leader. This section from the opening invocation to the Chorus's prayer ending 'In spite of our gender' comprises the Entry-Song (*parodos*) of the Chorus. It is modelled loosely on the actual procedure at the start of meetings of the Athenian assembly, comprising a prayer for divine approval of its deliberations and a curse on those who are enemies and betrayers of the community as a whole. Both prayer and curse are followed by a choral ode or song reinforcing the sentiments just expressed. There is humorous adaptation to suit the particular occasion (i.e., the Thesmophoria festival) and the gender of the celebrants. The opening invocation represents the

longest unbroken passage of prose in extant Aristophanes (the other significant example, in *Birds*, is also a prayer, but it contains frequent interruptions).

41. *Divine Maiden*: Demeter's daughter, Persephone.

42. *city was contested by the gods*: The reference is to the story that Athena and Poseidon competed for the possession of Attica, Athena emerging victorious on account of her gift of the olive tree.

43. *Persians or Euripides*: The Persians are the Medes who, with an empire extending into the Ionian seaboard in Asia Minor, were longstanding enemies of the Greeks. They were the only enemy mentioned by name in the assembly curse; here, the addition of Euripides' name suggests that the women view him as an inveterate foe.

44. *cabbage-woman's son*: The joke that Euripides' mother, Cleito, was a seller of greens in the marketplace is found throughout Aristophanes (see, e.g., *Frogs* 840). The origin of the joke is unclear; there is evidence to suggest that she was in fact well born.

45. *Wherever there's a stage*: Mica means not only Athens but other parts of the Greek world where Athenian tragedy was performed. Aeschylus, for example, produced plays in Sicily, and shortly after the date of *Women*, Euripides and then Agathon went to the court of King Archelaus of Macedon.

46. *It cannot be ... our guest from Corinth*: A quotation from Euripides' *Bellerophon* (fr. 664). In Euripides' play, a character describes Stheneboea's desire for Bellerophon, who was a guest of her husband King Proetus, by saying that whenever she drops something she toasts their 'guest from Corinth'.

47. *Whence come ... thy cheek*: The source of this quotation is not known.

48. *An old man ... wife*: A line from Euripides' *Phoenix* (fr. 804).

49. *Molossian dogs*: From the northwest of the Greek mainland, noted for their ferocity and size. They were used both as sheep-dogs and guard-dogs.

50. *Laconian ones with triple teeth*: Keys made in Laconia (i.e., Sparta) were more elaborate than ordinary keys, making their locks more secure.

51. *sticky end ... some other way*: There may be an allusion here to Euripidean heroines who use poison. The phrase 'perhaps by poison' occurs twice in Euripides in connection with such women. Medea also advocates murder by poison (*Medea* 384–5).

52. *saying that there aren't any gods*: Euripides was, like Socrates, sometimes accused of atheism. The accusation probably arose partly from his interest in philosophy and partly from the attribution to him of views expressed by some of his characters, such as Bellerophon, who rejects the gods in at least one speech (*Bellerophon* fr. 286), and Hippolytus, who spurns Aphrodite and goes back on an oath (*Hippolytus* 113 and 612).
53. *special order of twenty wreaths*: This may be a reference to the celebrations after the Dionysia festival, at which such wreaths were worn. The remark suggests that the woman is not as badly off as she claims.
54. *For we're alone ... these things*: Quoted from Euripides' *Telephus* (see note 11), from the main speech by Telephus in the debate among the Greek leaders, after the case against him has been made. The situation in which Mnesilochus speaks in defence of Euripides is closely comparable, although he shows little of Telephus' oratorical skills.
55. *He did me ... Apollo*: The description suggests a small sanctuary of Apollo, or at least an altar with a sacred laurel bush nearby. Needless to say, engaging in a sexual act in such a place would have been seen as sacrilegious.
56. *bit of garlic ... this time*: A woman meeting her lover would not have eaten garlic because it would have given her bad breath. 'Wall Duty' was the overnight guarding of the long fortified walls extending from Athens to its harbour at Piraeus (necessitated by the Spartan presence at nearby Deceleia).
57. *same bend halfway along*: Presumably the old woman knows this because she also nursed the husband as a child.
58. *We suffer nothing worse than we deserve*: Also adapted from Euripides' *Telephus* (fr. 711), probably from the same speech by Telephus which Mnesilochus quotes earlier.
59. *ancient proverb ... ugly head*: The proverb in question suggests that a scorpion may lurk under any stone. The line that follows is taken from Euripides' *Melanippe in Chains*, except for the final remark ('except ... womankind'), in which the Chorus-Leader briefly steps out of character.
60. *he never writes a play about a virtuous woman like Penelope*: As it happens, the respective heroines of the two Euripidean tragedies parodied extensively in the second half of the play *are* presented as virtuous.
61. *we give the meat ... Apaturia*: The Apaturia festival involved men organized into groups called phratries (based on common

ancestry) attending several meat-based feasts. Much of this meat was provided by the participants (hence the opportunity for their womenfolk to steal some).

62. *killed her husband . . . sent him mad*: These examples may refer to contemporary cases but there are, nonetheless, similarities with certain well-known tragic situations. The woman killing her husband with an axe resembles Clytemnestra's murder of Agamemnon. The woman giving her husband a dangerous drug with unintended, catastrophic results is similar to Deianeira's accidental poisoning of Heracles, as presented in Sophocles' *Women of Trachis*; she was tricked by the centaur Nessus, whom Heracles had mortally wounded, into thinking the poison was a love-potion. The third example, which follows directly, has no mythological paradigm.

63. *I'll make you . . . eat*: He implies that she has been eating on the sly; the women were meant to fast during part of the festival.

64. *breathless with excitement*: Cleisthenes' role in the comedy corresponds to that of Odysseus in Euripides' *Telephus*, who comes in with urgent news about the presence of an intruder in a meeting of the Greek leaders. His first line is mock-tragic. His last sentence and the Chorus's subsequent reply are tragic in style, as are most of the lines subsequently uttered by the Chorus in this scene.

65. *Cleonymus*: Politician frequently abused by Aristophanes, especially in his early plays. He was an ardent supporter of Cleon and was regularly taunted for having dropped his shield in battle; see *Wasps* 19–20 and note.

66. *Cothocidae*: Deme near Eleusis. It is unclear why Mnesilochus gives this answer.

67. *shuttle service across the Isthmus*: A reference to the grooved track built across the Isthmus of Corinth (*c.* 600 BC) for transporting goods, and later ships, between the Saronic and Corinthian gulfs.

68. *snatches* MICA*'s baby*: The following scene is based on a scene, or possibly an offstage event, from Euripides' *Telephus*, in which the hero Telephus saves himself by taking Agamemnon's baby son Orestes hostage (the same scene is also parodied in *Acharnians*, where the 'baby' is not a baby but a coal-basket). The entire scene is full of elevated language and the Chorus's diction is tragic throughout. Following Barrett's translation, the first few lines of the lyric section have not been put in rhyming verse.

69. *I shall engrave . . . bleeding veins*: Mnesilochus' words are tragic, possibly taken from *Telephus* or another Euripidean play.

70. *Cretan clothes . . . Persian booties*: Part of an attempt to disguise the wineskin as a child.
71. *getting on for . . . four festival years*: Mnesilochus is suggesting not only that the wineskin is too big to be a 'baby' but also that it has been taken to a number of festivals.
72. *slay the victim*: Mnesilochus' motive may be simply to have a drink himself.
73. *Palamedes*: One of the Greek leaders at Troy and famed for his ingenuity and for the invention of writing. His cleverness earned him the enmity of Odysseus, who contrived to have him killed. Euripides' *Palamedes* is the second play in a trilogy about the Trojan War (the first play of which is the surviving *Trojan Women*) produced in 415 BC. It dealt with the execution of Palamedes through false accusation (by Odysseus) and an unfair trial. Prior to his execution the condemned Palamedes manages to send news of his plight to his brother Oeax by writing on oar-blades which he threw into the sea; one of these washed up on the shores of his homeland and brought news of his fate to his father, who later brought about the wreck of much of the Greek fleet as it returned home, by way of revenge. The play may be used here partly to poke fun at the excessive cleverness of Euripidean plot devices.
74. *O hands . . . hopeless plight*: The ode is probably not based on a specific passage from *Palamedes* but an imitation of Euripidean tragic lyric in general.
75. *as they are mentioned*: What follows is a series of jokes about various well-known figures that employ mostly made-up female names whose meanings mock the men's respective shortcomings. Charminus was a general in 412–411, who had recently been defeated by a Spartan fleet off Syme, north of Rhodes, and lost six ships in the process. Cleophon, who was a general in 428, was a regular target of comic poets (see, e.g., *Frogs* 1504, 1532). Here he is simply described as more unsavoury than Salabaccho, a well-known prostitute.
76. *Hyperbolus' mother*: Hyperbolus was a demagogue who came to prominence after the death of Cleon. He was a favourite target of comic playwrights and appears as a central figure in three plays by contemporaries of Aristophanes. His mother is also a major target in at least two of the three plays mentioned above, and is described variously as old, drunken and sluttish.
77. *Helen*: Euripides' play, performed the previous year (412) along

with *Andromeda*, which is used later in this play. Both plays would therefore still be fairly fresh in the minds of the audience. *Helen* involves a familiar variant on the Trojan myth, by the poet Stesichorus, in which Helen was never in Troy – Hera sent a phantom Helen there instead – but transported to Egypt under the protection of King Proteus. The play is set seven years after the end of the Trojan War, when Proteus is dead and his tyrannical son Theoclymenus means to marry Helen by force. The shipwrecked Menelaus arrives and, after he and Helen recognize one another, the couple plan their escape with the help of Theoclymenus' prophetic sister. The extensive parody and adaptation of *Helen* which follows draws primarily on three scenes: the prologue (a monologue by Helen); a scene between Menelaus and the palace door-keeper (already somewhat comic in the tragedy); and the recognition scene between Menelaus and Helen. Much of the exchange between Euripides and Mnesilochus comprises lines borrowed directly from these scenes (sometimes adapted), but even lines that are not taken from *Helen* are largely tragic in style. For precise details about which lines from *Helen* are used through this scene see the table in Sommerstein's edition of the play (1994), p. 212, which also gives the speaker (and, in some cases, the addressee) in the tragedy and the extent to which lines are adapted.

78. *between Hell an' high water*: The original contains a pun on the mention of the name Helen.
79. *Egypt's dark-clogged citizens*: Adapted from Helen's opening monologue (*Helen* 1–3). Aristophanes uses a variant on the epithet 'dark-clothed' meaning 'fond of dark emetics', suggesting that the Egyptians were constipated (according to Herodotus, they were very fond of emetics and enemas). Mnesilochus' borrowings up to 868 are from the same monologue.
80. *Hecate*: Goddess associated with magic and the underworld.
81. *Phrynondas*: A name proverbial for roguery.
82. *Scamander's banks*: Scamander was a river near Troy often mentioned by Homer in the *Iliad*.
83. *What lord ... resides*: Quoted from *Helen* 68 (spoken in the tragedy by Teucer rather than Menelaus). Mnesilochus' reply is adapted from *Helen* 460, where it is spoken by a female janitor (in a scene that is largely humorous anyway).
84. *Proteas*: Critylla, who fails to recognize the parody of *Helen*, supposes that Mnesilochus is falsely claiming to be in the house

of Proteas. A man of this name was a general in the 430s, and it is likely that this is the Proteas to whom she is referring; nothing else is known of him.

85. *Theonoë*: Daughter of King Proteus and a prophetess. In Euripides' play, she assists Menelaus and Helen in their escape.

86. *let me see your face*: The following exchange imitates the recognition scene between Menelaus and Helen. The language mixes snippets from various parts of *Helen* with general tragic phraseology.

87. *from your rags I see*: The Greek text for this is uncertain; it is unclear whether the joke about Menelaus' appearance refers to his rags or the presence of greenery. For jokes about Euripides' fondness for presenting heroes in rags, see *Acharnians* 412–39, *Frogs* 842, 1063–6. For jokes about his mother being a seller of greens, see *Women* 387, *Frogs* 840. Menelaus in *Helen* regularly refers to his ragged clothing but makes no mention of seaweed. Still, Aristophanes may have added seaweed to the costume of Euripides-playing-Menelaus to facilitate a joke about his mother; the fact that Mnesilochus is a friend and relative of Euripides does not prevent him making jokes at the latter's expense.

88. *tie him to the plank*: Mnesilochus' fate suddenly becomes grievous. Being fixed to a plank by means of an iron collar and clamps for the wrists and ankles was a means of execution known as *apotumpanismos*, in which the victim would be tied fast but without being pierced so as to take an agonizingly long time to die.

89. *O saffron dress . . . rescue any more*: Mnesilochus' expression of despair contains tragic language. His address to an inanimate object at a moment of despair is also characteristic of tragedy.

90. *Pauson*: Painter who specialized in caricature; he is mentioned by Aristotle (*Poetics* 1448a). The joke supposes he was so poor that he routinely fasted.

91. *to the audience*: The lyrics accompanying dancing sometimes involved the lampooning of well-known citizens (see, e.g., *Frogs* 420ff.).

92. *Far-Shooter, Lord of the Lyre*: Both epithets of Apollo.

93. *Cithaeron's fountains*: Cithaeron, a mountain close to Thebes, was where the infant Oedipus was exposed on his parents' orders, although the shepherd to whom the task was entrusted subsequently rescued him. Dionysus was also closely associated with

Mount Cithaeron. His mother, Semele, was the daughter of Cadmus, a king of Thebes.

94. *shout in da sky*: The character of the Scythian is the fullest surviving example of the portrayal of a 'barbarian' in Old Comedy. In the Greek text his speech is defective both in terms of pronunciation and grammar; this is only reflected approximately in the translation.

95. *Euripides appears*: While it is possible that Euripides at this point makes a trial run on the stage-crane (*mēchanē*) it seems much more likely that he just appears momentarily in the wings. Not only does the text suggest that he emerges briefly and furtively – the crane was not suitable for brevity or furtiveness – but the use of the crane at this point would undermine Euripides' spectacular aerial appearance as Perseus later in the scene (1098). The stage-crane, a device used in tragedy, was probably invented fairly late in the fifth century. Evidence for its use is somewhat limited. It seems likely that it was associated specifically with Euripidean tragedy; there is no conclusive evidence for its use by Sophocles (or Aeschylus). Its main purpose, it seems, was for presenting gods descending from Olympus (e.g., Iris in Euripides' *Heracles*) or heroes in flight, such as Bellerophon on Pegasus in Euripides' *Bellerophon* (a spectacle parodied by Aristophanes' hero Trygaeus in *Peace*) and Perseus in *Andromeda*.

96. *As Andromeda*: What follows is an extended parody of Euripides' lost play *Andromeda*. Like *Helen*, *Andromeda* was a play of rescue and romance produced in 412. One of Andromeda's parents – either Cepheus, king of Ethiopia, or his wife Cassiopeia – had offended Poseidon, who sent a flood and a sea-monster to destroy their land. Cepheus learnt that Poseidon's anger could only be appeased by leaving his daughter Andromeda chained on the shore as a victim for the monster. She awaited her fate accompanied by her own voice, echoing from a nearby cave, and a sympathetic chorus of maidens. Perseus, however, returning (in the winged sandals given to him by Hermes) from slaying Medusa, saw Andromeda and fell in love with her. He killed the monster, using Medusa's head, and saved Andromeda in return for her hand in marriage. After this, the play's action is unclear, but there seems to have been some conflict between the would-be-weds and Andromeda's parents. Aristophanes' parody uses two scenes out of their original sequence: the first involved heroine and chorus; the second, the tragedy's opening scene, comprised Andromeda's voice being echoed.

The opening of Mnesilochus' lyrics, adapted from *Andromeda* (fr. 117), is probably modelled on Andromeda's first words to the Chorus. In the rest of the monody, some lines, whether quoted (or adapted) from *Andromeda* or a patchwork of tragic language, are suited to the tragic Andromeda; others are pertinent to Mnesilochus' own situation (e.g., 'With that Scythian watching me', 'I must get back to my wife'); others still are applicable both to Andromeda and Mnesilochus (e.g., 'Pitiless, ah me, / Was the hand that bound me').

97. *Glaucetes*: A glutton who was regularly satirized in comedy. His name may also be appropriate here because of its marine connotations (*glaukos* can mean 'grey-green' or 'sea-coloured').

98. *ECHO*: Probably not an actual character in Euripides' *Andromeda*. Here, however, the way in which Mnesilochus greets her – as if they are face to face, and without undue surprise – suggests that she is present onstage, although she does speak to the Scythian from offstage later on in the scene. It seems unlikely that the part of Echo was played by the character of Euripides. Unlike Euripides when he is disguised as Menelaus and Perseus, Echo offers no assistance or encouragement whatsoever to Mnesilochus; in fact, quite the reverse. It is also unlikely that Echo was played by the *actor* playing Euripides, as he would already be in the costume of Perseus at this point. It is improbable that he would be able, or expected, to change into the costume of Echo only to have to make an almost instant change back into the Perseus costume, as well as being attached to the stage-crane – not an easy task, as the device required its own special operator – for his aerial appearance.

99. *I worked together with Euripides*: Echo is referring openly to the production of *Andromeda* in 412.

100. *Gods . . . I bear*: Euripides' speech is largely quoted (and adapted) from a monologue by Perseus in *Andromeda* (fr. 123–5). In the exchange that follows he uses some quotation, some general tragic pastiche and some contrastingly blunt comic language.

101. *Gorgas da writer*: It is not clear to whom the Scythian is referring. The Greek word for 'writer' (*grammateos*) properly means 'secretary'. There was a man named Gorgus who died in a naval battle in 411 and who may have held the position of *grammateos* to some state body or other. It is, however, possible that the Scythian means Gorgias, the famous sophist (memorably portrayed by Plato in the dialogue named after him), although this would

require him to use the word *grammateos* to mean rhetorician, which is not all that likely.

102. *To use new schemes upon a witless fool*: Quoted from Euripides' *Medea* 298.

103. *a serious offer*: The women (in the form of the Chorus) accept Euripides' offer of a truce readily, despite being so implacably hostile to him earlier. Such inconsistency is not uncommon in Aristophanes (compare Dionysus in *Frogs* 1471).

104. *stay inside dem clothes*: He warns Mnesilochus not to develop an erection at the sight of the dancing-girl. Presumably in the original performance there would have been humorous use of the phallus worn by comic actors (as there is at 643ff., when Mnesilochus is being exposed as a man), not only in the case of Mnesilochus but also the Scythian.

105. *pointing the wrong way*: This misdirection of the 'barbarian' Scythian is loosely comparable to a scene in Euripides' *Iphigenia among the Taurians*, produced in 413 or 412, in which the (Greek) Chorus-Leader misinforms a barbarian messenger – he has come to inform his master, King Thoas, about the escape of Iphigenia, Orestes and Pylades – of the king's whereabouts. There is also a resemblance to the scene in Euripides' *Cyclops* in which the Chorus of Satyrs plays 'blind man's buff' with the blinded Cyclops while Odysseus escapes.

FROGS

1. *buskins*: High laced-up boots worn by tragic actors.

2. *Phrynichus . . . Ameipsias*: Contemporaries of Aristophanes. Phrynichus' *Muses* came second to *Frogs*. Ameipsias' *Revellers* won first prize over Aristophanes' *Birds* in 414; he also competed favourably against *Clouds* in 423. Little is known of Lycis.

3. *comic porter scene . . . one in every comedy*: *Frogs* itself is no exception: the action until 627 is, among other things, an extended comic routine involving luggage carrying and role swapping between master and slave.

4. *Juice*: Instead of the expected 'Zeus'. 'Juice' also links Dionysus to wine (the joke in the Greek text refers to a drinking festival in Dionysus' honour).

5. *sea-battle . . . I'd be a free man now*: All slaves who took part in the Athenian victory at Arginusae (406 BC) were subsequently freed and granted full citizen's rights.

6. *lion-skin . . . regiment*: Heracles' string of questions about

Dionysus' effeminate dress resembles Mnesilochus' questioning of Agathon in *Women* (136ff.). Both passages are adapted from Aeschylus' *Edonians* (fr. 61), in which Dionysus is questioned by Lycurgus.

7. *Cleisthenes*: An effeminate, apparently beardless man, regularly mocked for being cowardly and a passive homosexual. He appears in *Women*, dressed in women's clothing, to expose the disguised Mnesilochus.

8. *Andromeda*: Exotic, romantic play by Euripides, in which the hero Perseus rescues Andromeda from a sea-monster and wins her for his bride; it is parodied extensively in *Women*. Dionysus' remark is one of the very first references to solitary, recreational reading in the ancient world.

9. *Molon's size*: Molon, a well-known actor, was a very large man.

10. *Please!*: The ancient Greeks saw sexual relations between men and boys as permissible in certain circumstances, but frowned on them between men. They particularly reviled men who adopted a passive role in homosexual relationships.

11. *little brother*: Heracles and Dionysus are half-brothers; both are sons of Zeus by mortal women.

12. *many are gone . . . bad*: Dionysus quotes Euripides' *Oeneus* (fr. 565).

13. *Sophocles' son, Iophon*: Little is known about the work of Iophon. Tragedians often belonged to theatrical families, e.g., Aeschylus and Euripides.

14. *slippery customer*: Euripides' slipperiness is probably inferred from the wiliness of his heroes such as Telephus and Palamedes.

15. *took life in his stride*: Sophocles was known for his affable and sociable nature.

16. *Agathon*: He won the tragic competition in 416, possibly at his first attempt. He was noted for his effeminacy and homosexuality; his work was known for its distinctive stylistic innovations. He appears as a character in *Women* and in Plato's *Symposium*.

17. *king of Macedon*: At some time prior to 405, Agathon followed Euripides to the court of King Archelaus of Macedon.

18. *Xenocles . . . Pythangelus*: Two tragedians; nothing is known of Pythangelus but Xenocles was from a well-known theatrical family. His father, Carcinus, is regularly mocked by Aristophanes, including in the finale of *Wasps*, where Xenocles and his brothers perform a ridiculous tragic dance routine.

19. *choir of swallows*: From Euripides' *Alcmene* (fr. 89).

20. *Ether, bedsit of Zeus*: Parody of Euripides' *Melanippe the Wise* (fr. 487) with 'bedsit' replacing 'abode'.
21. *the tread of Time*: Occurring in Euripides' *Bacchae* (889), produced posthumously in 405, but a similar phrase occurs in his earlier *Alexandros* (fr. 42).
22. *tongue . . . committed*: Clumsy paraphrase of Euripides' *Hippolytus* 612: 'My tongue did swear, but my heart is not under oath.' The line was well known; see *Frogs* 1471 and *Women* 275–6.
23. *Seek not . . . your own*: The line resembles a number of Euripidean lines without being obviously linked to any one (although it may be from an unknown source).
24. *cold feet*: Hemlock supposedly drains the body's warmth, starting with the extremities.
25. *torch race*: An event in the Panathenaea and other Athenian festivals.
26. *ferryman . . . two obols*: The ferryman is Charon. His fare was usually one obol but here Aristophanes has doubled it, either because of the return fare or to reflect wartime inflation.
27. *Theseus introduced the idea*: Probably a reference to Theseus' journey to the underworld with Pirithous. Pirithous had wanted to wrest Persephone from Hades, but was punished for his presumption by being kept captive in the underworld; Theseus remained with him out of loyalty. The two were later rescued by Heracles when he came to capture Cerberus (his final labour). The rescue was the subject of a (lost) play *Pirithous* either by Euripides or Critias.
28. *Morsimus*: Son of the tragedian Philocles and great-nephew of Aeschylus. A tragedian himself, he was the butt of several critical remarks by Aristophanes.
29. *Cinesias*: Dithyrambic poet, regularly mocked by Aristophanes for using pretentious polysyllables and being gaunt and incontinent (possibly due to disease).
30. *People initiated into the rites of the Mysteries*: The Chorus comprises initiates of the Eleusinian Mysteries, who were believed to lead a blissful, toil-free existence in the afterlife in a special part of the underworld which had daylight like that of the upper world.
31. *two drachmas*: One drachma equalled six obols.
32. *Charon . . . couldn't care less*: Dionysus calls Charon three times, imitating the custom of calling upon the dead three times as a final farewell. He then complains that Charon, whose name is

linked to the word *chaire* meaning 'welcome' or 'farewell', is not very welcoming.

33. *FROG-CHORUS*: *Frogs* is unique among Aristophanes' plays in having two separate choruses, the Frog-Chorus and the Initiate-Chorus (*Lysistrata* has semi-choruses of old men and women but these appear together, and collectively comprise a single chorus). The Frog-Chorus may only have been audible and not visible (see 205), but equally it may have appeared onstage; the difficulty of hearing offstage singers also counts against their non-appearance. When *Frogs* was produced, strained finances made it hard to find people willing, or able, to serve as *chorēgos*; as a result, each competitor was assigned two *chorēgoi*. While this makes it seem unlikely that Aristophanes could have asked for *two* choruses, the fact that the Initiate-Chorus, dressed in rags, was inexpensive to fit out – the Chorus themselves refer to this (see 406ff.) – means it may have been possible to present a second chorus without exceeding budget.
34. *festival days*: The festival is the Anthesteria, celebrated in the sanctuary of Dionysus-in-the-Marshes (south of the Acropolis, possibly by the river Ilissus). The sounds of the Frog-Chorus are closest to those of the marsh frog (*Rana ridibunda*).
35. *Empusa*: Female creature that could change form at will. She was associated with Hecate, the divine patroness of witchcraft.
36. *appealing . . . front row*: Here Dionysus appeals directly to the priest of Dionysus Eleuthereus ('the Liberator'), who sat in the front row of the theatre.
37. *Lord Heracles . . . my name*: Heracles was often invoked in distress as an averter of evil. Here Dionysus supposes that Xanthias is referring to him as Heracles because of his disguise. He warns him not to do so, possibly because of the Greek belief that if an evil spirit or creature knows an individual's name, its power over that person is greater.
38. *Hegelochus . . . heave no more*: Hegelochus was a tragic actor, who famously accentuated the Greek word *galên* – from a line of Euripides' *Orestes* (279) – incorrectly, so that instead of meaning 'tranquil' it meant 'weasel'. Since the joke belies exact translation, I have kept Barrett's alternative.
39. *Oh dear . . . brought me down*: Dionysus' sentiments are tragic but the language and metre are not. Xanthias, in his subsequent reply, uses the Euripidean phrases Dionysus quoted earlier (100ff.).
40. *Diagoras*: Confirmed atheist who mocked religious practice; he

was prosecuted for divulging the closely guarded secrets of the Eleusinian Mysteries. He may be mentioned here to defuse any danger of Aristophanes' comic version of Eleusinian hymns seeming sacrilegious or disrespectful.

41. *CHORUS*: What follows is the parodos, or Entry-Song, of the play's main Chorus (as distinct from the subsidiary Frog-Chorus). Their hymn to Iacchus (a deity who had come to be identified with Bacchus/Dionysus) has metrical and stylistic similarities with the hymns to Dionysus sung by the Maenad-Chorus in Euripides' *Bacchae*.

42. *Persephone ... daughter of Demeter*: Demeter and Persephone were the other main deities (besides Bacchus/Dionysus) connected with the Eleusinian Mysteries.

43. *wonderful smell of pork*: Xanthias' exclamation refers to the smell of suckling pigs, which were sacrificed during the initiation ritual; but the Greek word *choiros* is also – invariably in Aristophanes – a double-entendre for the female genitalia (like English 'pussy').

44. *noble and grand*: The original specifically mentions the comic playwright Cratinus, an older contemporary of Aristophanes. Aristophanes mocked Cratinus (as a drunken incontinent) while he was alive, but treated him with deference after his death. The description of him in the original Greek as 'Cratinus of the bull-devouring tongue', on account of his grand style, is complimentary; 'bull-devourer' was a title of Dionysus, the god of drama.

45. *customs inspectors ... on the sly*: The original refers to one Thorycion, who was accused of illicit trade.

46. *Some people ... cutting his pay*: Dramatists were paid honoraria for being selected to compete in the Dionysiac festivals. Here Aristophanes alludes to certain unnamed politicians who proposed cuts, possibly due to wartime financial pressures.

47. *persons caught short ... chorus*: The original, which contains crude scatological imagery (omitted here), refers to the dithyrambic poet Cinesias, who was regularly accused of incontinence.

48. *Princess of Spring*: Persephone, whom Pluto abducted to make queen of the underworld. Her mother, Demeter, unaware of her fate, mourned her so much that she neglected her duty as goddess of the crops. In the ensuing crisis, the truth emerged and Persephone was allowed to return to the upper world, but only for part of the year as she had tasted food (pomegranate) from the underworld. Winter represents the part of the year Persephone

spent in the underworld, during which Demeter continued to be mournful, while the coming of spring represents Persephone's yearly return to the upper world.

49. *the shrine*: The Temple of Demeter at Eleusis, about twelve miles northwest of Athens. Initiates into the Mysteries took an image of Iacchus in a procession from Athens to Eleusis.

50. *My clothes . . . cuts down on expenses*: Initiates traditionally wore old or torn clothes. Here the Chorus joke that their ragged costume has helped the play's *chorēgos* save money.

51. *Archedemus*: Key political figure in 406/5. He prosecuted one of the generals at the battle of Arginusae and may have been instrumental in condemning the other generals to death. He was known by the soubriquet 'Bleary Eyes'.

52. *Cleisthenes . . . hair*: The translation plays down the crudeness of these lines, in which Cleisthenes (see note 7) is described as depilating his rectum, grieving over the loss of a male lover, whose name and home town are altered to something like 'Shaftus of Stiffwick'.

53. *Callias*: Wealthy patron of intellectuals and womanizer, who allegedly ran a *ménage à trois* with his wife and mother-in-law. The translation plays down the coarseness of the original, in which Callias is called the son of Hippo*cin*us (changed from Hippo*nic*us), suggesting the sexual urges, or endowment, of a horse.

54. *doorkeeper of Hades*: This character is usually called Aeacus, although he is not named in the text. Aeacus, a son of Zeus, was a hero of exemplary standing; he fathered the two heroes, Peleus and Telamon, who in turn fathered Achilles and Ajax respectively. He is usually described as sitting with Minos and Rhadamanthys, and judging the souls of the dead. His role as doorkeeper may be traceable to a lost tragedy, *Pirithous*, in which he challenges Heracles on his descent to the underworld.

55. *My bowel is empty*: The Greek (*enkekhōda*, 'I've shat myself') is a comic adaptation of a religious formula (*ekkekhutai*, 'it is poured out') used when a libation is poured during a sacrifice. The libation would be followed by an invocation to the god to whom the sacrifice is being made (hence Dionysus' remark, 'Call on the god'). The irony here, of course, is that he himself is a god.

56. *Theramenes*: Politician whose career began under Pericles; he came to prominence as someone who established but later

supplanted the oligarchic revolution of 411. His opportunism led to his being called 'the Buskin' (a shoe that fits either foot). He also had a hand in the harsh treatment of the generals at the battle of Arginusae in 406.

57. *Cleon*: The demagogue who came to power after Pericles. He died in 422 (and so had been a resident of Hades for some time). Aristophanes savaged him in several early plays, including *Knights* and *Wasps*.

58. *Hyperbolus*: Politician frequently reviled by Aristophanes and other playwrights of Old Comedy.

59. *in court . . . day's out*: Cleon's influence over the lawcourts forms the background to *Wasps*.

60. *Hipponax*: Poet of the sixth century BC.

61. *spouting swallow . . . Thracian*: Cleophon, a primary target of comic poets around the time *Frogs* was written, was a general in 428 but came to prominence after the oligarchy of 411 was overthrown and democracy restored. Consistently opposed to peace with Sparta, he was tried on dubious grounds and executed in 404. He may have had some family connection with Thrace, but is likened to a Thracian swallow here because he declaims in warlike fashion (Thrace was associated with belligerence).

62. *Phrynichus*: Joined the oligarchic revolution despite originally having been a radical democrat; assassinated in 411, shortly before the downfall of the oligarchic regime. He is not to be confused with the early tragedian, or contemporary comic playwright, of the same name.

63. *allies from Plataea*: The Plataeans were granted Athenian citizenship after their city was destroyed by the Spartans in 427.

64. *Cleigenes*: Radical democrat opposed to peace with Sparta; he may have owned a bathhouse or laundry. Other politicians with business interests were similarly mocked (e.g., Cleon 'the Tanner', Hyperbolus 'the Lamp-maker').

65. *the right to have his dinner . . . honour*: These privileges may allude to the right accorded to winners of certain festivals to take meals at public expense in the Prytaneum (the building housing the sacred hearth of the state) or to the additional award of *proedria*, only given occasionally, which entitled the recipient to the best seats at the theatre and other public events.

66. *eye to eye with the Athenians*: There were later claims of friction between Aeschylus and the Athenian public of his day, but their reliability is questionable (not least because they may be inferred from the present passage). It is not surprising that Aeschylus

should be at odds with the Athenians of Aristophanes' day, who are characterized as degenerate.

67. *take up their seats*: Other non-speaking characters may have come on at this point – dancing-girls, attendants, perhaps even a collection of the distinguished dead.

68. *Ah, how impressive . . . stone*: Describing Aeschylus.

69. *Neatly . . . what you mean*: Describing Euripides.

70. *son of the seed-goddess*: Aeschylus parodies a line from a play of Euripides (fr. 885) which probably involves Achilles being addressed as 'the son of the sea-goddess' (i.e., Thetis). The joke rests on Aristophanes' regular slur that Euripides' mother Cleito was a seller of greens (see, e.g., *Women* 387); while the origin of the slur is unclear, there is evidence to suggest that Euripides' mother was of good birth. Euripides is regularly criticized in Aristophanic comedy for making his characters speak in more ordinary, less elevated language and for presenting heroes in pitifully reduced circumstances.

71. *Do not inflame . . . rage*: Probably a parody of a line of Aeschylus.

72. *cripple-merchant*: As well as wearing rags, a number of Euripidean heroes appear lame or injured. In *Acharnians*, Euripides himself gives a list of such characters, including Phoenix (blind), Philoctetes (gangrenous foot), Bellerophon (lamed by a fall) and Telephus (septic war wound).

73. *black lamb*: Black lambs were sacrificed to appease storm-gods.

74. *Cretan arias . . . incest*: Euripides was fond of solo songs particularly in his later plays. It is not entirely clear why these should be described as Cretan; perhaps they refer to songs from plays with a Cretan setting such as his *Cretans* or *Cretan Women* (both lost). Euripides' *Aeolus* (also lost) involved an incestuous union between half-brother and half-sister, while his *Cretans* deals with an even more unsavoury union between Minos' wife, Pasiphae, and a bull (resulting in the birth of the Minotaur).

75. *Telephus*: Controversial, presumably, even by Euripides' standards.

76. *My plays . . . hand down here*: After Aeschylus' death, his plays were granted the unique distinction of being eligible for re-performance in the tragic competition against the work of living tragedians (for reference to such a performance, see *Acharnians* 9–11).

77. *O Demeter . . . your mysteries*: Aeschylus invokes Demeter not only because he was initiated into the Mysteries but because he was a native of Eleusis, the site of her main temple. The invo-

cation is also fitting in the presence of a Chorus of Initiates and Dionysus, one of the main deities connected with the Mysteries.

78. *Hail, Ether . . . Nostrils*: Euripides is shown as rejecting traditional gods in favour of gods of his own (as was Socrates in Aristophanes' *Clouds*). While the charge of worshipping new gods was often levelled at intellectuals, there is no evidence to suggest that Euripides (or Socrates) rejected traditional divinities. The main point here is to contrast the avant-garde Euripides with the traditional Aeschylus.

79. *Phrynichus*: Older contemporary of Aeschylus; the tragedian was known for his imaginative choreography (sent up in the finale of *Wasps*) and melodious lyrics.

80. *Niobe . . . Achilles . . . not a word*: Euripides refers to two lost plays of Aeschylus, *Niobe* and *Myrmidons*. In the former, Niobe boasted that she had more children than Leto, mother of Apollo and Artemis, whereupon Leto sent her divine twins to kill all twelve (or fourteen) of Niobe's children, leaving her maddened with grief and suicidal. The latter, part of a trilogy based on the *Iliad*, focuses on Achilles' grief at the death of Patroclus. Both plays involved main characters sitting onstage in prolonged silence.

81. *device painted on the ships*: In *Myrmidons*, the emblem of a hippocock (a creature that was part horse, part bird) painted on a Greek ship is described as dripping into the sea after Hector has set fire to it (while Achilles is still refusing to fight).

82. *And there was I . . . Eryxis*: The context of this joke is unknown.

83. *Cephisophon*: Member of Euripides' household (possibly a slave) who was alleged to have collaborated on his plays and to have had sexual relations with his wife, although there is no reliable evidence for either rumour.

84. *first character . . . origin*: Nearly all of Euripides' plays begin with a prefatory speech elucidating background events. The plays of Sophocles, by contrast, tend to open with dialogue or exchange between two characters, while Aeschylus' plays start in various ways including monologue, exchange and choral ode.

85. *better than your own*: Another joke about the (supposedly) humble origins of Euripides' mother (see note 70).

86. *I should keep off . . . if I were you*: Dionysus is alluding to the fact that Euripides left democratic Athens for the court of King Archelaus of Macedon (where he remained until his death) in 408 BC.

87. *Phormisius . . . Megaenetus*: A man called Phormisius is

mentioned in *Assemblywomen* and another comic fragment. Nothing else is known of Megaenetus.

88. *Cleitophon*: Probably the man of the same name who appears in Plato as a friend of the sophist Thrasymachus.

89. *You see this, famed Achilles*: A line from Aeschylus' *Myrmidons* (fr. 134), possibly the opening lines of the play but, at any rate, almost certainly addressed to Achilles by the Chorus.

90. *oxhide, seven layers thick*: Alluding to the Homeric Ajax, who is regularly described in the *Iliad* as carrying a huge, impenetrable shield made of seven layers of oxhide.

91. *Seven Against Thebes*: The only surviving work of a Theban tetralogy (*Laius*, *Oedipus*, *Seven Against Thebes* and the satyr-play *Sphinx*), produced in 468/7, deals with the attempt by one of Oedipus' sons, Polynices, to capture Thebes from his brother Eteocles (with six other princes). The two had agreed to rule in yearly alternation but after the first year Eteocles refused to cede power. The play culminates in a duel (offstage) in which the two brothers die simultaneously. The subsequent attempt by Antigone to bury her brother Polynices, against the orders of the new king Creon (her uncle), forms the action of Sophocles' *Antigone*.

92. *Persians*: Aeschylus' earliest surviving play, produced in 472, is unusual in treating a historical rather than a mythological subject.

93. *Orpheus*: Legendary singer and musician, who tried but failed to rescue his wife Eurydice from the underworld.

94. *Musaeus*: Legendary figure from Eleusis, to whom were attributed poems on the origins of the cosmos, hymns and divinely inspired oracles.

95. *Hesiod . . . harvesting*: Hesiod wrote *Works and Days*, a didactic poem about agriculture and the farmer's life, at a date close to that of the Homeric poems.

96. *Homer . . . equipment*: Besides being considered the greatest poet, Homer was regarded as a source of battle tactics (Alexander the Great always kept a copy of the *Iliad* by his bedside for this purpose).

97. *Pantacles*: There is one other reference to a man of this name by another comic playwright (Eupolis, fr. 318) also suggesting that he is stupid.

98. *Lamachus*: Successful general in the early part of the Peloponnesian War, presented as a blundering soldier in *Acharnians* but

mentioned in a more positive light in *Women* three years after he died fighting courageously.

99. *Patroclus*: Appears in Aeschylus' *Myrmidons*. Fragmentary evidence suggests that the play presented the relationship between Achilles and Patroclus as homosexual (in contrast with Homer's ambivalence). Here Aeschylus perhaps has in mind the messenger-speech in which Achilles is told the courageous nature of Patroclus' death.

100. *Teucer*: Half-brother of Ajax. It is unclear which plays of Aeschylus he appeared in, but he may well have featured in any that were about Ajax.

101. *Phaedra . . . Stheneboea*: Phaedra appears in two versions of Euripides' *Hippolytus* (we only have the second). Stheneboea appears in *Bellerophon* and another play named after her. The two women's stories, as presented by Euripides, involve similarities: both are married but fall in love with other men (Phaedra with her stepson Hippolytus and Stheneboea with Bellerophon, a guest of her husband's); both make false accusations against the men who reject their infatuations; both commit suicide. Aeschylus seems to deplore such female characters not only for openly expressing uncontrollable sexual feelings – this was generally deemed unacceptable in freeborn women – but for wrongly accusing innocent men.

102. *experience of Aphrodite . . . in the end*: A reference to the alleged relationship between Euripides' wife and his collaborator Cephisophon (see note 83).

103. *took poison straightaway*: Aeschylus means either that noble women have committed suicide because they are so appalled at Euripides' portrayal of Stheneboea's immoral behaviour towards Bellerophon or that they have committed suicide in imitation of Euripides' Stheneboea.

104. *We have a duty . . . right and proper*: The view of poetry as having a predominantly moral function is common in Greek attitudes to art. It is visible in Plato's wary attitude to poetry in the *Republic*, and is perhaps implicit in the use of the term *didaskalos* ('teacher') for a dramatist, although this usage may have had more to do with the dramatist's role of instructing the performers. Moral and political advice also forms a key part of the contest between Aeschylus and Euripides.

105. *ship levy*: Wealthy Athenians had to pay for, and command, a warship as a form of compulsory public service. Exemption could

be obtained only if the person in question could propose someone richer who had not yet been required to perform the service; if the proposed man wished, he could contest the claim in court. Aeschylus is suggesting that in such cases men try to outdo each other in evoking the sympathy of the jury by wearing tattered clothes – like Euripidean heroes.

106. *bawds*: Probably referring to the nurse in *Hippolytus*, who tried to arrange an adulterous union between Phaedra and Hippolytus (see note 101).

107. *giving birth in temples*: In *Auge*, the eponymous heroine, a priestess of Athena, gave birth to her son Telephus (by Heracles) in Athena's sanctuary.

108. *sleeping with their brothers*: In *Aeolus*, Aeolus' daughter Canace had sexual relations with her half-brother Macareus.

109. *life is not life*: From Euripides' *Polyidus* (fr. 638). The remark was made by a mother, possibly Pasiphae (see note 74).

110. *For I have come back . . . return*: The opening lines of *Choephori*, the second play of the *Oresteia* trilogy, which deals with the killing of Clytemnestra and Aegisthus by Orestes and Electra to avenge their murdered father Agamemnon. The same story is treated in two plays called *Electra* by Sophocles and Euripides respectively.

111. *subterranean function*: Hermes was responsible for guiding souls of the dead to Hades. In the *Odyssey*, he escorts slaughtered suitors to the underworld in this capacity.

112. *Orestes . . . those in power*: In all three plays that treat this story, by Aeschylus, Sophocles and Euripides respectively, Orestes returns to Argos without the knowledge of Clytemnestra and Aegisthus.

113. *A happy man . . . mortal men*: The opening two lines of Euripides' *Antigone* (lost).

114. *your iambics . . . I'll show you what I mean*: Aeschylus' point is that Euripides' trimeters have a predictable word-break at a particular point in the line. Iambic trimeters comprise three feet, or units, each with four metrical quantities arranged in iambic sequence. The predictable word-break comes after the first quantity of the second foot (i.e., the fifth quantity out of the twelve in the line). Aeschylus inserts the same seven-quantity-long phrase after each such word-break. In this translation, during the 'oil-flask' section, the Euripidean word-break comes after the fifth syllable of an English iambic hexameter (which is equivalent to

a Greek iambic trimeter because the Greek foot or unit is four iambic quantities rather than our two).

115. *Aegyptus ... reaching Argos*: These lines may be the opening from one of two plays by the name of *Archelaus* (on Archelaus see note 17).

116. *Dionysus ... to the dance and*: The opening of *Hypsipyle*. The play concerns the fifty daughters of Danaus, who all vowed to murder their husbands, the sons of Aegyptus, because they had been forced to marry. Hypsipyle, however, was in love with her husband and spared him.

117. *No man ... lowborn and*: The opening of Euripides' *Stheneboea*.

118. *Cadmus ... town of Sidon*: The opening of the second of two plays by Euripides entitled *Phrixus*.

119. *Pelops ... speedy horses*: The opening lines of *Iphigenia Among the Taurians*. The play deals with the visit by Orestes and his friend Pylades, who were exiled after murdering Clytemnestra and Aegisthus, to the land of the Taurians. Upon arrival they are seized and about to be sacrificed only to be spared by Orestes' sister Iphigenia. She, it turns out, was saved by Artemis from being sacrificed at Aulis, and transported to the land of the Taurians, where she became the priestess of the goddess.

120. *'Tis said ... full harvest*: These lines, which allow Aeschylus to interrupt *twice*, are from Euripides' *Meleager*. Oddly, they do not seem to be the opening lines, which are known from other sources.

121. CHORUS: This brief choral passage contains two short blocks of lines that are somewhat repetitive. It is possible that one set was used in the original production in 405 and the other in the restaging of the play the following winter; both are included here.

122. *Achilles ... rescue*: A patchwork of Aeschylean lines. It begins with two lines from *Myrmidons* (fr. 132), the second of which is repeated nonsensically after each new line. The lines from *Myrmidons* are originally spoken by envoys pleading in vain to the implacable Achilles. Euripides makes fun of Aeschylus' fondness for dactylic rhythm (the metre of Homeric epic) and of his overuse of refrains.

We who dwell ... Hermes: From *Ghost Raisers* (fr. 273), a play about Odysseus' visit to the underworld.

Lord Agamemnon ... hear my words: Of uncertain origin (fr. 238).

Silence . . . temple doors: From the *Priestesses* (fr. 87), a play whose Chorus were priestesses of Artemis.

I am empowered . . . travellers: From *Agamemnon* 104.

123. *Of how the twin-throned kings . . . phlatto-thrat*: This section combines short quotations stitched together from the same choral ode from *Agamemnon* quoted a few lines earlier but with three lines from other plays.

Of how the twin-throned kings . . . Hellas' manhood: From *Agamemnon* 108–9.

Did send the Sphinx . . . baleful days: Probably from the satyr-play *Sphinx*.

With spear . . . bird of omen: From *Agamemnon* 111–12.

To be the prey . . . hounds: From an unknown play (fr. 282), though the lines resemble the *Agamemnon* passage.

And those who fought with Ajax: Possibly from the *Thracian Women*, which deals with the death of Ajax.

Phlatto-thrat: Perhaps a humorous misrepresentation of the stringed accompaniment used in Aeschylean choral lyrics.

124. *A bit of Persian from Marathon*: Aeschylus had fought in the battle of Marathon (490 BC).

125. *Meletus*: Composer of erotic verse and drinking songs (probably sixth century BC).

126. *Caria*: In southwest Asia Minor; associated with emotive pipe music.

127. *castanets*: This may be an allusion to Euripides' *Hypsipyle*, in which the eponymous heroine amuses the infant Opheltes by singing to him and using castanets (the borrowings from *Hypsipyle* in the ode itself support this).

128. *DANCING-GIRL*: This silent character may have been an old hag or an unpalatable young woman. At any rate, she would have been ridiculously dressed.

129. *Not in the Lesbian mode, I take it*: This remark may have two connotations: first, that the dancing-girl's music is not in the dignified style of the high lyric poets of Lesbos, such as Terpander; secondly, that she does not – or, if she is very unattractive, has never been asked to – perform fellatio (the word in the Greek text, *lesbiazein*, is very close to the verb *lesbizein* meaning to perform fellatio). The term 'Lesbian' had no connotations of female homosexuality at this time.

What follows is a parody of Euripidean choral lyrics. The basic metre is aeolic. While the passage is metrically coherent and the language predominantly tragic, its sense and stylistic excesses are ridiculous. The presence of trivial subject-matter – spiders and their webs – and non sequiturs render the whole parody grotesque and ludicrous.

130. *You halcyons ... droplets*: The opening lines from Euripides' *Hypsipyle* (fr. 856).

131. *Where the flute-loving ... dark-blue rams*: From Euripides' *Electra* 435ff.

132. *Gleaming delight ... child*: Based on Euripides' *Hypsipyle*. The first two lines belong together (fr. 765), while the last line seems to look to a climactic moment when Hypsipyle is reunited with one of her sons.

133. *Did you notice that foot ... That one too*: Aeschylus tries to point out a Euripidean metrical feature he dislikes (one which he exemplifies in the last line of his lyric parody) but Dionysus takes the word 'foot' literally, and looks at the feet of Euripides' 'Muse'. There was, in the original production, clearly some sort of visual humour involving the 'Muse' at this point. After saying 'Fling your arms', she probably does this herself to one of the characters onstage (Dionysus or Euripides are the most likely candidates).

134. *Cyrene*: Well-known prostitute, to whom Aeschylus refers subsequently; she is mentioned in *Women* (98).

135. *what his solo arias are like*: Such long monodies, without corresponding strophe and antistrophe, are a distinctive feature of late Euripidean tragedy (see, e.g., *Orestes* 1369–1502). Aeschylus aims to show how Euripides brings 'everyday things' (*Frogs* 959) onto the stage. The elevated style of the monody quickly descends into the ridiculous, dealing as it does with the mundane theft of a cockerel (possibly a retort to Euripides' earlier criticism of Aeschylus for mentioning a cock in a tragedy in 935). There is also parodying of general Euripidean characteristics and (adapted) quotation of specific passages. Euripidean idiosyncrasies include a preoccupation with night, visions and dreams ('dire dream ... shadowy Hades ... sable night ... horrific sight ... Shrouded in blackness ... this dream'), a fondness for oxymoron ('shining gloom ... life and yet no life') and melodramatic repetition ('Murder, murder ... bereft, bereft ... falling, falling').

136. *Spi-i-i-nning some flax ... round*: These lines resemble the description of Helen in *Orestes* 1431–3.

137. *O Cretans ... arrows*: The first line of this stanza (possibly more) is taken from Euripides' *Cretans*. The reference to Cretans with

their bows and arrows may also allude to the Athenian police force, known as 'Archers'.

138. *If only the Argo ... its way*: Euripides quotes the opening line of his *Medea*.

139. *The watery vale ... graze*: Aeschylus quotes from his *Philoctetes* (fr. 249).

140. *Persuasion ... the word*: Euripides quotes from his *Antigone* (fr. 170).

141. *Of all the gods ... no gifts*: Aeschylus quotes from *Niobe* (fr. 161).

142. *Achilles threw ... a four*: The origin of this line is uncertain. Humour arises from bathos. The opening words 'Achilles threw', which anticipate something weighty such as a boulder, are followed by a low-scoring throw in a dice game (the game involved throwing three dice, three sixes being the highest score).

143. *He lifted up ... iron*: Euripides' line is from *Meleager* (fr. 531).

144. *Chariot ... was piled*: Aeschlyus' line is from *Glaucus of Potniae* (fr. 38).

145. *hundred Egyptians couldn't lift that lot*: The Greeks associated the Egyptians with hard labour.

146. *One's so wise, and the other I just love*: It is not clear here which remark applies to which poet. The question has been debated since antiquity.

147. *Alcibiades*: Nephew of Pericles, belonging to the distinguished clan of the Alcmaeonids. Known for his aristocratic airs, physical beauty and (supposedly charming) lisp, he was friends with Socrates and was by far the most flamboyant, controversial and unpredictable of the Athenian leaders of his day. After his arrest (along with several others) in 415 for profaning the Mysteries, he escaped and went over to the Spartans, whom he helped to gain the upper hand in the war until he fell out of favour because of an alleged affair with the wife of one of the Spartan kings. In 411 he had dealings both with the oligarchs who seized power in Athens and with the Persians. The following year, as general, he defeated the oligarchs and had some success against the Spartans at sea, as a result of which he was reinstated in Athens in 407. But Alcibiades' enemies stripped him of his position and he withdrew to a fortress in the Hellespont. At the time of *Frogs*, uncertainty remained as to what should be done about him.

148. *one speaks so discerningly ... distinctly*: It is not clear which description applies to which poet; it is hard even to tell whether or not Aristophanes intends the remarks to be ambivalent. The

two Greek words *sophōs* and *saphōs* have various different nuances: *sophōs* can mean wisely, discerningly, cleverly, shrewdly, and so on; *saphōs* can mean lucidly, eloquently, distinctly, emphatically or, merely, well. The fact that the adjective *sophōs* is also used of one of the poets in line 1413 – there, as here, it is unclear to which of the two it is applied – does not make matters any clearer.

149. *I have something I'd like to . . . if we do the opposite*: The Greek text here comprises two sets of lines, one belonging to the original script and the other to the revised script (for the play's second production). Barrett primarily follows Stanford's 1963 edition of the text but with some omissions and alterations. Here I have followed the revised script according to A. H. Sommerstein's 1996 edition. For discussions of textual problems with the passage, see the commentary on the relevant lines in K. J. Dover's 1993 edition of the text, and also A. H. Sommerstein's argument in *Tragedy, Comedy, Polis*, eds. A. H. Sommerstein et al. (Bari, 1993).

150. *They must regard . . . wealth is woe*: Aeschylus' advice, namely to be prepared to concede land and trust in naval superiority, is very similar to that of Pericles (according to Thucydides in his *History of the Peloponnesian War*), given nearly thirty years before *Frogs*.

151. *I'll judge . . . soul desires*: The line, which is tragic in rhythm and style, is very probably a Euripidean quotation.

152. *It was my tongue that swore*: Dionysus quotes the first half of Euripides' *Hippolytus* 612 (with greater accuracy than his earlier attempt in 101–2).

153. *What's shameful . . . view it?*: Another Euripidean line from *Aeolus* (fr. 19). By changing the last word slightly, from *chrōmenois* ('those who do it') to *theōmenois* ('those who view it', i.e., the audience), Dionysus gives the line a metatheatrical twist. Euripides' disbelieving question in the previous line may also be taken from a Euripidean play.

154. *Who knows . . . death is life?*: From Euripides' *Polyidus* (fr. 638). This line, which is alluded to earlier (*Frogs* 1038), is particularly apt as the action among the dead seems every bit as lively as the world above.

155. *To fritter . . . a fool*: Euripides and Socrates are seen as key figures of the intellectual avant-garde, a group that suffers much ridicule from comic playwrights.

156. *Nicomachus*: A man of this name was involved in the codification

and public inscription of the laws in 410 and 403; this may be him.

157. *Myrmex . . . Archenomus*: Both unknown.

158. *Adeimantus*: Cousin of Alcibiades; he was general in 406/5.

159. *Spirits of the darkness . . . his way*: Adapted from Aeschylus' *Glaucus of Potniae* (fr. 36).

160. *To the city's counsels . . . lend*: Adapted from the *exodos*, or Exit-Song, of *Eumenides* (1012–13), the final play of Aeschylus' *Oresteia* trilogy, in which Athena wishes the citizens of Athens well.

read more

PENGUIN CLASSICS

PROMETHEUS BOUND AND OTHER PLAYS
AESCHYLUS

PROMETHEUS BOUND / THE SUPPLIANTS / SEVEN AGAINST THEBES / THE PERSIANS

'Your kindness to the human race has earned you this.
A god who would not bow to the gods' anger – you
Transgressing right, gave privileges to mortal men'

Aeschylus (525–456 BC) brought a new grandeur and epic sweep to the drama of classical Athens, raising it to the status of high art. In *Prometheus Bound* the defiant Titan Prometheus is brutally punished by Zeus for daring to improve the state of wretchedness and servitude in which mankind is kept. *The Suppliants* tells the story of the fifty daughters of Danaus who must flee to escape enforced marriages, while *Seven Against Thebes* shows the inexorable downfall of the last members of the cursed family of Oedipus. And *The Persians*, the only Greek tragedy to deal with events from recent Athenian history, depicts the aftermath of the defeat of Persia in the battle of Salamis, with a sympathetic portrayal of its disgraced King Xerxes.

Philip Vellacott's evocative translation is accompanied by an introduction, with individual discussions of the plays, and their sources in history and mythology.

Translated with an introduction by Philip Vellacott

www.penguin.com

read more

PENGUIN CLASSICS

LYSISTRATA AND OTHER PLAYS ARISTOPHANES

LYSISTRATA / THE ACHARNIANS / THE CLOUDS

'But he who would provoke me should remember
That those who rifle wasps' nests will be stung!'

Writing at a time of political and social crisis in Athens, Aristophanes (*c.* 447–*c.* 385 BC) was an eloquent, yet bawdy, challenger to the demagogue and the sophist. In *Lysistrata* and *The Acharnians*, two pleas for an end to the long war between Athens and Sparta, a band of women and a lone peasant respectively defeat the political establishment. The darker comedy of *The Clouds* satirizes Athenian philosophers, Socrates in particular, and reflects the uncertainties of a generation in which all traditional religious and ethical beliefs were being challenged.

For this edition Alan H. Sommerstein has completely revised his translation of these three plays, bringing out the full nuances of Aristophanes's ribald humour and intricate word play, with a new introduction explaining the historical and cultural background to the plays.

Translated with an introduction by Alan H. Sommerstein

www.penguin.com

read more

PENGUIN CLASSICS

HOMERIC HYMNS

'It is of you the poet sings . . .
at the beginning and at the end
it is always of you'

Written by unknown poets in the sixth and seventh centuries BC, the thirty-three *Homeric Hymns* were recited at festivals to honour the Olympian goddesses and gods and to pray for divine favour or for victory in singing contests. They stand now as works of great poetic force, full of grace and lyricism, and ranging in tone from irony to solemnity, ebullience to grandeur. Recounting significant episodes from mythology, such as the abduction of Persephone by Hades and Hermes's theft of Apollo's cattle, the *Hymns* also provide fascinating insights into cults, rituals and holy sanctuaries, giving us an intriguing view of the ancient Greek relationship between humans and the divine.

This translation of the *Homeric Hymns* is new to Penguin Classics, providing a key text for understanding ancient Greek mythology and religion. The introduction explores their authorship, performance, literary qualities and influence on later writers.

'The purest expressions of ancient Greek religion we possess . . .
Jules Cashford is attuned to the poetry of the Hymns'
Nigel Spivey, University of Cambridge

A new translation by Jules Cashford with an introduction by Nicholas Richardson

read more

PENGUIN CLASSICS

MEDEA AND OTHER PLAYS EURIPIDES

MEDEA / ALCESTIS / THE CHILDREN OF HERACLES / HIPPOLYTUS

'That proud, impassioned soul, so ungovernable now that she has felt the sting of injustice'

Medea, in which a spurned woman takes revenge upon her lover by killing her children, is one of the most shocking and horrific of all the Greek tragedies. Dominating the play is Medea herself, a towering and powerful figure who demonstrates Euripides's unusual willingness to give voice to a woman's case. *Alcestis*, a tragicomedy, is based on a magical myth in which Death is overcome, and *The Children of Heracles* examines the conflict between might and right, while *Hippolytus* deals with self-destructive integrity and moral dilemmas. These plays show Euripides transforming the awesome figures of Greek mythology into recognizable, fallible human beings.

John Davie's accessible prose translation is accompanied by a general introduction and individual prefaces to each play.

'John Davie's translations are outstanding . . . the tone throughout is refreshingly modern yet dignified' William Allan, *Classical Review*

Previously published as *Alcestis and Other Plays*.

Translated by John Davie, with an introduction and notes by Richard Rutherford

www.penguin.com

read more

PENGUIN CLASSICS

THE LAST DAYS OF SOCRATES PLATO

EUTHYPHRO / THE APOLOGY / CRITO / PHAEDO

'Nothing can harm a good man either in life or after death'

The trial and condemnation of Socrates on charges of heresy and corrupting young minds is a defining moment in the history of Classical Athens. In tracing these events through four dialogues, Plato also developed his own philosophy, based on Socrates's manifesto for a life guided by self-responsibility. *Euthyphro* finds Socrates outside the court-house, debating the nature of piety, while *The Apology* is his robust rebuttal of the charges of impiety and a defence of the philosopher's life. In the *Crito*, while awaiting execution in prison, Socrates counters the arguments of friends urging him to escape. Finally, in the *Phaedo*, he is shown calmly confident in the face of death, skilfully arguing the case for the immortality of the soul.

Hugh Tredennick's landmark 1954 translation has been revised by Harold Tarrant, reflecting changes in Platonic studies, with an introduction and expanded introductions to each of the four dialogues.

Translated by Hugh Tredennick and Harold Tarrant with an introduction and notes by Harold Tarrant

www.penguin.com

read more

PENGUIN CLASSICS

ELECTRA AND OTHER PLAYS SOPHOCLES

AJAX / ELECTRA / WOMEN OF TRACHIS / PHILOCTETES

'Now that he is dead,
I turn to you; will you be brave enough
To help me kill the man who killed our father?'

Sophocles's innovative plays transformed Greek myths into dramas featuring complex human characters, through which he explored profound moral issues. *Electra* portrays the grief of a young woman for her father Agamemnon, who has been killed by her mother's lover. Aeschylus and Euripides also dramatized this story, but the objectivity and humanity of Sophocles's version provided a new perspective. Depicting the fall of a great hero, *Ajax* examines the enigma of power and weakness combined in one being, while the *Women of Trachis* portrays the tragic love and error of Heracles's deserted wife Deianeira, and *Philoctetes* deals with the conflict between physical force and moral strength.

E. F. Watling's vivid translation is accompanied by an introduction in which he discusses Sophocles's use of a third actor to create new dramatic situations and compares the different treatments of the Electra myth by the three great tragic poets of classical Athens.

Translated with an introduction by E. F. Watling

www.penguin.com

read more

PENGUIN CLASSICS

THE GREEK SOPHISTS

'In the case of wisdom, those who sell it to anyone who wants it are called sophists'

By mid-fifth century BC, Athens was governed by democratic rule and power turned upon the ability of the individual to command the attention of the other citizens, and to sway the crowds of the assembly. It was the Sophists who understood the art of rhetoric and the importance of being able to transform effective reasoning into persuasive public speaking. Their inquiries – into the gods, the origins of religion and whether virtue can be taught – laid the groundwork for the next generation of thinkers such as Plato and Aristotle.

Each chapter of *The Greek Sophists* is based around the work of one character: Gorgias, Prodicus, Protagoras and Antiphon among others, and a linking commentary, chronological table and bibliography are provided for each one. In his introduction, John Dillon discusses the historical background and the sources of the text.

Translated by John Dillon and Tania Gergel with an introduction by John Dillon

www.penguin.com

read more

PENGUIN CLASSICS

THE POLITICS ARISTOTLE

'Man is by nature a political animal'

In *The Politics* Aristotle addresses the questions that lie at the heart of political science. How should society be ordered to ensure the happiness of the individual? Which forms of government are best and how should they be maintained? By analysing a range of city constitutions – oligarchies, democracies and tyrannies – he seeks to establish the strengths and weaknesses of each system to decide which are the most effective, in theory and in practice. A hugely significant work, which has influenced thinkers as diverse as Aquinas and Machiavelli, *The Politics* remains an outstanding commentary on fundamental political issues and concerns, and provides fascinating insights into the workings and attitudes of the Greek city-state.

The introductions by T. A. Sinclair and Trevor J. Saunders discuss the influence of *The Politics* on philosophers, its modern relevance and Aristotle's political beliefs. This edition contains Greek and English glossaries, and a bibliography for further reading.

Translated by T. A. Sinclair
Revised and re-presented by Trevor J. Saunders

www.penguin.com

read more

PENGUIN CLASSICS

THE BIRDS AND OTHER PLAYS ARISTOPHANES

THE KNIGHTS / PEACE / THE BIRDS / THE ASSEMBLYWOMEN / WEALTH

'Oh wings are splendid things, make no mistake: they really help you rise in the world'

The plays collected in this volume, written at different times in Aristophanes's forty-year career as a dramatist, all contain his trademark bawdy comedy and dazzling verbal agility. In *The Birds*, two frustrated Athenians join with the birds to build the utopian city of 'Much Cuckoo in the Clouds'. *The Knights* is a venomous satire on Cleon, the prominent Athenian demagogue, while *The Assemblywomen* considers the war of the sexes, as the women of Athens infiltrate the all-male Assembly in disguise. The lengthy conflict with Sparta is the subject of *Peace*, inspired by the hope of a settlement in 421 BC, and *Wealth* reflects the economic catastrophe that hit Athens after the war, as the god of riches is depicted as a ragged, blind old man.

The lively translations by David Barrett and Alan H. Sommerstein capture the full humour of the plays. The introduction examines Aristophanes's life and times, and the comedy and poetry of his works. This volume also includes an introductory note for each play.

Translated with an introduction by David Barrett and Alan H. Sommerstein

www.penguin.com

read more

PENGUIN CLASSICS

THE REPUBLIC   PLATO

'We are concerned with the most important of issues, the choice between a good and an evil life'

Plato's *Republic* is widely acknowledged as the cornerstone of Western philosophy. Presented in the form of a dialogue between Socrates and three different interlocutors, it is an inquiry into the notion of a perfect community and the ideal individual within it. During the conversation other questions are raised: what is goodness?; what is reality?; what is knowledge? *The Republic* also addresses the purpose of education and the roles of both women and men as 'guardians' of the people. With remarkable lucidity and deft use of allegory, Plato arrives at a depiction of a state bound by harmony and ruled by 'philosopher kings'.

Desmond Lee's translation of *The Republic* has come to be regarded as a classic in its own right. His introduction discusses contextual themes such as Plato's disillusionment with Athenian politics and the trial of Socrates. This new edition also features a revised bibliography.

Translated with an introduction by Desmond Lee

www.penguin.com

THE STORY OF PENGUIN CLASSICS

Before 1946 … 'Classics' are mainly the domain of academics and students, without readable editions for everyone else. This all changes when a little-known classicist, E. V. Rieu, presents Penguin founder Allen Lane with the translation of Homer's *Odyssey* that he has been working on and reading to his wife Nelly in his spare time.

1946 *The Odyssey* becomes the first Penguin Classic published, and promptly sells three million copies. Suddenly, classic books are no longer for the privileged few.

1950s Rieu, now series editor, turns to professional writers for the best modern, readable translations, including Dorothy L. Sayers's *Inferno* and Robert Graves's *The Twelve Caesars*, which revives the salacious original.

1960s The Classics are given the distinctive black jackets that have remained a constant throughout the series's various looks. Rieu retires in 1964, hailing the Penguin Classics list as 'the greatest educative force of the 20th century'.

1970s A new generation of translators arrives to swell the Penguin Classics ranks, and the list grows to encompass more philosophy, religion, science, history and politics.

1980s The Penguin American Library joins the Classics stable, with titles such as *The Last of the Mohicans* safeguarded. Penguin Classics now offers the most comprehensive library of world literature available.

1990s The launch of Penguin Audiobooks brings the classics to a listening audience for the first time, and in 1999 the launch of the Penguin Classics website takes them online to a larger global readership than ever before.

The 21st Century Penguin Classics are rejacketed for the first time in nearly twenty years. This world famous series now consists of more than 1300 titles, making the widest range of the best books ever written available to millions – and constantly redefining the meaning of what makes a 'classic'.

The Odyssey continues …

The best books ever written

PENGUIN CLASSICS

SINCE 1946

Find out more at www.penguinclassics.com